REDEVELOPING WORKING POOR COMMUNITIES AND NEIGHBORHOODS

A GENERAL GUIDE

J. MURUKU WAIGUCHU

AUSTIN & WINFIELD
SAN FRANCISCO, 1993

Library of Congress Cataloging-in-Publication Data

Waiguchu, J. Muruku.
    Redeveloping Working poor communities and neighborhoods: a
general guide for rebuilding poor urban communities and neighborhoods/
by J. Muruku Waiguchu.
    276 p.
    Includes bibliographical references and index.
    ISBN 1-880921-25-1: $ 29.95
    1. Community development, Urban--United States. 2. Urban poor--
United States.   I. Title.
HN90.C6W33   1992   93-18918
307.1'416'0973--dc20   CIP

Editorial Inquiries:

Austin & Winfield, Publishers
534 Pacific Avenue
San Francisco, CA 94133
Fax: (415) 434-3441

Order Fulfillment:

Austin & Winfield, Publishers
P.O. Box 2529
San Francisco, CA 94126
Fax: (415) 434-3441

Table of Contents

Preface

What the book attempts to do

In this book, we propose ways and means of empowering working poor Americans so that they can be more self supporting. Empowering would be accomplished by linking what the individual working poor gets in the form of public assistance to physical rehabilitation of his/her neighborhood. The book argues that the reason for providing public assistance to the working poor ought to be (where and if it is not) to bring about a discernible degree of individual self improvement which then translates into more individual self reliance. More importantly, it is further argued, the individual thus improved should become a home and/or business owner in and within a contiguously set pattern of home ownership and occupation with similarly situated local small business establishments which are locally owned and managed. Process of self improvement and ownership should ideally take place simultaneously. Ownership, we maintain, creates stakeholders who can reasonably be expected to worry about what happens to their communities and neighborhoods.

The reasons for the book

Apart from the contribution that this book may make to the existing pool of knowledge on how to assist and empower the working poor, we wrote this book because of what we perceived to be a real need for a more practical and realistic reference material for those of us who are guiding and supervising students in the inner city communities and neighborhoods or happen to be involved in various activities and programs intended to help working poor to take initiative to improve their living conditions. A second reason for writing the book was our desire to influence (or, at the very least question) the beliefs and philosophies which appear to undergird our public assistance policies and practices in providing services to those of our fellow citizens who are physically and mentally fit. The point here is that public assistance to the physically and mentally able should be timed and predicated on yielding certain pre-defined results in the improvement of both the individual recipient and his/her neighborhood physical setting. A third reason was our desire to add our voice to the view that social and human service creation and delivery for the working poor is (or rather, should be) viewed and practiced as a temporary activity and not as a permanent career ladder occupation or profession for the nonworking poor. Instead, the working poor themselves (as service recipients and consumers) should be converted - through education and training - to service providers who, as time goes on, would also give way to other similarly trained public assistance recipients. In the context of this scenario, the bottom line would be that those thus trained and replaced would move on to other situations and opportunities suitable to their newly acquired skills and work experience even as others from the ranks of the working poor/service recipients succeed them. And the cycle would go on and on. The idea here is, of course, that we would thus minimize the power and durability of the current stifling-and-suffocating-publicly-funded bureaucracy which too often seems to feed off the working poor!

The importance for something which can and will work in our depressed inner city communities and neighborhoods should never be underestimated. It is like nothing works. Our efforts, as a society to help the working poor have been and continue to be many and wide ranging. One does not have to be a rocket scientist to appreciate the fact that most of these efforts have not made much difference in the lives of the working poor. There are not many communities or neighborhoods that one can now cite as living examples of what has been redeveloped during the past several decades. In other words, most, if not all, of these past efforts have fallen far short of actually redeveloping our inner city areas or making the working poor Americans less dependent. It is because of that perceived failure that we decided to write this general guide for those who labor and toil endlessly in that effort to empower our working poor to do for themselves what you and I try to or do for them.

About the book

The point is to empower the working poor to overcome, or, at the very least, minimize the hugely adverse effects of poverty. The book starts by suggesting a linkage of both the human and physical dimensions of poverty followed by suggestions of key aspects and sources of influence/power available to and readily usable by the working poor. Empowering the working poor (that is, using what is already available in the way of voting, involvement, education and, most importantly, wise use of their limited consumer dollars) is here posed as the energizing mechanism - the engine - which will propel the working poor to positions of relative influence in their community and neighborhood affairs. To give these traditional sources of power and influence functional reality, certain things must be done. First thing to do is to convert the working poor from public assistance dependents to stakeholders in their communities and neighborhoods. This would be done by making working poor who are currently public housing tenants home, apartment or condominium owners. Ideally, home owning should go hand in hand with establishing, owning and managing other neighborhood based economic establishments. Lack of realistic or practical consideration in selecting and locating economic activities in the working poor communities and neighborhoods continues to be self defeating.

Also clearly overlooked in the effort to redevelop inner city poor areas, is the role of community and neighborhood based institutions and facilities such as the schools, or the restructure and reorientation of social and human services to be more effective in helping individuals to change from public dependence to self dependence. Effective and constructive system of community communication is a necessary condition for the rebuilding of the working poor neighborhoods. Such a network of communication will indeed facilitate cooperation among the working poor, motivate and support group and individual efforts in creating, sustaining and enhancing self reliance.

I want to thank Marty Laurence, Jackie Pope and Philip Clay for their generosity and useful comments, suggestions and criticisms of earlier drafts of this book. I also want to express gratitude to my students in the community development class for enriching my perspectives and their strong and candid views and comments with specific regard to issues surrounding the notion and practice of neighborhood empowerment and home ownership.

Finally, I am grateful to my wife, Dorothy, for her efforts in helping prepare this manuscript and, of course, maintaining an enlivening company.

J. Muruku Waiguchu
Paterson, New Jersey
1992

Perspectives in Rebuilding Working Poor Communities and Neighborhoods

Poverty and the neighborhoods

The relationship between the state of being poor and the social and economic conditions in the inner city neighborhoods is in many ways similar to that of the chicken and the egg. The eternal question as to which came first, the chicken or the egg, resonates very well with the parallel question of which came first: inner city poverty or the collapse of the inner city neighborhoods. Did poverty cause the collapse of these neighborhoods or was it the collapse of the neighborhoods that caused poverty? Which came first? Thinking about poverty unavoidably leads to thinking about particular areas where the poor live. And, conversely, thinking about the areas where the poor live, one has to confront poverty face to face. The two go together. We cannot have one without the other and, similarly, we cannot improve one without improving the other. And yet, it seems as though this is exactly what we have tried to do in our past efforts to rebuild poor communities: fight poverty and provide public assistance without physical improvement.

1

We may therefore begin by wondering whether or not there are any good, clean and livable poor neighborhoods anywhere? And, to continue wondering, if the poor have always lived in the bad neighborhoods (as we suspect), could it ever be possible (and desirable) for a poor person to have and live in a good, clean and safe neighborhood? Is the condition of being poor incompatible with living in a good neighborhood? Or, could the poor neighborhoods ever be made more livable and safe? And, whether any of all this were ever possible, who should do what for whom? What would charity and the service providers do if the poor were empowered to provide for themselves? These and other questions suggest some of the issues which must be faced and hopefully resolved in order to rebuild our depressed communities and neighborhoods. By raising and discussing these issues, we hope to clarify and suggest better and sustainable ways of improving living conditions of the less fortunate amongst us.

But even before we are able to determine which came first (poverty itself or collapse of the neighborhoods) and without being certain that it could ever be resolved, we must reckon with the fact that the working poor exist and they live in the poor neighborhoods. Perhaps the point is moot as to which came first. But given the fact that the poor exist, we have taken the common ground that both the poor and their neighborhoods exist and that it does not make good sense to improve one without improving the other simultaneously. It is precisely on this point that we find fault with the current and past efforts to assist the working poor. That is, improving their human needs has never been sufficiently linked to improving where they live or vice versa.

The poor are poor for many reasons and circumstances which are not discussed in this book. What we have done is simply acknowledge (which is really over-doing it) that poverty and the poor exist as different sides of the same coin and that they constitute a serious societal problem for which solutions are sought. Semantically, the analogy of the two-sided coin refers to the fact that poverty cannot exist without poor people and vice versa.

2

Similarly, the condition of being poor must necessarily encompass both the human and the physical dimensions. We further suggest that, as a general proposition, working poor people, by virtue of being poor, do not own much in their neighborhoods and as such they would tend to have no particular invested interests in where they live. Because they do not have much (or anything) at stake, they are not likely to take all the necessary care of their communities and neighborhoods.

Pertinent literature on life in the poor inner city neighborhoods seems to suggest that living in such poor and blighted neighborhoods may have a chilling and depressing effect on those who live there. May be it is natural to feel that way when one lives in a place that does not reflect well on them. Accepting this assumption leads to the feeling that inner city neighborhoods no longer provide the kind of community-belonging support that they once did. To put the idea differently, there is less functional harmony between inner city residents and their run down physical environment. How the individual working poor person can improve his or her life in the same neighborhood where he or she now lives, succinctly captures both the essence and reasons for this book.

The book lays out the conceptual framework for redressing individual, group and environmental problems arising from the condition of being poor and the collapse of the inner city neighborhoods and goes on to make concrete suggestions on how to correct the problems arising from this situation. Like families, neighborhoods are the basic units of a society. Societal institutions, norms and values have their greatest meaning and impact within neighborhoods. These visible and often invisible entities we call neighborhoods provide the social and organizational context within which residents, young and old alike, grow, live and function in accordance with certain (stated or unstated) precepts and practices. Without such guiding precepts and their corresponding sociocultural fabric and patterns, community people, and especially the young ones, are without common guides and yardsticks for

3

functioning as productive members of one community (Warren:51-61, Whyte, Jr: 378-386).

A key element of being poor, we submit, is living in communities and neighborhoods where there are few or no particular precepts and practices by which to live and function for both individual and group stability and benefit. And, where and when such precepts and practices may exist, majority of such neighborhoods often lack the wherewithal with which to assimilate or, for that matter, force their tenets on their residents and especially the young ones. The inability of neighborhoods to provide structural and behavioral guidance makes such neighborhoods dysfunctional.This dysfunctionalism, we believe, constitutes both the essence of poverty in today's inner city neighborhoods and the conditions for which we seek solution. Furthermore, the predicament of the poor neighborhoods has not been made easier by our traditional insistence on monetary income as the main, if not the only, measure of and relief for poverty. This idea leaves out much to be desired. In fact, it is also self defeating in that no society can ever have enough money for every working poor person!. Without a nurturing and supportive set of neighborhood mechanisms, the lives and welfare of the less fortunate amongst us are likely to remain and unstable.

To redress the type of community and neighborhood concerns and problems common to the South Bronxes, Central Wards and the Watts of America, we propose to link human and physical redevelopments. That is, helping the individual who is on public assistance should be linked or tied to qualitative (and perhaps quantitative, too) improvement of that individual's physical setting and vice versa. We do not seek job training, for example, for the working poor without also improving where the working poor now live at the same time. Neither do we seek to assist an individual without simultaneously insisting that they be more self reliant. That is, to be more self reliant is to increasingly shoulder the greater burden of their own maintenance. We propose to link individual or community redevelopment

4

activities and programs to various public assistance programs. For instance, we may propose to tie housing to home ownership or income transfer to self employment. We seek such linkages as a way of creating more comprehensive, complementary and sustainable strategies to halt, if not reverse, the deterioration of both the individual working poor and the urban poor neighborhoods. To this end, we have made some proposals in chapters six, seven and eight which we believe will help solve many of the more endemic problems facing inner city and minority neighborhoods.

The idea of redeveloping communities and neighborhoods

The concept of redeveloping communities and neighborhoods implies that these communities and neighborhoods were once developed and now (as the term implies) they have to be redeveloped - meaning that something had to have happened to make a second development necessary. (Wadley:82). We, of course, know that something happened. We are planning to develop them again because, as communities and neighborhoods, they are unable to provide the kind of support that neighborhoods have traditionally provided for and to their residents (Palen:245). While describing this inability in a preceding section, we used the term collapse to mean the near complete breakdown of the social, cultural and economic fabric of these communities and neighborhoods. Unlike the past efforts in community development, the specific type of community redevelopment or rebuilding we have proposed in this book has three linked features. These are (a) human development which is linked to (b) the physical rehabilitation of the neighborhood setting which, in turn, is linked to (c) locally based ownership and management of both residential properties and economic resources and establishments.

Operationally, the idea of rebuilding a neighborhood is, to borrow an expression from Chicago's *Center for Neighborhood Technology* (1986:6), to establish a working community which we interpret as a neighborhood whose residents generally work within and outside their neighborhood; own their homes; own, operate and support their local businesses; have pride in their community and neighborhood; share social bonds and cultural life in the community; and are civic, that is, willing and able to participate and influence the local and state public policy processes. In short, we envisage community and neighborhood redevelopment as representing that process by and through which we can qualitatively change what Donald Warren has described as *the anomic neighborhood to the integral neighborhood* (Warren :61-63). A more complete discussion of these types of neighborhoods is found in chapter three.

The idea and practice of rebuilding communities and neighborhoods constitute the essence and point of this book. The book is not about poverty per se. It is about the ways and means of enabling working poor Americans first to withstand and secondly to overcome that type of human and physical devastation brought about by poverty. Therefore, instead of probing and presenting the causes and consequences of poverty in America (as much of the literature on the subject has and continues to do), we have outlined, pin-pointed and embraced poverty as the problem we seek to resolve. Towards that end, we have identified that segment of low income Americans
(the working poor) whose human, social and economic inabilities and instabilities seem to aggravate both the rates of and numbers in poverty. Our thesis is that stabilization of the working poor would go along way in stabilizing both the individual person and his/her neighborhood. Such stabilization, we contend, will not only restore but also maintain reasonable degrees of neighborhood viability. Additionally, such stabilization would be expected to make two other improvements. First, it will at least keep the working poor above abject poverty and, secondly, it will close the social and economic cracks through which the lower middle class and the low income people may slip back into abject poverty.

Purpose of the book

This book seeks to delineate ways and means by and through which working poor people can be empowered to be more self reliant. This is done by specifying and recasting prevailing ideas and practices of community development to constitute a general guide for rebuilding the poor inner city communities and neighborhoods. The book therefore adds to the existing pool of knowledge of ways and means of empowering the less fortunate among us to be more self supporting. To the extent the book does fulfill that purpose, it justifies its raison d'etre for being a useful tool for teaching and general reference. We believe there continues to be a great need for a text that looks at the problems of the working poor from a bottom up perspective. In this sense, the book fulfills textual and reference purposes for those academic programs dealing with empowerment of the working poor, community and neighborhood redevelopment, public and community service, political economy of poverty, public management in inner city neighborhoods, urban studies, African-American Studies, nonprofit management and more important, as a general guide for students interning in the working poor neighborhoods.

Additionally, the book is likely to be equally useful to other professional and paraprofessional areas in the public, private and nonprofit sectors. In particular, the book would be useful to most, if not all, of the public, private, nonprofit and religious groups and agencies involved in helping to improve conditions of living in the inner city communities and neighborhoods. The book represents a typical and yet a handy guide and reference for municipal and county agencies and officials, a variety of service providers, community development corporations, church and civic groups, banks, foundations, advocacy groups and fraternal organizations interested in assisting the working poor to be more self supporting.

The concept of the working poor

The term working poor is critically important to the purposes of this book. Conceptually, the term helps us understand and sort out various levels, attributes and dichotomies of poverty in America. Operationally, the term helps us focus on and target our activity proposals to particular segment(s) of our communities. The working poor are important to this effort because the book is about how to make them more self reliant and their neighborhoods more viable places for them and their families.

That segment of Americans we have referred to as the working poor is, for lack of a more precise measure, made up of working individuals whose annual incomes were between $9,500 and $14,999 in 1988. The 1988 poverty threshold was roughly about mid-way between the above income ranges. And as would be expected, corresponding thresholds for subsequent years has differed and will differ according to both inflation and the annual adjustments. But the most noticeable attributes of the working poor are manifest in their income ranges, where they live and their economic standing. Their annual incomes fall within the above income range or subsequent ranges as measured by poverty threshold. The working poor would either be employed or self employed during the year or part thereof but their incomes are generally low enough to permit only very limited upward mobility. This description of the working poor is not intended to be exclusive. There are times and situations when given incomes, even when higher, may not adequately cover the basic needs of a given family. (See Figure I)

Positioning the working poor

In order to accurately depict the social and economic position of the poor and low income people on whom we have focused in this book, we have created a schema (Figure I) to illustrate and depict how we view the interactions and the relationships amongst the various income bracket groups both as economic and residential entities. The schema categorizes American

Table I
Income Bracket Schema

Group A: $75,000 and over	*** Wealthy
Group A2: $35,000-74,999	*** Middle Class
Group B: $25,000-34,999	*** Lower Middle Class
Group B2: $15,000-24,999	*** Low Income
Group C: $ 9,500-14,999	*** Working Poor
Group C2: $ 5,000-9,499	*** Working & Nonworking Poor

society into three main income bracket groups each of which has a subgroup. A case in point: income brackets A and A2 represent the wealthy and middle class Americans; B and B2 represent the lower middle class and low income Americans while C and C2 represent the working poor and the poor in general. Although some consideration has been given to segments of income groups B2 and C2 whose social, economic and living circumstances may at times be similar to or overlap with those of income group C proper, our principal focus henceforth is on income group C who are also considered to be working but poor. Note also that these income bracket groups have been similarly reflected on Figure VIII. Although some working poor may be found in neighborhoods designated as II and III, the proper working poor would be found in neighborhoods designated as I.

To accompany the above schema and to create the proper context for topics discussed in the chapters, we have, in addition, developed and borrowed a number of themes and assumptions to provide the necessary conceptual and organizational cohesiveness to the book. These themes and assumptions serve as the grounds and bases on which we make proposals and deviate from some of the traditional approaches to community development. But before stating these themes, let us take note of what some literature say about the working poor.

A glimpse at the literature on poverty

But before we introduce the leading themes and assumptions in this book, let us note in passing that although we are blessed with voluminous literature on poverty - examining, analyzing and measuring its various facets, we have not been as fortunate in getting adequate literature focusing on various aspects of policy implementation and other operational considerations relative to the problem of poverty in America. And, even with such wealth of literature, an admonitory remark by Alice Rivlin is very much in order. Referring to the researchers' fascination with number tricks and formulae, she admonishes that even with fancier statistical manipulation of inadequate data from traditional sources, one may not always improve on the knowledge about policy choices. (Aiken & Kehrer:31).

Among the more recent studies of poverty in America, we consider Jencks & Peterson's *The Urban Underclass* (1991), to be a good example. In its discussion, analysis and summaries of contemporary literature dealing with the problems of poor during the decade of the 1980's, this book appears to chart a middle course between Wilson's *The Truly Disadvantaged* (1987) and Murray's *Losing Ground: American Social Policy,1950-1980* (1984). These are some of the often cited and influential scholarly materials available on the subjects of the poor, low income Americans and public welfare. It does not seem to us that these or the rest of the scholarly literature available out there would be particularly suitable guides for use as either reference materials by inner city interns or the local policy maker or, for that matter, materials that the head of a neighborhood agency could readily use to organize or empower community individuals and groups to engage in neighborhood redevelopment and self help activities.

Indeed, if we consider operational requirements of various community based projects in the inner city areas, we should not be surprised to find that local officials, agency heads, service providers and community people in general tend to have serious difficulties using much of the academically generated research materials. And, as it has been suggested, unless recast or retranslated, academic research materials are not particularly suitable for immediate application for two reasons. First, disciplinary and theoretical jargons common in such literature impede lay understanding. Second, most research materials either lack policy implications or do not make operational recommendations. Additionally, it is not unusual for academic cynics to make disparaging remarks and reviews about applied research which, unlike academic research, attempts to address an institutional audience that seeks to act on problematic situations. (Staudt, 1991:86). The emphasis here is on the actual and potential difficulties encountered by the working poor and their allies in using and/or applying academic research materials to practical situations at the local and in the poor neighborhoods.

The leading themes and assumptions

Now, to turn back to the themes which permeate much of our discussion in this book, it bears repeating here that these themes provide the frameworks within which we make proposals for rebuilding our depressed inner city neighborhoods. In some ways, the themes and assumptions we have outlined here are based on common sense and in other ways, they reflect existing literature on poverty and community development programs and activities. In the latter case, we have taken to heart that type of literature

11

which is more conceptual, grassroots oriented, prescriptive and less statistically induced or modelled. In this regard, our thinking and assumptions have been influenced by Donald Warren's *Black Neighborhoods*, Michael Sherraden's *Assets and the Poor*, Daniel Fusfeld's *The Basic Economics of the Urban Racial Crisis*, James Blackwell's *The Black Community* and Chicago's community-based *Center for Neighborhood Technology*. It goes without saying that we have borrowed from many others too.

The five major themes and underlying assumptions we put forth pertain to(a) the primacy of neighborhoods as the starting point in the process of rebuilding the inner city poor neighborhoods, (b) the idea of linking support programs and activities, (c) the recognition of the fact that the poor will always be with us and that we cannot provide effective assistance to or for them without their involvement, (d) the idea that the point of rebuilding neighborhoods is to make the poor more self reliant, and, (e) the notion that in order for neighborhood redevelopment to be sustainable, there must be home and business ownership and management at the local neighborhood level.

Rebuilding must start at the neighborhood level

Whether we are fighting poverty or rebuilding inner city blighted communities, the logical starting point should be at the neighborhood level. Community life has traditionally been based on and within neighborhoods and without viable neighborhoods, such community life would be impossible. We have dedicated a whole chapter on neighborhoods. In a preceding section, we emphasized the idea that the collapse of traditional neighborhoods and their support systems created many social and economic problems for the poor amongst us. This assumption, on our part, leads us to the proposition that for any assistance to the working poor to have the desired effect, it would be

12

necessary that we also improve the physical location of the poor along with any other improvement we may make to the individual. Accordingly, our efforts and the proposals we have made to rebuild depressed communities and neighborhoods are based on and in neighborhoods - neighborhoods as places where people live!

The linkage imperative

The concept and the theme of linkage run through this entire book. We argue that linking all the efforts, resources and facilities required for rebuilding the poor communities is a pre-requisite to effective neighborhood development. We therefore link people to neighborhoods and neighborhoods to people, programs to people and then people to programs and neighborhoods. It is necessary and useful that we eliminate both conceptual and operational dichotomies we seem to have created over the years between the individual and neighborhood.

We seek as much complementarity, if not integration, of all human and physical development programs and activities intended to benefit the working poor and their neighborhoods. People live in communities and neighborhoods which are made up of and for people. It is not feasible to have neighborhoods without residents or have residents without neighborhoods. It is for this reason that we consider our past and current efforts to assist the poor or redevelop depressed inner city neighborhoods to be fundamentally flawed. The flaw is in the fact that there has not been proper linkages between human improvement activities and the physical rehabilitation of the particular neighborhood.

The working poor are a permanent feature of our society

A third theme is that that group of our fellow citizens we have designated as the working poor are going to remain with us. They are not going to disappear. If we accept that they are not going to disappear, we must also reckon with another distinct possibility that if all things remain equal and in the context of US income distribution as mapped out in our schematic construct (Figure I), we would expect those designated as income group C to pretty much remain what and where they are economically. We would not expect their income to double up in any foreseeable time to upgrade them to lower or middle class people. Neither would we expect them to ever uproot themselves and follow the middle class to the suburbs! Regrettably, we have to consider them to be economically stuck exactly where they are - at least for the foreseeable future. This unfortunate economic circumstance prevents them from fleeing to anywhere else. Ironically, this unfortunate circumstance makes them uniquely suited to form the bases for redeveloping our depressed communities and neighborhoods.

The primacy of self reliance

Our fourth theme deals with our affirmation of what we consider to be the natural balance between what the public support can and should do for the individual on one hand and what the individual can and should do for self-support on the other hand. Just as there are moral and legal reasons for public and charity support for the poor, there are corresponding individual responsibilities that are inherently residual to the individual. Among them is the individual responsibility to control, shape, or, at the very minimum, help shape one's destiny and those external forces that impact on oneself. In other words, effective assistance to and for the working poor must be based on the efforts of the individual to help and improve oneself.

Throughout this book, we have argued that the working poor should

14

be allowed to or let do for themselves what you and I do or try to do for them. Let us start by acknowledging the realities and the facts about poverty in the inner city neighborhoods. Even though we have devoted the next chapter to the problem of poverty, we must mention here that poverty in the poor, African American and Latino neighborhoods is alive and well. See Figures II, III and IV in Chapter Two. It is our view that all attributes and dimensions of poverty in some neighborhoods must be confronted. Painful as it may be, we must acknowledge that the current state of social and economic disarray in the inner city communities and neighborhoods cannot be exclusively explained by simply citing the exodus of white, and later, black middle class. This would be rather simplistic. Taken to its conclusion, this line of thinking would suggest that the working poor, unless helped, cannot help themselves. We are not persuaded by this view and the philosophy on which it is based. It would be too patronizing and diminishes individuals who otherwise could do some things for themselves but are now discouraged by those of us who insist on *doing* for and *giving* them as opposed to *encouraging* them to or insisting that they *do* for themselves.

Additionally, we should acknowledge that the failure of inner city neighborhoods has been made worse not just by the much blamed flight of the middle class but perhaps more so by the failure of the working poor themselves to take charge of their lives and communities by doing the little things which count and often make huge differences in one's neighborhood. Being poor is a lame excuse for not voting or attending school board's meeting or guiding young boys and girls or cleaning up one's vicinity or performing such other neighborly chores as would be expected of a good neighbor. That these neighborhoods have failed to provide community based support mechanisms cannot and should not all be blamed on the exodus of the middle class. This situation, we suggest, is also reflective of inability and/or unwillingness on the part of the poor and working poor themselves to take part in shaping their lives.

15

The necessity for neighborhood ownership and management

The fifth theme and its underlying assumption is that there must be neighborhood based ownership and management of economic and residential facilities and institutions as a prior condition for sustainable redevelopment of the poor inner city neighborhoods. We have made what we think is a compelling argument for home and economic ownership by the working poor citizens in their own neighborhoods. Our reasoning in this matter is arguably simple and to the point. That is, we cannot rebuild our inner cities with absentee landlords; neither can we depend on transient individuals to put the necessary effort and time to improve where they live. As indicated in the chapters on empowerment and home ownership, both Warren and Sherraden have given us some sound points and arguments on how ownership motivates owners to be more involved and participatory in the affairs of their communities and neighborhoods.

Until Jack Kemp, former HUD Secretary, came along with his ideas of making the working poor home owners, it was pretty much a non-subject. Even the nonprofit groups and agencies appear to have provided little, if any, advocacy for using ownership as a strategy for assisting the working poor and rebuilding inner city neighborhoods. Furthermore, neither the academic and urban research communities nor public bureaucracies appear to have put enough thinking and articulation to this idea of using home ownership by the working poor as a basis for both empowerment and rebuilding our depressed areas. Besides being piecemeal, traditional urban development strategies appear to have paid no attention to the importance of community based ownership and management of locally based resources. Put differently, this is to say that neighborhood economic and residential ownerships should be linked with and to the operation of the same in the particular neighborhood of their location. Home ownership must go hand in hand with and

16

simultaneously linked to economic ownership and operation. It is in such this linked ownership and local based management that we can realistically expect (a) the working poor to avoid sliding back into the bottom of poverty and (b) to sustain momentum in rebuilding our communities and neighborhoods.

Some definitional perspectives

The jargon we use to describe and define those programs and activities designed and intended to assist the poor to improve their neighborhoods and the quality of life need some clarification. Invariably, anti-poverty efforts may be expressed in such terms as community action, neighborhood revitalization, preservation or restoration, housing development or renovation, job training, and urban renewal and development.These terminologies are more descriptive than programmatic although some of them may often refer to the same public or private support effort. A diversity of individuals and groups (ranging from policy makers, scholars and practitioners to community activists) have contributed to the use and proliferation of these terminologies.

Our particular concern here is one of caution that the continued use of these different terms to describe what is basically the same phenomenon is not permitted to obfuscate and confuse what is essential in rebuilding or redeveloping our depressed communities and neighborhoods. Without some common understanding of neighborhood issues and problems, there would be less room for common understanding as to what should be done, how it should be done, who should do what, when and how. We suspect that this lack of common understanding of the issues and what could and should be done may often de-empower the working poor.

For instance, if we look at two recent and widely discussed theses of poverty - one by Charles Murray and the other by William Julius Wilson - it is not clear at all what we should do. On one hand, Murray does not appear to support any assistance to the poor while Wilson appears to support massive assistance to all poor people. Murray's thesis seems to suggest that if the government did not support the poor, young, handicapped and the unemployed, we would have less poverty as well as fewer poor people. (Murray:1984). After what is easily an excellent elucidation of the problems of the poor, Wilson has (in one of his chapters) suggested some public policies favoring full employment, unemployment insurance, family support, community revitalization and emphasis on greater inner city ethnic diversity. (Wilson:1987)

Turning to the other key terms used in this book, the reader should note that most of the key terms have been defined when and where used or in the context in which they appear. However, it is important that we mention here that the terms "community" and "neighborhood" are widely used throughout the book and that they are intended to complement one another and operationally convey the same meaning. They are not only the most common and useful terms in this book but also provide organizational and geographical cohesiveness to the programs and activities which constitute the essence of rebuilding our depressed neighborhoods. Moreover, the terms do also depict both the physical and demographic settings within which ownership and operation of resources and facilities are carried out.

One other attribute of the term "neighborhood" that requires a mention here is our attempt to operationalize this concept. That is to say, to make the idea of a neighborhood more practical. In this regard, we have embraced and expanded Donald Warren's definition and description of neighborhoods as being equal to *elementary-school districts - roughly one square-mile - area usually comprised of 1,000 families* (Warren:51-53). We prefer to expand this definition of the neighborhood for several reasons. First, the school district is already established and from time to time, we shall refer to it as the *school neighborhood*. Secondly, the school district is already an operational entity which citizens understand. Thirdly and though somewhat expanded, the school

18

district has an identifiable geographical and demographical size which is assumed to be able to accommodate certain community and neighborhood activities. Because school districts already exist and are widely used all over the country, there is no need to re-invent some other community or neighborhood entity for such community functions as meetings, voting, sports and other civic functions and activities.

Organization of the book

This book is made up of eleven chapters. In the first four chapters, we set the stage for redeveloping working poor communities and neighborhoods. This is done by posing poverty as the problem which must be solved by making the working poor more self reliant. To make the working poor more self supporting, we suggest a linkage of the public assistance they get as working poor persons to engaging in physical improvement of the neighborhoods where they now live. We include empowerment of the working poor in this phase of setting the stage because we regard it as the engine power without which the vehicle cannot move. Finally, there is a need to plan and implement programs and activities for rebuilding these communities.

The middle three chapters deal with the proposals we have advanced as the solutions to the problems of the working poor. These three chapters spell out what must be done, who should do what, where and in what sequence to rebuild the working poor neighborhoods. What must be done comes in two forms. First, those particularly involved, the working poor, must be converted to stakeholders in their communities and neighborhoods. This would be done by and through home and economic ownership. Secondly, realistic income generating activities and programs must accompany neighborhood based ownership.

Because we are dealing with poor people, the last two chapters articulate and outline the type of support that neighborhood rebuilding efforts will need in order to succeed. These support mechanisms include neighborhood based system of communication to inform and motivate individual and group self-reliance, neighborization of social and human services to provide bridges and sustenance for individual and group during the transition period - from public dependence to self-dependence.

Summary of the chapters

The first chapter highlights the problem and nature of community and neighborhood redevelopment, states the purpose of the book, outlines basic themes on and around which the book is based and organized, provides definitions perspectives. Chapter two explores the nature, extent and impact of poverty in America with particular reference to the working poor. Because of its impact on both inner city residents and neighborhoods, poverty is posed as the central problem to be resolved in order to rebuild the depressed areas. In addition to laying out the physical setting of neighborhoods, chapter three makes a serious attempt to operationalize the concept of 'neighborhood'. It explores the key functions, attributes and types of neighborhoods and how these relate to the rebuilding effort or needs and aspirations of the working poor.

Chapter four makes the case for empowerment. It enumerates numerous sources and types of power and influence for the working poor to tap. The main theme though is that before the working poor can be counted on to make complete use of these sources of power and influences, they must be empowered. Empowerment is viewed as a pre-requisite to effective and sustainable redevelopment of depressed areas. The chapter concludes by discussing some actual and potential difficulties that the working poor and people of color are likely to encounter while attempting to be empowered.

Chapter five on the other hand outlines and discusses the process and some techniques of community planning and the implementation of community planning. For the purpose of this book and as a general guide, a survey of community needs and resources or, simply, community resource assessment, is intended to precede community planning. Establishing programmatic goals and objectives, will facilitate program linkage and implementation.

Perhaps the single most important point made in this book is the proposal for home ownership by the working poor discussed in chapter six. Home ownership empowers the working poor by making them owners who, like other owners anywhere, can be counted on to care for, maintain and rebuild where they live. Home ownership is considered and presented as the basis for sustainable neighborhood redevelopment. Accompanying home ownership is economic ownership and operation which is discussed in chapter seven. The point here is that sustainable rebuilding of our inner city poor areas requires that the majority of the residents in these areas own where they live as well as having a major say in the major economic decisions of the community. While home ownership breeds neighborhood roots which roots sustain interest and commitment in the neighborhood, economic ownership and management creates sustenance without which no community or neighborhood can survive. Supplementing ideas and themes discussed in chapter seven, chapter eight outlines alternative types and sources of community investment such as "sweat equity."

Chapter nine is on communication for neighborhood redevelopment. Because of the overwhelmingly negative reporting and depiction of the working poor areas and especially where and when such areas are black and latino, it is necessary to counter the negative reporting by positive reporting. In particular, the chapter suggests a neighborhood based communication network to counter or minimize the damage caused by the mainstream media abuses of the working poor and people of color. Positive communication about the working poor and their neighborhoods will go a long way in building pride in themselves, their neighbors and their neighborhoods.

Chapter ten, on social and human services, visualizes these services as bridges (and temporary mechanisms to support the working poor during the transitional period) from dependency to self reliance. The chapter argues that social and human services should be understood and practiced as a society's mechanism for transforming the working poor from their current social and economic dependency on to more self supporting status.

The final chapter presents outlines and brief discussions of some thirteen common sense-based basic steps that any neighborhood can and should use to rebuild itself. These are, in our view, the real ABC's for inner city neighborhood redevelopment. Given that we are talking about and have targeted the working poor, there cannot be many and better substitutes for common sense. Indeed, some of the proposed steps are applicable to all types of neighborhoods. But the important variable here is to ensure that the content and direction of local public policy reflects these basic steps.

The Problem of Poverty in America

Introduction

Existence of poverty in some American urban communities and neighborhoods is not a new phenomenon. Over the years, the existence of poverty has given rise and rationale to a variety of efforts to curb it or to assist those who have been entrapped in it. Some of the efforts have sought to curb poverty by focusing on the individual while others have focused on the physical setting. Relief of individual poverty has generally attempted to transfer resources to the poor person in the form of cash grants, vouchers, goods and services, employment and/or training so as one can make their own income. While it is natural to anticipate certain types of outcomes as a result of training or retraining done, it is not always clear what it is one expects or should expect when an individual is eligible and receives assistance in the form of cash, vouchers, or goods and services.

Similarly, when the effort to relief poverty focuses on improving or changing the physical environment where the working poor live, it may take different forms. In many instances, improving the physical setting where the working poor live is and has been synonymous with low income housing development. Here, too, it is not clear as to what it is we expect to happen after the poor person has been thus housed. It would seem reasonable though that one should expect some type of an outcome from the effort thus made. The notion of connecting or linking assistance - training or subsidies or income transfers - to some specifiable outcome is the real task of this book. Implicit in assisting a poor individual (where that individual is physically and mentally fit) is the expectation that, even when not so specifically stated, the individual thus assisted or benefited will some how use such assistance or its results to overcome the prevailing difficulties or at least learn to deal with them in a manner that improves his/her living conditions. By its very nature, the search for improved living conditions requires that the changes and improvements thus made on the person of the poor individual be correspondingly replicated in the physical setting or environment of that individual. This is the linkage that we seek in this book.

The primary purpose of this chapter is therefore to determine and identify the working poor and why they are considered essential to the continuing effort to rebuild poor urban neighborhoods and communities. In Chapter one, the working poor were defined as those Americans whose annual incomes remain below the official poverty threshold even though they may have worked throughout or most of the year. The process of identifying the working poor starts with some highlights of the main attributes and parameters of poverty in America. These characteristics include the meaning and threshold of poverty, its extent and distribution as well as the efforts that have been made to reduce poverty. After identifying the working poor, the chapter also attempts to sketch out a niche for the working poor within the American free enterprise system.

Definitional and historical perspectives on poverty

Contemporary American responses to incidences of poverty appear to be continuously influenced by many religious ideas and beliefs, values and attitudes as well as laws emanating from the ethnic mosaic that makes America what it is. Some of the prevailing attitudes and values are said to have emanated from Christian and Buddhist traditions as well as the English Public Poor Relief Provisions of 16th century." (Weaver and Magid:8). In religious terms and in some sectors, poverty has at times been equated with "sanctity" as may be "exemplified by the austerity of priests, monks, and nuns." In secular terms, and as was provided under some amendments to the English Poor Law, "pauperism was equated with crime and treated accordingly by punitive and repressive measures." (Weaver and Magid:8). But the type and nature of the poverty to which we are referring here is an enormously complex phenomenon with religious, social, political and economic implications and dimensions.

One side of our interest in poverty here is in that condition of living in which there are individual and neighborhood social, political and economic deficiencies. To that end, we have adopted and amended Robert Straus's definition of poverty. He has described poverty as the "deprivation of those minimal levels of health, housing, food, education and recreation compatible with the contemporary technology, beliefs and values of a particular society in a specific locality." (Weaver and Magid:7). While adopting this definition, we have substituted the term "absence" for "deprivation." The significance of the word `absence' is that while one may be deprived of something, it is also possible that one may, on their own, fail to make use of available resources and opportunities in which case the notion of deprivation may be a misnomer.

The other side of our interest in poverty is in posing it as the multidimensional problem we face as a society. It is from this perspective that the book draws its meaning, namely, that it represents an effort to set out, describe and detail the process by and through which the said problem can and should be tackled. Much as we must not disclaim our basic interest in the subject of poverty (because it constitutes the problem we seek to resolve), we must reiterate that this book is about how we may go about the process of curbing poverty. That being the case, let us start by providing a brief summary of historical influences which appear to have shaped and sustained our thinking on the matter of poverty.

Robert Straus points out that much of contemporary American thought and approaches to the existence of poverty has been greatly influenced by the ideas and views of Thomas Malthus, Karl Marx, Herbert Spencer and William Graham Sumner. These are nineteenth century personalities and philosophers. Only two, Spencer and Sumner barely made it to twentieth century - one to 1903 and the other 1910. Straus has summarized their views as follows:

> Poverty (as seen by Thomas Malthus) was the result of an inexorable law of nature - the tendency of population to outstrip the means of subsistence. Karl Marx viewed poverty as inherent in the capitalistic economy which he saw as a method of exploiting the poor and maintaining the vast majority of the people in a precarious economic existence. Herbert Spencer, influenced profoundly by Charles Darwin, found poverty to be the result of natural forces in the struggle for existence, with the fittest surviving and the unfit tending to be eliminated.
>
> According to W. G. Sumner, the 'forgotten man' is the real victim of poverty. Sumner's forgotten man, however, played a very different role from that of the destitute...[he] described his forgotten man in situational terms. When A observes that X has a problem, Sumner noted, A discusses it with B; then A and B propose a law whereby A, B and C or, more frequently, C alone shall be obliged to do something for X. C, not X, is the forgotten man and, in Sumner's terms, the real victim of poverty. "(Weavery & Magid:9).

Perhaps it should not be surprising at all that most of these ideas and attitudes towards the poor are still current and that they easily bring back the memories of the 1980's when it was fashionable not only to ignore the poor but also to heap scorn on them at times. Going by what appeared in the media, one is confronted by hordes of academic and public commentators (especially those of conservative persuasions who share almost identical views with William Graham Sumner regarding poverty in America. Elaborating on Sumner's ideas further, Straus adds that:

> C is the simple, honest laborer ready to earn his living by productive work; he is independent, self- supporting and asks no favors. Every particle of capital which is wasted on the vicious, the idle, and the shiftless [X], is taken from the capital   available to reward C who is the independent and productive laborer." (Weaver and Magid: 9-10)

It would therefore seem to us that prevailing American ideas (and, therefore, the accompanying efforts) to fight poverty and assist the poor have not yet overcome historical myths, stereotypes and influences which have often distorted clear understanding of the nature of poverty in general and in particular among people of color.

In a book that should be a required reading for those academic researchers and public policy makers who deal with the problem of poverty and design our system of public welfare, Michael Sherraden (1991:35-45) has delineated what he considers to be the two main theoretical approaches to the problem of poverty in America and the ensuing attempts to alleviate that poverty. Citing much of the rather voluminous literature available on this subject, Sherraden identifies and contrasts those theories which focus on individual behaviors and those which focus on social structures as the basis of understanding and explaining the incidence of poverty. In passing, it may be noted that this theoretical delineation, though not in the same format, somewhat corresponds to our earlier remarks on linkages between the individual poor person and his/her physical setting.

It is not our intention to discuss these theories in any particular details. Our purpose is sufficiently served by simply identifying them as alternative ways of understanding and explaining poverty. Such cursory reference to Sherraden's work does not, of course, do any justice to the book. It is an excellent and succinct discussion of how the poor could be assisted to own assets. He has grouped together those theories which use individual behaviors or attributes (e.g socioeconomic class, geography, race, ethnicity, gender) as bases for examining and explaining the nature, origin and pattern of poverty. These theories include theories of choice, expectancy, attitudes, motivation and human capital. And a quick scrutiny of the theories reveals that they are mainly based on the assumption that individuals make decisions according to their interests and choices. Allowing for minor variations and emphases here and there, the premise underlying and tying these views together is that poverty is related to an individual's behavioral attributes and shortcomings. Also, of noteworthy is the fact that most of these views, as presented by Sherraden, are closely associated with the names of Malthus, Darwin and Sumner.

Turning to Sherraden's second group of theories, these theories attempt to explain poverty in terms of what the social system does to the individual behavior. The main thrust of these theories is that prevailing societal structures at a given time are unfair to poor people and that particular conditions in society at given times and places are the causes of poverty. This line of thinking suggests that unproductive or undesirable behaviors are caused by structural attributes of society. In other words, unproductive behaviors should be related to the rise of poverty. Among the theorists associated with structural views of poverty, Sherraden has mentioned Karl Marx and his followers, Max Weber, the New Dealers, Michael Harrington of *The Other America* and William Julius Wilson of *The Truly Disadvantaged*.

In addition to recognizing the need to *integrate* and/or *link* these two major systems of thinking about the poor and poverty, Sherraden also laments that "only limited progress has been made in this direction". (1991:38). The limited amount of integrative work done in this respect is attributed to Max

28

Weber, Ralf Dahrendorf and William Julius Wilson. (1991:39).

While we are still worrying about ways to integrate individual and structural focused theories of poverty, we want to revisit Robert Straus' view of American individualism and its implications. (Weaver & Magid:10). He points out that historically, Americans have always valued individualism and, stemming from the value of individualism, there has always been this tendency of looking at the individual rather than the group. Without having to declare our agreement or disagreement with Straus' observation that the values of rugged individualism do indeed appear to contradict the norms which support a publicly funded search for a solution to a group problem of poverty, we must affirm what we consider to be the natural balance between the public and individual domain. That is, the natural balance between the public support and the individual self-support. Just as there are moral and legal reasons for public support for the poor, there are corresponding individual duties and responsibilities that are inherently residual to the poor individual. Among them is the individual responsibility to control, shape or, at the very minimum, help shape one's destiny and those external forces that impact on oneself. In other words, effective assistance to and for the poor must be based on the poor individual's efforts to help and improve oneself.

Measuring poverty

Although there were attempts to measure poverty dating back to the turn of the century (Sherraden:21), it was not until 1959 that official poverty data was first collected, tabulated, defined and used to establish a national poverty threshold. At the time, there were almost 40 million Americans classified as poor because their annual income fell below the newly established

Figure II

Number and Percent of Poor Americans:1974-1990

Year	Number	%
1974	23.370	11.2
1976	24,975	11.8
1978	24,497	11.4
1980	29,272	13.0
1982	34,398	15.0
1984	33,700	14.4
1986	32,370	13.6
1988	31,878	13.1
1990	33,585	13.5*

Source: US Dept of Commerce, Bureau of the Census.
Money Income and Poverty Status in US: 1988. p.12.
*US Dept. of Commerce, Current Population Reports
Consumer Income, *Poverty In the U.S: 1990*, 8/91, p.4

poverty threshold. Insofar as measures of poverty reflect minimum cost of goods and services needed by individuals to maintain a decent standard of living, we consider such measures reasonable. In measuring poverty, the OMB makes year to year adjustments for inflation to the poverty thresholds (established in 1959) and based on official consumer price index (CPI). Using this criterion, the number of Americans falling below the poverty line had declined from 39.9 million in 1959 to 24.1 million in 1969 - a decrease of about 40 percent. (Bureau of Census: 1988:12). That decline in poverty rates during the 1960's was at least partially due to government expenditures for the war on poverty programs. As shown on Figure II, both the rate and the numbers of poor Americans fluctuated from a low of 11.2 percent in 1974 to a high of 15 percent (numbering some 34.4 million Americans) in 1982. The number of poor Americans have remained well above 30 million throughout much of the 1980's. Indeed, one observer has described the decade of the 1980's as the era of the *capitalist blowout* when the rich got richer and nearly everyone else paid the price! (*NY Times Magazine*: 6-17-90:26). Obviously, those affected most were the traditionally poor in the black and latino communities.

Distribution of poverty by race

Figure III highlights poverty rates and poverty distribution among the three major racial groups in America for 1979, 1985 and 1990. Although both the numbers and rates of poverty among the races appear to correspond to the general pattern of poverty in the US, it is clear from these data that over these years and beyond, black people and other people of color have not fared as well economically as whites. There can be no argument that the reasons for these discrepancies are many and varied. But among such reasons, we consider racial discrimination against people of color to be the principal factor for the disproportionate number of African Americans living at poverty level. Another reason may be found in the fact that poor people (regardless of ethnic background) have a tendency of not functioning in their best economic interests when they need to. For instance, even as consumers, they do indeed possess the power of their spending dollars which they generally do not use for bargaining purposes. In 1988, there 21.7 million whites, 7.1 million blacks and 4.3 lations within the $5,000 to $14,999 income bracket. The mean family income for all three ethnic groups in the $5000 to $14,999 income bracket was:

Figure III

The Number of Poor by Race: 1979, 1985 and 1990

Race	1979 No.	1979 %	1985 No.	1985 %	1990* No.	1990* %
Nonwhite	10.7	36.8	8.9	31.3	9.8	31.9
White	16.8	8.9	22.9	11.4	22.3	10.7

Source: Edwin Mills & Bruce Hamilton, *Urban Economics*, Glenview, Ill.,Scott, Foresman & Co.,1989:169-171
*US Dept. of Commerce, Current Population Reports Consumer Income, *Poverty In the U.S: 1990*, 8/91,p.4

about the same. (Bureau of Census, 1988:41). What has been and continues to be significant is the rate of poverty among these groups. For instance, in 1979 and 1985, there were, respectively and proportionately, four and three nonwhite persons within the official poverty threshold for every one white person in poverty.

Additionally, it should be noted that poverty is not confined only to the inner city areas and neighborhoods. Actually, there is poverty in all types of neighborhoods. In 1990, 59.0% of the nation's 12.7 million poor residents of poverty areas (poverty area is defined as an area of high concentration of poverty) lived in poverty areas while 28% lived outside metropolitan areas and 13% lived in suburban poverty areas. More than any other poor group, poor Blacks were more likely to be concentrated in the central city poverty areas. (Current Population Reports: Consumer Income: Poverty in the US:1990, p.6).

Figure IV

Suburban Poverty Per Capita

Suburban Town	Income in $	Population	% Black
Alorton, IL	5,795	2,720	68
Bell Gardens, CA	5,337	37,030	79
Camden, NJ	6,304	82,440	53
Centerville, IL	6,341	4,400	89
Coachella, CA	6,185	13,350	1
Compton, CA	6,777	93,850	75
Cudahy, CA	5,170	21,020	1
East St.Louis, IL	5,973	49,250	96
Florida City, Fl	6,490	6,510	60
Ford Heights, Il	4,943	5,240	99
Huntington Park, CA	6,298	55,050	0
Kinlock, MO	6,823	4,920	99
Robbins, IL	7,037	8,800	98
South El Monte, CA	7,100	17,980	0
Venice, IL	6,581	3,810	70

Source: *NorthStar News and Analysis Vol.1, #.2* 8/1989,p.6.

As Figure IV indicates, there are suburban communities whose 1985 poverty and poverty rates far exceeded that of some traditional areas of poverty. The one variable though that appears to remain constant in these instances is that the majority of these suburban poverty areas are either predominantly or wholly black or latino which fact keeps them in line with the national trend in poverty rates among African Americans and Latinos. It is also in keeping with our earlier point that when considering poverty and poverty rates among African Americans and Latinos, race must be taken as one of the principal factors.

A second principal factor (discussed in the chapter on empowerment) is reflected in our amended definition of poverty. Here, we refer to the inability or unwillingness of the poor to use available resources and opportunities to their advantage. Much as we agree that the poor have been indeed deprived, it is difficult to accept the idea that the poor and minorities have taken full advantage of all that is available or could be available to them including the proper use of their raw political potential or consumer dollars. (Jencks & Peterson:357-71)

ink fighting poverty to neighborhood redevelopment

Fighting poverty and community redevelopment should be linked. The person who lives in a depressed neighborhood is inseparably tied to the physical environment that surrounds him. It is not practical to successfully (although numerous attempts have been made) rehabilitate one and not the other. And yet, that seems to be the thrust of many of the current and past public assistance programs and activities. As viewed here, fighting poverty (or assisting the poor) is inseparably entertwined with the search for the physical improvement and redevelopment of the poor neighborhood.

Among the many social, economic, technological and legal

developments that have taken place in United States during the last three decades or so, three of them are of particular interest to us because of their relevance and impact on both the number of poor and rates of poverty. One, the development or emergence and crystallization of a publicly supported segment of Americans amongst whom a disproportionate number of black and latino citizens is included. (This, the so called *underclass*, is well discussed by Wilson, 1987 and Jencks & Peterson, 1991). But unlike these and the other authors (e.g. Murray), we consider racial discrimination to be the main reason for the over-representation of blacks and latinos both in absolute numbers of poor and rates of poverty.

The second and the third developments, reflected in Figure V, are the urbanization and deindustrialization of America and the subsequent urban congestion, decay and flight of manufacturing jobs. As Figure V indicates, central city population decreased by 25% while suburban ring population increased by over 40% between 1950 and 1980; manufacturing based employment in the central cities decreased by over 27% while suburban based manufacturing employment increased by almost 47%. Similar decreases and increases are evident in retailing, wholesaling and services. As if this out-of-central city movement wasn't bad enough, the emigration of jobs and employment opportunities to foreign countries made a bad situation worse. While a central city resident may have contemplated following a job to the suburbs, that very thought was totally out of question when the plant relocated to Taiwan or Mexico. (Mills & Hamilton: 1989: 38-67; *Star Ledger*: 7/23/89 & 11/8/87:81).

Undoubtedly, these developments have negatively impacted on both the content and quality of life in the poor neighborhoods. Apart from the deindustrialization of American central cities, the flight of employment opportunities to out-of-state and overseas and the debilitating use of drugs and crime rates, the quality of urban life has additionally been worsened by suburban gentrification (See Figure IV), environmental pollution, the farm

34

crisis and the disappearance of the small farmer, the public debt, and the withdrawal of federal block grants. These are some of the major factors which have contributed to the general decline of the quality of life in the urban areas. (Fusfeld:41-44; Ford Foundation, 1989:50-67). Although each one of the factors cited has been and continues to be important in its own way, particular emphasis must be given to `plant closings' because of their immediate and particularly pernicious and disabling effect on the working poor and the minorities.

Table V

Urbanization of America
Population & Employment in Selected SMSA's :1950-1980

Item	1950		1960		1970		1980	
	C.C.	S.R.	C.C	S.R.	C.C.	S.R.	C.C.	S.R
Popul.	53.3	42.7	49.2	50.8	43.1	56.9	39.9	60.1
Employ.								
-Mfg	63.3	36.7	56.5	43.5	51.0	49.0	46.1	53.9
-Retg	74.4	25.6	65.3	34.7	52.2	47.8	46.6	53.4
-Serv	80.8	19.2	75.2	24.8	64.2	35.8	58.2	41.8
-whsl	87.1	12.9	80.4	19.6	65.5	34.5	57.3	42.7
Total	70.1	29.9	63.1	36.9	54.6	45.4	49.5	50.5

Key:C.C.=Central City; S.R.=Suburban Ring; Pop. in millions
Source:Edwin Mills & Bruce Hamilton, *Urban Economics*, Glenview, IL ,Scott, Foresman & Co. 1989: 89.

A note on fighting poverty in America

In reviewing America's attempts to fight poverty and/or redevelop the depressed neighborhoods and communities, one is immediately struck by the numerous instances of repeated attempts to revive the past as the answer to contemporary problems of poverty and community development. The last 30 years (start with Harrington's *The Other America* through President Johnson's *war on poverty* and on to the damn-the-poor Reagan's era) have witnessed varying efforts to help the poor and their communities. Partly spurred by Harrington's widely read book, the civil rights movement, and urban riots of the 1960's, the economic hopelessness among the poor, the moral imperatives of the situation, and political considerations, the federal government took the first serious measures to rectify the problems of urban America in the mid-1960's.

Starting in the mid-1960's, the federal government offered several categorical grant programs to urban communities across the country. The programs

> included Urban Renewal, Model Cities, programs for constru-
> ction of water and sewer facilities administered by HUD,
> loan programs for various rehabilitation projects, loan prog-
> rams for public facilities and other prescriptions to cure the
> ailing cities. (Stutz: V-5-B).

When these programs were translated into anti-poverty activities, they not only generated a great deal of local political activities and controversies but also helped train some poor people, rehabilitate some buildings, supplement and support local school education offerings, relocate displaced poor people and families when the neighborhood housing projects were torn down, and create jobs sometimes through payroll padding and at other times through genuine economic development initiatives.

As for the cost of these programs, we do not have a final figure, if there is one. But in a number of instances, it has been estimated that in 1964 alone, $31 billion were earmarked for federal anti-poverty programs and $54.6, $98.0, $152.9, and $149.9 billions for 1968, 1973, 1978 and 1983 respectively. (Task for Force Economic Growth and Opport. 1965:1, Levitan : 1990 :31). President Reagan terminated anti-poverty and other revenue sharing programs when he came to office in 1981. These cut backs had the effect of increasing both the numbers and rates of poverty during the latter part of the 1980's. But even before these Reagan cut backs came into effect, we should note here that the number of poor families increased from 5.3 million to 6.85 million between 1971 and 1981 (a 29% increase) while the rate of poverty increased by 12% during the same period. (Current Population Reports, Consumer Income: Poverty in the US: 1990:P.7).

There are two points that should be noted with regard to public expenditures on poverty. First, even if we accept that the above expenditures were inadequate (as indeed many have argued), the simple fact is that almost five hundred billion dollars were spent in five years for purposes which were intended to be rebuilding of our decayed neighborhoods and helping the poor. And, as much as one can determine, most urban neighborhoods have become worse during the same period, and, as the numbers show, we continue to have more and more poor Americans who are actually poorer. And, without having to subscribe to most of the ideas and conclusions advanced by such "blame-the victim" scholars as Sowell, 1975, Murray, 1984, etc, we are compelled to concede in their favor the general conclusion that neither the poor themselves nor the depressed neighborhoods appear to have been well served by these expenditures. Shouldn't somebody have expected some tangible results from such expenditures?

The second point is actually a question. And the eternal question that one would always want to ask and answer is: what if a fraction of that one half trillion dollars was given in lump sums to those determined to be deserving and working poor to start or engage in self-employment activities of their choice? We visualize indefinite possibilities here. Among them, we may include ownership and creation of assets (properties, equipments, skills, etc.) by and for the working poor. (Sherraden: 1991:189-191). But for something like this to happen, two things must change. First, society's ingrained beliefs about the poor must change. (Other views on these beliefs have already been explored in the preceding section on definitional and historical perspectives on poverty). And, two, our public and nonprofit bureaucracies (which we suspect - not accuse - of actually maintaining and feeding off the working poor) would have to change too. The pertinent literature on the poor is truly enormous (American Assembly, 1969; Tabb, 1970; Task Force on Econ. Growth and Opportunity: 1965; US Chamber of Commerce, 1965; Harrington, 1962; Levitan: 1969,1987, 1990; Wilson: 1987; Jencks, 1991). But we have made no attempt to discuss much of it in this book other than refer to it as it may help us define and delineate various attributes and parameters of community and neighborhood redevelopment. Poverty is not the subject of this book. It is the problem to be resolved and the book represents the attempt to layout and articulate the process of resolving the said problem. But the literature on community and neighborhood redevelopment, especially as that literature pertains to the African American and Latino neighborhoods, is either nonexistent or scant. Perhaps even scantier is the literature on Latino community development. With the probable exception of when lumped together with other minorities, there is hardly any literature to speak of on the development of Latino neighborhoods and communities.

Parts of the poverty literature we reviewed can be classified into one of three general orientations. One type is the standard academic literature which, as Staudt suggests, is rarely suitable for application partly because it is addressed to other academics and is heavily loaded with disciplinary jargon and language varies from discipline to discipline. The other part of academic litarature is that its "policy implications and recommendations, if they exist at all, are often limited." (Staudt:86). If Staudt is correct, then, one can safely assume that a significant portion of academic literature has been of much less value to the working poor and/or the local neighborhood program executive than is generally acknowledged.

As a second orientation in the poverty literature, we have determined that much of the research and writing produced by conservative scholars and think tanks has that clearly detectable strain of *blaming-the-victim* for being poor or black or female or all of them - failing to acknowledge and rectify those other factors which may have helped the poor to be or remain poor. This strain of fault finding theme (especially for people of color) appears to permeate throughout much of this type of literature. Thomas Sowell, Charles Murray and Daniel Patrick Moynihan would appear to fit in this orientation although Moynihan can at times appear as supporting our third orientation.

With regard to the third orientation, we find this literature to be essentially in opposition to the second orientation. The premise here, although almost never so explicitly stated, appears to be based on the notion that the working poor bear no responsibility in changing their condition or their uplift from poverty. It is similar to an *exempting-them* school of thought. Put in others words, this thinking would seem to exempt the working poor from bearing the primary responsibility in or of influencing and championing actual and possible solutions to their current predicaments. This type of literature may be exemplified by annual reports by such civil rights organizations as the Urban League, NAACP, religious groups, unions or such scholars as William Tabb, Patrick Moynihan and others. In contrast and as already said, our thesis in this book is that sustainable community and neighborhood development must be based on property owning working poor individuals and that such individuals must assume primary roles in the effort to improve their living conditions.

But before concluding this section, it would be helpful to revisit some points we have already mentioned. In particular, and as already implied, that we have little or nothing to show for the effort and resources expended over the years to fight poverty, one may be excused for wondering : how was this so called war on poverty lost? Granting the fact that there may not be a single or two explanations ,perhaps the experience of one state may suggest one of the clues. In this regard, Ohio's Office of Local Government Services, trying to assess the impact of their efforts and programs in 1978 seems to suggest one or two possible explanations. They noted that

While the intentions were well-founded, the substantial
changes programs sponsors promised failed to materialize
for a number of reasons. Each program operated independe-
ntly of the others, applications were frequently bogged down
in red tape and regulations and many cities distrusted the
federal programs, fearing they would forfeit local control of
improvement programs. (Stutz:V-5-B).

In recent years, many states have started requiring that able bodied recipients of public assistance go back to school or enter some training program or get a job (Rodgers, 1988:14-35; Levitan, 1990:167-175; Levitan, 1987:99-129). While these requirements may ultimately help make some of the individuals thus involved more self-supporting, one should not construe such measures, taken during economic hard times or under political pressure, as sufficient and sustainable substitutes for a national public policy which links and systematizes all programs and activities designed to assist the working poor.

Also noteworthy, and a subject we plan to discuss in later chapters is the fact that our public assistance philosophy and practices are geared to providing for the poor and the needy. We seek to transfer income from public coffers to individual pockets. And because it is only a transfer, it cannot, by its very nature, make permanent changes to the recipients. In fact, current welfare policy does not only fail to empower the poor to own anything, it prohibits ownership by the poor.

Finally, it is important to understand that whatever strategy one may use to rebuild depressed communities and neighborhoods, one must decide whether to recreate the past or try something different or new. And if the decision is to recreate the past, one must take into account the fact that more than 80 percent of us live in some type of an urban community now (Mills & Hamilton, 1989:38-43) and that urban life and communities of the 1980's and 1990'a are constantly besieged by drug wars and crime, homelessness, toxic waste, deficits and insolvent municipal governments. In more specific terms, attempting to rebuild a neighborhood with these types of problems requires

40

that we specify what it is we want. Do we want to:

(a)   re-industrialize the deindustrialized urban areas,
(b)   bring back the industries and job opportunities that
        fled the country,
(c)   clean up and rehab. the neighborhoods and leave it
        at that,
(d)   bring back the skilled and economically able of our
        citizens to urban areas,
(e)   eradicate and/or control drug lords and
        their merchandise,
(f)   or, may we ask, is any of this or all of it   what we
        should describe as community redevelopment?
        Or, exactly what is it that we should do?

Because there may not be complete answers to the questions we have posed, we suggest, as a starting point, that the search for a more practical and sustainable community redevelopment should be predicated on prior determination of whether it would be possible and desirable to re-establish or revive those industries which either left town or closed down. Most depressed communities have and continue to expend their limited resources and efforts to rehabilitating old buildings and neighborhoods in an attempt to lure some of the runaway or new businesses. While this sort of thing is laudable, there is no evidence available to us to suggest that it can be done and sustained in the low income urban communities. Whatever new or old strategy we may eventually pursue, it should be remembered that these communities and neighborhoods were once able to support themselves. But for a variety of reasons, they have now ceased to be viable communities and neighborhoods for living and raising families.

To reverse this situation, our options are clearly limited to (a) recreating the past, (b) keep on doing what we have been doing during the last 30 years, (c) develop or create something entirely different, or (d) redefine the problem, select, combine and refocus both the past and contemporary programs for assisting the poor and minorities. This book focuses on the last option listed above.

41

The Working poor

Counting the working poor

The ultimate value of this book is to suggest some specific ways and approaches by and through which we can reduce both the number of poor Americans and the prevailing rates of poverty. We have specified rebuilding communities and neighborhoods across urban America on basis of home ownership by that segment of our poor population which works throughout and/or much of the year. We have attempted to distinguish the working poor from the poor. In defining poverty as the absence of minimal levels of life essentials such as health, housing, food, education and recreation, we intended to convey the idea that while these essentials can be and, in fact, have been denied to certain groups and individuals, there are situations and times where and when working keeps you below the poverty threshold. When that happens and you have worked throughout or most of the year, you become a working poor.

For instance, of the 65.84 million families in the US in 1988, 4.45 million [or 6.8 percent] had a mean income of $7,500 while another 5.8 million [or 8.8 percent] earned between $10,000 and $14,999 annually. In raw numbers, these were 13.4 million persons in the first instance and another 16.9 million persons in the second instance making a total of 30.3 million persons whose lives depended on annual incomes that were less than $ 15,000. In 1988, there were 32 million poor people which translated into a 13.1% rate of poverty. The average poverty threshold for a family of four was $ 12,091 in 1988. (Census Bureau: 88:12).

Figure VI indicates that an average of 40% of the working poor worked during each of the preceding five years. Extrapolating from the data presented in Figure VII, it is determined that almost 66 % of the employable working poor

42

Figure VI

Number of working poor: 1986-1990

Year	Total no. of working poor	No. worked f/pt time	%	No. did not work	%
1990	21.8	8.8	40.4	13	59.6
1989	20.5	8.4	41.0	12.1	59.0
1988	20.9	8.4	40.2	12.5	59.8
1987	21.3	8.4	39.4	12.9	60.6
1990	21.3	8.9	41.8	12.4	58.2

Source: Bureau of Census,*Current Population Reports*, Consumer Income *Poverty in the US: 1990*, Series P-60, No.175., 8/1991. p.8

in 1989, over 41% were employed. To be sure, being a working poor is still being poor. But one must acknowledge that although the working poor make below poverty wages, they do pay their rents (subsidized or not) every month and every year. They do not own the apartments or the homes or the tenements in which they live. They are not able to buy a home or a condominium through the conventional market system because they are poor and yet they have been able to pay monthly rentals for the duration of their tenancy even if their rents may have been subsidized. This is the population targeted by this book. We have targeted them because we do believe that these working poor can and will do more for themselves with the resources that are currently expended on them or on their behalf than government agencies can or have been able to do for them thus far! The State of Washington has been piloting a similar idea where they give the unemployed one half of their annual benefits in a lump sum so that they can engage in self employment initiatives of their choice (*NY Times*, 5/16/90:1)

Figure VII
The Working Poor in 1989
(Number in Millions)

Number of poor aged 15 yrs and over	20.5	
Number of poor not employable	6.95	(33.9%)
Number of poor employable & worked	8.43	(41.1%)
Number of poor employable but didn't work	5.13	(25.0%)

Number of poor who worked year-round	7.0	
Number who worked full-time	4.6	
Total no. who worked part and full time	11.6 or 56.6%	

Source: Mishel & Frankel, *The State of Working America: 1990-91* Economic Policy Institute, Armonk, NY: M.E. Sharpe, 1991, p.180: Figure 6.17.

Neighborizing the working poor

A neighborhood view of the preceding account and numbers, may be accurately depicted by the following family's life. This family of three had a 1991 combined annual income of $14,990. The husband worked for $4.25 per hour for 43 weeks in 1991 and the wife worked for $4.00 for 48 weeks in 1991. He made $7,310 and she made $7,680 as both of them worked only parts of the year earning minimum or below minimum wages. They live in a two-bedroom apartment on the first floor of a 16-floor high-rise apartment building. There are ten such high-rise buildings standing or built adjacent to one another in this section of the the city.

For the two-bedroom apartment, the family's out of pocket monthly rent was $359 in 1991 while the actual monthly market rental value was $908. In other words, this family's monthly rental subsidy was $577. If the family's annual income was $10,000, the corresponding figures would have been as follows: market rental value would have remained the same ($908); out of pocket $210 and subsidy $698. Now, let us examine the higher income of $14,990 and see its possibilities. Without subsidy, the annual market rental value for this two-bedroom apartment would be $ 10,896 which was equivalent to 73% of the family's annual income. With the subsidy, they paid $4,308 which was only 28.7% of their income. To assist the family's cost of housing, the public paid $ 6,924 which was 46.2% of the annual cost of housing in 1991. To get this family's actual annual income equivalence, it would be necessary to add to these figures the cost of such other items as child allowance ($400), food stamps ($1,680), medical ($600) and utility expenses ($336) - which we estimate to be approximately $3,016). When all is added (and it is only an estimate) this family's income comes to about $24,930.

The 1920 households in this section or neighborhood are comprised of 7,680 people who live in these ten high-rise apartment buildings. Of the 1920 households 768 (40%) are one parent households, 921 (48%) two parent households, and the rest, 231 (12%) include others such as grand parents, seniors, aunts and uncles. Estimates are that of the 1920 house-holds, 1005 (52%) are working poor. That is, they work at least some part of the year and are also on some type of public assistance, at least some part of the year. The rest, that is, 644 (34%) are wholly on public assistance, 231 are seniors, handicapped and others. The remainder 40 (2%) households are either ineligble or have not sought and received public assistance or subsidy. Most of the working people poor who live in this neighborhood make less than $ 8,000 a year. They occupy such positions as may be found in the maintenance area, cleaning, janitorial, automobile garage, car washing, teacher aides, food, cooking and kitchen areas. Other characteristics of the poor and working poor neighborhoods including history, size, uses, behavioral and attitudinal traits are discussed in the next chapter.

The notion and practice of self reliance

Although conventional wisdom as well as human moral imperatives teach and expect us to assist and uplift the less fortunate amongst us, we want to add that providing assistance may not always be the best thing for the working poor. We argue and propose that the best way to assist the poor and the working poor in particular, is to make them self dependent so that they can do for themselves what others do or try do for them. But this is easier said than done. The first thing that one should note is that the working poor do not own any assets. Secondly, they are almost always paid less than other workers because they may lack job opportunities or the requisite skills or motivation or a combination of these. Or, perhaps, the condition of being poor and the way the society views the poor, may indeed, invite comparatively low wages.

It goes without argument that the cost of living does not make allowance for being a working poor or low income. The poor do not own supermarkets or apartment buildings. They pay as much, if not proportionately more, as the rest of us do. Those who own apartment buildings or operate supermarkets in the inner city neighborhoods, do so because they make profit. Like any good business operation anywhere, owning and operating residential and economic establishments in the poor communities and neighborhoods entitles the investors to a fair return for their investment. But the need for a fair return on the investment should be viewed in the context of inner city economic realities: high operating expenses, high crime rates, high rates of public dependence, unemployment and plenty of underutilized manpower.

When underutilized manpower, public dependence and unemployment are the general characteristics of a poor neighborhood, we can and in fact should make a case for introducing and linking minimum wage to asset building. Most wages in the inner city poor neighborhoods are either minimum or very near the minimum wage rates. It is not, therefore, a matter of choice as it is a fact of life. One way of dealing with it as a fact of life, is to change or increase it as has been proposed already. Another way would be to deal with it in some creative ways. To make minimum wage a more viable alternative to public assistance, it must be clearly linked to some complementary self-supporting activity such as owning a home or a business.

It is not enough to just extol the virtues of minimum wage without linking it to self-support building programs.

A self-supporting activity for a working poor family like the one described in the preceding section, is when and where the earned income is combined with the specific public entitlement to create the basis for acquiring and accummulating such assets as a home. Sherraden's idea of asset building reflects and emphasizes among other things such items as real property, savings, machines and equipment, durable household goods and so on. (p.100-105). How the person making minimum wage may end up owning any hard asset is discussed in lengthy details in chapters six, seven and eight.

Another likely and possibly persuasive side of the minimum wage debate is that an employer is entitled to as inexpensive manpower as the market can provide. Without that, no one can stay in business. The businessman, who, in this case, is also the employer of the minimum wage earner, is entitled to take the necessary measures to reduce his/her operating expenses. One way of doing that may be in the greater use of minimum wage earners as long as such workers are available and willing to take the offer. There are, of course, situations and chances of the working poor getting exploited by some employers. But again, this is where and when public policy intervenes. Government's proper role in this and similar situations is to make and enforce fair rules and regulations to govern the relationship between ownership, use and management of community based residential and economic institutions on one hand and those who work and patronize such facilities on the other hand.

It is in this sense that we believe the working poor can and must be empowered to participate fully in the free enterprise system. When fully informed and empowered, the working poor will use their labor and their consumer dollars to conduct either individual or group bargaining for what they deem to be in their interests. Organized labor collective bargaining offers an excellent operational model of mutually beneficial interactions between the working poor and would-be employers.

Too much public assistance and dependence, like too much charity, is likely to stifle individual initiatives. Regardless of the historical cause of the prevailing conditions of social, political and economic imbalances or unfairness, the individual thus disadvantaged retains the primary role and responsibility in rectifying or correcting the problematic situation. Self reliance, even with difficulties and hardships, is still a more effective long term solution for the problem of poverty than continued dependence on public and private charity. Being a rich country is not a sound argument or reason for creating and maintaining a system of dependence based on charity or sympathy for the working poor.

In the following chapters, we have argued and proposed that the best way to develop or redevelop some of the most blighted inner city neighborhoods is to make those who live there owners of where they now live. We have further argued that ownership of a home or an apartment is not by itself a sufficient condition for a community or neighborhood redevelopment. It is necessary that such home ownership be linked to other community and neighborhood redevelopment projects and activities in order to bring about some balance and sustainability in community development. In the preceding chapter, we set out a number of themes and assumptions on bases of which our proposals for both residential and economic ownerships are discussed and, hopefully, sustained. The following chapter sets out the physical environment and parameters within which redeveloping of the inner city areas would have to be carried out.

The Neighborhoods

The concept of neighborhood

A neighborhood is a small territorial unit within a larger community in which there is some sense of local unity and identity. Because a neighborhood is a small area, it permits and facilitates close contacts and communication among it residents. (Theodorson:273). These contacts and communications among residents promote that sense of local unity and identity. Two or more neighborhoods constitute a community. A community, on the other hand, may consist of several neighborhoods. It may also be described as an area with some distinguishing attributes "which may include distinct ethnic or economic characteristics (such as) schools or social clubs or boundaries defined by physical barriers such as highways...or other natural features". (Blackwell: 75:16). Conceptually, a community may have all or most of the attributes of a neighborhood but lack the benefits of closer interpersonal contacts and communication. Determining the proper size of a neighborhood can be deceptively difficult. What may be numerically acceptable as a neighborhood may lack either economic or cultural viability. Too often, neither pure numbers nor cultural homogeneity are adequate indicators or measures of a neighborhood viability. During the recent past and at the behest of HUD's model cities programs of the 1960's and 70's, attempts were made in Akron, Ohio to establish numerical sizes of urban neighborhoods. Some of the recommendations emanating from these programs suggested that neighborhoods should have a minimum of 20,000 people. (Report of the Committee on Citizen Participation:1973:27).

In determining neighborhood boundaries, the Committee recommended that serious consideration be given to natural features, common problems and citizens' perception of such boundaries. Similar efforts were made in Dayton, OH, where a neighborhood was intended to consist of 35 precincts. A precinct is the smallest unit in an electoral or political party structure process. (Successful Citizen Participation:1978:III-2). Using Elliot and Ali's estimates of the numerical size of a precinct which may range from a low of 200 to a high of 1,000 voters, Dayton's proposed neighborhoods would have populations of between 7,000 and 35,000 people. (Elliot & Ali, 1988:82). The figure of 7,000 is closer to our estimates referred to below. Other attempts to establish numerical and geographical sizes of neighborhoods have been made in Birmingham, Alabama, San Antonio, Texas and Portland, Oregon with varying successes and diversity.

Before discussing how useful the size and demographic composition of a neighborhood should be for our present purposes, we should mention that without economic viability, the operational meaning of any neighborhood is rather hollow. Any serious effort to reclaim most of the depressed urban neighborhoods must take economic viability into consideration. A Chicago community based group involved in various aspects of community and neighborhood development points out that in one predominantly minority Chicago neighborhood with a below-average household income in 1985, there were 70,000 residents, 5,600 owner-occupied housing units, 22,600 renter-occupied units, $583.3 million total household income, $53 million weekly food bill and a $36 million yearly household gas and electric bill for 1983. (Center for Neighborhood Technology: 1986:6). As these figures would appear to suggest, this Chicago neighborhood has seemingly a bigger economy than that of most towns and cities in Illinois. Seventy thousand people (even if they have similar economic or ethnic identities), would be too many to have and maintain mutual contacts and communication as was suggested in our definition. It would seem to us here that a neighborhood of this size, while demographically viable, should be regarded more as a community - meaning that it has smaller and more functional units within itself - than a neighborhood. Similarly, Dayton, Oh., with the proposed neighborhoods of between 7,000 and 35,000 people and St. Paul, MN. with its recommended neighborhoods of 20,000 and above, would be somewhat larger than what we consider to be a viable size and less complex neighborhood.

Towards operational neighborhoods

In Figure I, we delineated <u>four</u> income groups which are intended to correspond to the <u>four</u> types of neighborhoods mapped out in Figure VIII. The idea is to place income groups in their respective neighborhoods and communities. Thus, the top income Groups A and A2 in Figure I would be residents of neighborhood numbers 4 and 3 in Figure VIII. Similarly, the Lower middle class and low income people in Groups B and B2 of Figure I would be residents of neighborhoods numbered 2 in Figure VIII. And, finally, income Groups C and C2 in Figure I would be residents of neighborhoods numbered 1. Neighborhoods 4 and 3 are by far the best neighborhoods while neighborhoods 1 (one) would be the poorest. Neighborhood 1 corresponds to Warren's *anomic neighborhood* discussed later on in this section.

Figure VIII should be understood to be a conceptualized representation of a city of 135,000 people who live and sometimes work within its 18 neighborhoods. This city is demographically diversified. One third of its residents are African Americans, another third is Latino and the other third is white. Although there are integrated neigborhoods with more or less similar economic abilities, residential patterns of this city do appear to correspond to the national norm of ethnic break down and neighborhoods with blacks and latinos living in the more blighted areas and whites living in the better sections of the city.

Without diminishing the ethnic and economic attributes of these neighborhoods, we emphasize the functional adequacy of these demographic entities as neighborhoods. Like most old American cities, this one, too, would be experiencing some declining fortunes. Its manufacturing industries would have either declined or left town. The commercial and downtown business district of this city would have been hit hard by lack of sufficient dollars circulating in its neighborhoods. Most people, including those who live in the neighborhood 1 go shopping in the surrounding suburbs and malls. As a result, the poor neighborhoods of this city have been negatively affected.

To make the concept of neighborhood more precise and operational, we believe Warren's definition of a neighborhood as [equal to] an elementary-school district - roughly a square-mile - area usually comprised of about 1,000 families (Warren:1975:51-69), would be (with some adjustments) a more operationally useful concept. Assuming a family of four or five (and the typical working poor family is generally larger than the corresponding middle class family), this would make a neighborhood of approximately 4,000-5,000 individuals. In some ways and specifically as potential consumers (because poor folk are consumers), a neighborhood of 1,000 families may be viewed as rather too small. Instead, we have enlarged Warren's school district by 50% and retained the same family size. This enlarged concept of neighborhood would have 1,500 families and population ranges of between 6,750 and 7,500 individuals. As would be expected, some of the neighborhoods will be larger than others.

Even as we readily concede that an average population of 7,000 may not be a very viable number economically, we consider it sufficient to sustain

Figure VIII

NEIGHBORHOODS:

The Physical, Residential, Commercial and Industrial Layout

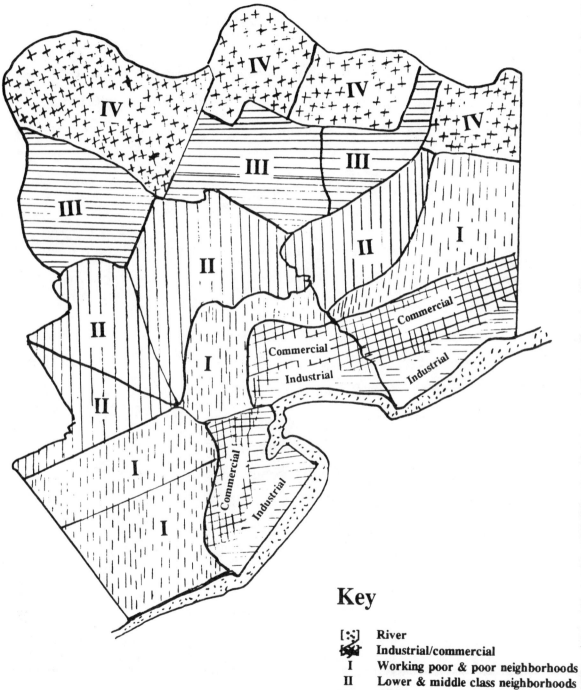

Key

[:·:] River
Industrial/commercial
I Working poor & poor neighborhoods
II Lower & middle class neighborhoods
III Middle class neighborhoods
IV Upper middle class neighborhoods

an owner-occupied neighborhood. For instance, the annual food bill for 1,500 families of four or five members would have been, at $150 per week per family in 1988, $46.8 million. Add to this figure other financial transactions in home maintenance, drug and hardware expenses, personal and property insurances, deli and restaurant operation, clothing and other wear items and you end up with a sizable amount. And, to borrow a term from the Center for Neighborhood Technology, this is no trivial matter. What this size of a neighborhood may lack in numbers may be made up in efficiency and manageability of neighborhood affairs.

The purpose of neighborhoods

Besides providing an organizational and geographical context for our operating themes outlined and discussed in chapter one, there are other fundamental functions of neighborhoods. Our discussion of such functions draws from Warren's conceptualization of neighborhood typologies. Although he has identified six key roles of neighborhoods in the lives of individuals and their communities, we refer only to one or two. One such a role is when and where neighborhoods serve as centers for interpersonal interaction. This is when neighborhoods provide frameworks for various local functions including interpreting and digesting events, acculturating and socializing their young ones, changing of values and translating the broader societal trends into a form that is meaningful and operational in terms of the local neighborhood. (Warren:54-55). Neighborhoods exert great pressure and influence on the inculcation and maintenance of basic community values.

Additionally, neighborhoods also provide a context for neighbors to exchange information or knowledge about anything ranging from raising children to figuring out how to compute income tax. Sometimes, neighbors do help their neighbors and, at other times, they do reach out to the larger society through neighborhood organizations. If these types of events take place, one can assume that neighbors have used their neighborhoods as a base for organizing to help themselves and others. (Warren:56-67).

We view the purpose of neighborhoods as described above to be one of cultivating and influencing community values and behavior among the residents and their neighborhoods. Traditional roles of traditional neighborhoods have become dysfunctional and failed to give the kind of support that individuals (poor or middle class) can only get from their neighborhoods. This failure was outlined in the chapter on poverty. Our interest in this chapter (and therefore in the book) is to attempt to suggest some ways of restoring the social stability of the old neighborhoods so that we can socially empower our working poor to pursue rewarding activities for their individual benefit and that of their neighborhoods. Social chaos and turmoil make other neighborhood pursuits difficult, if not impossible, to pursue. Using Warren's format, we have not only given brief descriptions of various types of neighborhoods but also identified the two types of neighborhoods on which we hope to focus. One is the good and working neighborhood and the other is the poor and blighted neighborhood.

Our description of neighborhood typologies begins by noting that the first type of neighborhood is close to being the ideal type of a neighborhood. This type of a neighborhood is not ordinarily accessible to the working poor. Our interest in this type of neighborhood is rooted in the fact that it has the type of neighborly attributes which we seek for the benefit of the working poor. This is the neighborhood Warren has been called the *integral*. He has labelled the poor and blighted neighborhood as the *anomic* neighborhood. The key point here is that most aspects of the integral neighborhood will not only cultivate and enhance social stability among the working poor but also provide the necessary physical setting for pursuing sustainable redevelopment of their neighborhood.

Our interest in the concept of a neighborhood is pegged, as it were, on its operational prospects for developing supportive environments for working poor people. Warren's casting of neighborhoods appear to have such attributes with the necessary operational readiness and adoptability. For instance, the school district is an established administrative entity which is recognized by most residents of the particular neighborhood. Most Americans live within some school district or parish somewhere. It is the place where they send their children to school. Oftentimes, children walk to school. It is their "school neighborhood". Residents know the teachers of their children and the teachers, in turn, know the parents and their children. As residents of particular school neighborhoods, one has to assume that these residents know and understand their physical and sociocultural environments - geographical and demographic - as well as how they relate to one another as neighbors in and around their particular school neighborhood.

Types of neighborhoods

The following delineations and descriptions of various types of neighborhoods have been influenced and guided by Warren's depiction of neighborhood typologies. (Warren:61-63). We accept Warren's idea that there exists overlapping between the meaning and operational use of the socioeconomic and political entities we describe as 'communities' and 'neighborhoods'. Put differently, that means that the two terms are often used interchangeably. We, too, have used the two terms to mean the same thing. Warren has delineated the following six types of neighborhoods. (Warren:18-24).

1. The integral neighborhood

The first type of neighborhood, labelled 'Janus-faced' is the *integral neighborhood*. Operationally, this type of neighborhood is able to simultaneously respond to and act on both internal and external situations. In this neighborhood, residents interact with one another and function cohesively within the neighborhood groups and organizations such as block clubs and PTA's. When and if the need arises, these neighbors not only turn out to help one another, but also unite to meet external challenges. In many ways, this type of neighborhood can be described as the ideal neighborhood where residents maintain internal and external ties for mutual benefits to their neighborhood and others.

Obviously, this is a good neighborhood. It comes through as a wealthy upper middle class neighborhood - classified as A and A2 in Figure I and number 4 in Figure VIII. It is certainly not where the working poor live. Nor is it where we are proposing they should live. But it has those neighborly aspects and attributes which the working poor would not only need but must also have before they can develop their neighborhoods to be more viable living places. Because of the neighborly characteristics of the integral neighborhood, we plan to use it as the model to emulate in rehabilitating the environmental and human conditions under which the working poor live.

2. The parochial neighborhood

The second type of neighborhood has been labelled the *parochial neighborhood*. This type of neighborhood, as Warren suggests, is a classic in certain ways. It has strong ethnic identities, homogeneous values and culture. Being so ethnic, homogeneous, cohesive and self-contained, this neighborhood unavoidably becomes insulated. It not only tends to duplicate institutions and structures of the larger society but also makes an attempt to provide for its residents' needs so that they do not have to go outside their neighborhoods to satisfy most of their needs. And although latino neighborhoods (like other minority neighborhoods) may be isolated by discriminatory practices, it appears to us that a number of latino urban neighborhoods do clearly manifest this type of insularity.

Unlike the integral neighborhood, parochial neighborhoods seem to us as the likely home of the poor, especially the immigrant poor. Indeed, the likely home of many working poor is such ethnic enclaves as Spanish Harlem or Chinatown. But because of other factors - some of which may be cultural, political, bias, legal or economic - the plight of the working poor in these neighborhoods has not been particularly visible. Sometimes, the working poor may not be exposed to the mass media. At other times, these neighborhoods do indeed provide the necessary assistance to their needy neighbors.

With regard to black neighborhoods, and without minimizing the existence of nearly all the attributes of parochial neighborhoods, the parochial designation may not be very accurate. For one thing, the practices of racial discrimination and segregation (so commonly and universally practiced against African Americans and their neighborhoods) have had particularly pernicious effects on black neighborhoods. Black neighborhoods are so economically and politically controlled, manipulated and exploited by the larger white society (Walton, 1975: 57-69) that it is unlikely that they could ever be viable without the residents first making full use of their political and economic power. This is something not just the blacks should do but also the working poor must do. They must agree to use the power of their votes and consumer dollars.

To summarize the parochial neighborhood, it should be noted that although the boundaries are imprecise, parochial neighborhoods may be easier to mobilize for or against a particular issue or situation because of the existing cultural, ethnic and value ties. Of great use to the working poor are the values, cohesiveness and neighborhood attachment characteristics of the parochial neighborhood. While de-emphasizing the insularity of the parochial neighborhood, these other attributes of the parochial neigborhood would be suitable means and efforts for rebuilding our blighted and run down communities and neighborhoods.

3. The diffuse neighborhood

In some ways, the *diffuse neighborhood* typifies both the spirit and practice of American individualism. Residents of this type of neighborhood are not poor; they appear to have more common characteristics with the middle class than with the poor. Their lives - especially social and cultural - are not necessarily tied or confined to their neighborhood. Some of the features of this neighborhood are similar to those of life in a dormitory. And although they appear to share similar social and economic background, this background does not appear to encourage many neighborhood face to face contacts.

Typically, this type of neighborhood appears to be similar to any new suburban or urban development. Or, for that matter, a public housing project in the inner city areas. There is potential here for shared values and homogeneity but there is little or no apparent neighborhood involvement. There also exists potential and susceptibility for external influences which may or may not be positive. Except where this type of neighborhood may be a result of new public housing development for the working poor and their dependents, it appears to have few or no redeeming features. There does not appear to be anything for the working poor to emulate here. The apparent lack of interest in community and neighborhood participation would appear to negate the entire effort set forth in our proposals.

4.The stepping-stone neighborhood

Warren has described this neighborhood as the *stepping-stone neighborhood*. This type of neighborhood may be known for its high degree of community activism by its highly mobile residents. People move in and out of the neighborhood frequently and, depending on who is moving in or out, one can expect varying degrees of involvement ranging from very involved to very uninvolved. As the name of the neighborhood suggests, community leadership in this type of neighborhood may be often motivated by ulterior motives. It is further noted that most active leaders in this type of neighborhood are those who are either motivated by career considerations or are attempting to pursue careers outside this type of neighborhood. In some ways, this would be a

59

changing neighborhood when the more mobile and more economically able would proceed on to presumably better situations. Those who may be left behind may be older or simply unwilling to move but not necessarily poor. Although this is the kind of neighborhood that could attract our working poor easily and in large numbers because of the prevailing mobility which creates additional space to be filled, we do not consider this neighborhood to be viable for community and neighborhood development. Unless otherwise stabilized (by halting this out/inward mobility), this type of neighborhood is not one on which we can build. It is too socially fluid.

One of our principal considerations in pursuing neighborhood redevelopment is stability of residential population. That is, we can count on those who have been empowered to be owners to stay on and take care of their properties. As stated previously, the working poor are preferred in this process of rebuilding of our run down neighborhoods precisely because they lack that economic and social mobility. Regrettably, they are stuck in the poor and non-stepping stone neighborhoods! This would not be a suitable model to emulate.

5. The transitory neighborhood

In many ways, *transitory neighborhood* is similar to the stepping-stone neighborhood. While the former experiences a high turn over of community leadership, the latter has a high residency turnover as families move in and out of this neighborhood. Family mobility may reflect economic changes or searches for better opportunities. But in either case, such mobility may in fact limit possibilities for one's involvement in their neighborhood. Rapid changes (for whatever reason) are not a good recipe for social and cultural stability saying nothing about economic stability. But the nature of change is such that not all parts of a neighborhood could change at the same time and rate. Some sections of a neighborhood do change faster than others just as the converse is true that other sections may change slower than others.

For a variety of reasons, residents of those sections of a neighborhood where the rate of change is faster tend to be more transient. It may be because they may not have had enough time to develop neighborhood attachments. Warren refers to these neighborhood residents as the newcomers. With regard to those sections of the neighborhood where change has been slower, residents would tend to have a more conservative outlook. They may have lived and raised families in the same house for years. They would be the old-timers who, unlike the newcomers, have attachment to and roots in their section of the neighborhood. Perhaps because of differences in outlook and time spent in the neighborhood, the old timers would naturally be more familiar with their neighborhood and its affairs. They would, too, be more likely to be involved and entrenched in running neighborhood and community affairs.

Where and when the old timers and the newcomers sit down to discuss their relationships, as they must in a transitory neighborhood, there may occur some tension and conflict because of uncertainty and anxiety as to what each side may be up to. In this type of a neighborhood, one would expect local institutions and services to be dominated by the old timers. There may be occasions when the newcomers may feel that they were not getting their fair share of community resources. At other times, the old timers may similarly feel as though the newcomers were being too pushy.

The transitory neighborhood appears to have two rather contradictory characteristics. On the one hand, the old timers, by virtue of their lengivity, represent the type of neighborhood stability that would be good for the working poor. On the other hand, the newcomers, by virtue of their newness, represent the kind of neighborhood instability we would want to avoid in seeking ways to empower the working poor. Viewed in these terms, a transitory neighborhood might attract the working poor who, in this scenario, would be joining the other newcomers. In fact, this scenario could be viewed yet as another stepping stone for the working poor on their way to other

61

stations in life. But a transitory neighborhood, by its very nature, does not appear to be a viable neighborhood model for empowering the poor.

For one thing, this neighborhood is changing and change has not always been compatible with stability. We therefore have linked newcomers to instability and old timers to stability. Transiency implies and carries with it certain properties of instability. Some neighborhoods might be too transient for the working poor. And for a neighborhood to be a useful tool for empowering the working poor, it must be stabilized first.

6. The anomic neighborhood

This *anomic neighborhood* is Warren's last type of neighborhoods. In most respects, this neighborhood is likely to manifest social and economic conditions similar to those of income groups C and C2 in our Figure I and neighborhood number I in Figure VIII. Chances of most residents of this neighborhood being the working poor are very good. This neighborhood gives you the image of a real ghetto where all the problems you would ascribe to or associate with a ghetto appear to be present. Like a typical ghetto, most residents of the anomic neighborhood are highly individualistic, keep to themselves and their different ways of life, avoid membership in local organizations and rarely, if ever, do they participate in neighborhood improvement activities. Theirs is not only a neighborhood with very little to protect but also a neighborhood which is open to many external influences. This neighborhood's ability to resist anything or solve its problems is thus reduced considerably.

Compared to the other types of neighborhoods, anomic neighborhood is probably the worst. In many ways, it represents much of what is undesirable and destructive in our poor neighborhoods. While this type of neighborhood is clearly not the model that we would like to emulate in rebuilding our depressed areas, it is certainly an excellent prototype of the neighborhood we would want to rebuild. Indeed, the suggested proposals for neighborhood redevelopment envisage a neighborhood similar, if not identical, to the anomic neighborhood.

Earlier on, we suggested that the neighborly attributes of the integral neighborhood would be very suitable in rebuilding such neighborhoods as the anomic neighborhood. It seems to us as a natural inclination that most people -regardless of economic status - would like to live in neighborhoods which are close or similar to the integral neighborhood and avoid, as much as possible, to live in the anomic type of neighborhood. Put in other words, and without making the case for the material abundance, the working poor Americans should seek and attempt to create or emulate a neighborhood similar to the integral neighborhood.

Approaches to neighborhood redevelopment

In the preceding chapter, we attempted to link the existence of poverty to both theoretical and programmatic efforts to control or eliminate it. The attempt to link the existence of poverty to a search for possible solutions is not only reasonable but very much in keeping with the natural tendency among human beings. Put differently, this is to say that because poverty exists amongst us, we make efforts to either control or eliminate it. Successful control and/or elimination of poverty translates into improved living conditions of those who live and toil under poverty. Improving living conditions of people who live under undesirable conditions is the essence of neighborhood and community development.

Now, there are two fundamental approaches of improving living conditions of people. The first approach focuses on the individual member of a neighborhood or community and the second focuses on the neighborhood or community to which the individual belongs. In the first instance, that is, when we focus on the individual, the idea and the ensuing effort include encouraging and assisting every neighborhood resident, through a variety of ways and means, to be active participants in the affairs of the neighborhood and community. Neighborhood residents are provided reasonable opportunities to pursue and maximize their individual potentialities to the best of their will, abilities and without having to negate or void their previous achievements or gains. In the effort to develop the individual resident, we have suggested home and business ownership and operation as the best way to get owner-residents involved in the affairs of their neighborhoods and communities. It is also the best way to develop the necessary neighborhood roots to ensure that you can count on them to stay.

The second approach addresses the matter of creating and providing opportunities for economic ownership by neighborhood residents and pursuit of their other ambitions. At the very least, every neighborhood must provide opportunities to its residents. This approach also requires that there be linkage between the operation of neighborhood based programs and activities (public and nonprofit) to service and enhance the principle of individual ownership of economic and residential facilities. In other words, such activities as business development, crime control, community and social services should be so structured and administered as to ensure the survival and growth of the new home and business owners.

A neighborhood which desires and aspires to be viable and self-reliant in producing and/or acquiring goods and services needed by its residents should ensure that individual initiatives and enterprise are permitted to make their fair contribution to community and neighborhood life and its vitality. Although ownership of economic and residential facilities is not and will not cure all the neighborhood ills, it is one sure way of motivating the new owners to live and participate in neighborhood and community affairs.

Community and Neighborhood Empowerment

Active involvement in [local block clubs and
other neighborhood organizations] has important
individual, community and societal functions.To
be sure, such neighborhood involvement may be
ot only an important source of psychological
well-being but also a critical instrument for
ommunity empowerment...

James S. Jackson

Introductory perspectives

The preceding chapters make two key points. The first point is the juxtaposition of poverty as the problem for which solution is sought. Towards that end, chapter two attempts to identify and depict the social and economic circumstances of the working poor as the problem which must be solved. The second point, described in the previous chapter, lays out the physical and demographical setting (or the geographical context) within which the said problems of the working poor must be tackled.

In this chapter, we introduce and use the concept of *empowerment* to serve as the driving force behind neighborhood redevelopment programs and activities. Our discussion of the concept emphasizes how empowerment can and must be realized and used. We stay with and emphasize the basic theme and assumption mentioned earlier on that community and neighborhood redevelopment must be clearly and directly linked to ownership and management of residential and economic establishments at the local neighborhood level. We also operationalized the concept of neighborhood - that is, determining the preferable physical layout or setting within which empowering activities and programs must take place.

For instance, owning a home in one's neighborhood is not only an important economic act but also an equally empowering act. Important as it is, owning a home alone is and cannot be an end unto itself. That empowering economic act of owning a home should be further linked to other forms of ownership - that is, owning and operating economic establishments in one's neighborhood and these too, should be linked to other community and neighborhood redevelopment programs and activities.

The act of owning and operating residential and economic enterprises presumes and anticipates the existence of certain fundamental interests, abilities and responsibilities within the community to control, guide and influence behavior of others to cooperate in the process of carrying out the wishes and policies of the community. Where and when this is not the case, attempts should be made to educate and encourage these attributes. In demur to this assumption, one may want to question this assumption on the grounds that the most universal and noticeable attribute of being a working poor is being powerless. To be powerless means reduced abilities (certainly not one's interests or responsibilities) of an individual or neighborhood to influence content, use or direction of public policy, economy, technology, social and cultural spheres of life. This lack of influence is generally due to many factors which may include deprivation and oppression, exclusion and discrimination, lack of education and skills, lack of leadership and organization, underemployment and unemployment and lack of self initiative. It may also be due to a lack of effective participation in both local politics and neighborhood civic affairs.

Most poor African American and Latino communities and neighborhoods have little or no influence over such community matters as local political control, local economy, sanitation, schools, zoning, street cleaning and maintenance, housing, community based professions, transportation, police services and such other vital community services. (Blackwell:193-215; *Review of Black Political Economy*, Vol.II No.1 1980:21).

Our consideration of empowerment emphasizes the natural linkage between the individual and his/her neighborhood. Community and neighborhood residents must accept their rightful and proper roles in the process of acquiring and exercising power. Being poor or a person of color may lead, and it often does, to all types of disenfranchisements. But it should never be the reason for self disenfranchisement! As indicated previously, we wholly embrace the precept that each individual, regardless of the attendant political, economic or racial circumstances, retains the primary right and responsibility for correcting the unfavorable situation in which he or she may be.

To be empowered, the individual must participate in the structuring and operationalizing of social and economic institutions in which power and influence are vested. But even as the poor and minorities accept their fair share of the responsibilities for changing their own neighborhoods, it is absolutely necessary that we acknowledge how formidable is the external control of the inner city and minority communities and neighborhoods by the white suburban-based political and economic structure. (Nat. Acad. of Sci. 1973:146-179). Furthermore, we interpret Tabb's discussion of the ghetto economy to suggest that poverty in black poor neighborhoods is both externally induced and controlled with the net effect being that such communities become de facto consumer colonies, reservations for the larger society or reservoirs of cheap labor. (Tabb:1970:21-34). Our point to be noted here is that neither free enterprise nor public assistance has been empowering to the poor and people of color in particular. Our explanation for this phenomenon is two fold. On one hand, the working poor and the African American in particular, have been excluded from gainful participation in the free enterprise system by legal, political and racial criteria while they, too, have failed to make full use of either the inherent powers of their consumer dollars or the ballots they already have to enhance their interests. On the other hand, public assistance, to extent that it could have enhanced self reliance or stabilized inner city neighborhoods, lacked proper linkages. It has been an end unto itself!

Defining community and neighborhood empowerment

The foregoing remarks pave the way for us to develop an operational definition of empowerment. We have used individual and/or community empowerment to mean the act and process of building and increasing neighborhood's influence or control over most or all of its social, cultural, economic and political life. In other words, community empowerment is the ability of community residents to make decisions and choices which are in their individual and collective interests as residents of a neighborhood and are in accord with the principles and practices of neighborhood based ownership and management of economic, social and political institutions and programs. Or, at the very least, neighborhood residents' ability to influence in their favor the process by and through which such decisions and choices are made. The emphasis here is on neighborhood institutions (social and economic) being of specific service to that neighborhood. And although a certain amount of neighborhood interdependence and interaction is actually unavoidable, the search and pursuit of as much community and neighborhood self sufficiency as possible should never cease.

While clarifying the meanings we attach to the terms used in this book, we pointed out that the idea of neighborhood redevelopment appears to betray the intent - that is, restoring neighborhoods to what they used to be. Communities and neighborhoods all across the nation have been redoing over what was done years ago. And although we have not established that the working poor ever owned homes or managed any economic firms, we believe our choices are very limited in conceiving and creating a more practical approach to rebuilding the inner city areas. The major theme and leading assumption in this chapter is on participation. We take the view that there cannot be sustainable improvement of the prevailing conditions in the inner city poor neighborhoods unless and until those who live there on regular and permanent basis are fully involved in the struggle for their own uplifting.

In selecting and presenting the strategies which we consider useful for both individual and neighborhood empowerment, we have not only drawn more and more from common sense and experience but also tried to be as practical as possible. The following then are some of the more suitable and recommended strategies.

Political empowerment

Political empowerment means acquiring and using political power and/or influence to one's advantage. To facilitate the discussion of this topic, we have examined the nature, exercise and constraints of political power and influence.

1. Nature and use of political power

Although it is likely to sound like an old cliche to the working poor and most people of color, political power comes from politics. And, politics is that process of creating and executing public policy by influencing and controlling sources of that power and authority. (Theodorson:1979:303). Power, it should be understood, is the ability or the capacity to get others do what they otherwise might not do. It thus encompasses the means of compelling and dominating the pursuit and articulation of societal and community goals, values and material objectives. (Kruschke & Jackson: 1987: 31-32). Put differently, this is to say that political power provides for the means by which to allocate, distribute, manage society's physical and human resources as well as regulating individual and community behavior.

The notion of "authority" is derived from the concept of power. We have used the term "authority" to mean the legitimate exercise of power. But an exercise of legitimate power may be in different forms such as political, knowledge, skill, professional or legal. Developing, implementing and administering public policy is the essence of exercising authority. When and if individuals or groups lack skills, political involvement or any other type of authority, their participation in and contribution to both public policy formulation and implementation are very limited. When this occurs, the individual or community thus affected are said to be powerless.

There exists formal and informal ways of acquiring and using political power in America. But the most common way of acquiring political power is through the political process. And, the essence of that process is the use of the "ballot" and taking part in community activities preceding and following the ballot. The following then are some specific ways for community and neighborhood political empowerment. Importance of these approaches is in the fact that they are the operational ends of political participation. They are concrete ways of creating and acquiring influence or power over some of neighborhood's internal and external affairs. They include any or a combination of the following.

2. Voting

This is the most traditional and the simplest form of empowerment. Although voting is often ignored or taken for granted, it is one of the cheapest and easiest way for the working poor to influence and/or control state and local policies. It is one possible way for any citizen - rich or poor - to influence his or her local community affairs.

It is not necessary for those individuals who need and must influence local public policies to be rich, middle or working poor. Possession and use of the vote equalizes the rich and the poor in this regard. A billionaire and a welfare recipient have one vote each. In order to vote, one must be registered and go to vote at the time and place of voting. When it is time to vote, the voter has one main guide: his or her individual and community interests. Regardless of what the other campaign issues and promises may be, the one thing that every voter should use as a guide is one's interests. Civic duties of particular community or neighborhood residents (who are also stakeholders) should converge with their individual needs and interests. And thus, their votes should serve them and their communities well. In the event this was not the case and there was a need for a general guide, use of what they consider to be their interests as home owners should be adequate for the community.

3. Participation

In the caption in the beginning of this chapter, James Jackson has emphasized the importance of community involvement to community and individual empowerment. Involvement in one's community is another traditional way for empowering community people. This approach requires residents to attend and participate in public meetings where one voices their views and articulates their interests as seen and perceived by them. This type of community involvement is generally referred to as political participation. Participation complements and gives meaning to voting. Voting is only the formal part of the process for electing the public policy maker. The other part

71

is ensuring that both the law and the policy emanating therefrom serve the needs and interests of one's community and neighborhood. By and large, this is the formal part of the process which is suitable for pressure groups. (Walton:160).

But political participation at the community and neighborhood levels (especially in the poor and minority areas) is aptly a matter of ensuring proper and fair implementation of public policies and equitable enforcement of local laws and regulations. (Walton:123-131). Community and neighborhood level political participation should be especially focused or refocused on ensuring efficient and fair implementation and administration of public policies with regard to equitable distribution of local resources, effective law enforcement and ensuring effective learning at neighborhood school(s).

4. Local political affiliation

In the process of creating, implementing and administering public policy, America operates on the basis of some loosely organized and generally undefined political associations, alliances and groups called democrats, liberals, republicans, conservatives and independents. For effective participation in the public policy process, the working poor and people of color must be involved in or affiliated with one or more of these political labels or groupings within a group.

Alternatively, one may wish to create a different political label as indeed some have already done. (Walton:121-131). Difficult as it may be for the working poor and minority citizens to meaningfully participate in the American party politics, there are no better alternatives available. Take, for example, the case of a Long Island town whose black and hispanic population was 10% in 1989. When blacks complained that the town administration had "turned a deaf ear and a blind eye to a large segment of electorate," the presiding supervisor of the town snapped back at them that he would make no commitments or promises. He let them know that "this is politics!". (N.Y.

Times, 7/5/1989:B4). The point of the presiding supervisor cannot be missed. It was that he could discount the black vote or their participation at public meetings. That, as town supervisor admonished, is the American political reality! Participate or be left out!

But our insistence on some political affiliation or association with the existing political party structure, should not be allowed to obscure the historical indifference and hostility that the major parties have shown toward African American and Latino citizens. (Walton:70-78). Our point though is that the poor and the minorities must overcome any obstruction to their participation in the political process. It is not necessary in 1990's to be rich or middle class before one can participate in the neighborhood affairs of the political party of their choice. Neighborhood residents must participate in that political process which controls and distributes their tax dollars, cleans their streets and runs their local school(s).

If they would prefer to be independent, by all means be independent but be politically involved. People belong to and participate in political parties because they want to acquire something or protect or enhance what they already have. There is no good reason why the poor and the minorities cannot do what others do to acquire and retain power!

It should however be realized that there is likely to be resistance by political stalwarts to any attempt by those seeking empowerment to take or share power in any manner or shape. Some political education for the neophytes might be advisable because it would be unlikely that local political officials would support or embrace community empowerment where and when such empowerment may reduce their influence on and over local decision making and resource allocation. It may therefore not be a good strategy to be too independent of the local political establishment unless the working poor in this case constitute a large, organized and voting group. Otherwise, it may be more effective to be one of the boys and work from within. But as long as community residents remain politically involved and voting, there is little doubt that the elected officials will think twice before ignoring active voters. Politicians may be guilty of many crimes but ignoring active voters is not one of them!

Safety

The first strategy is safety for people and their property. It is the starting point in community and neighborhood development. Safety means protection from crime and criminals at homes and neighborhoods for the home owners, apartment building owners and their tenants, the children, the neighborhood business owner and his/her premises and certainly the visitors and patrons. Although our intention here is not to rank these strategies in any particular order of importance, we suspect that the need for security takes precedence over other strategies. This, of course, does not alter our principal focus on the linkage and simultaneous implementation of these strategies for community and neighborhood redevelopment, providing community and neighborhood safety may utilize any number of different approaches and techniques. These may include the traditional use of alarms, group monitoring and patrolling, guards and police, pressuring civic officials to clean up drugs and prostitution, running workshops on self security procedures and techniques, and finally following and joining forces with other home owners or business people in those activities that may enhance mutual safety.

Recently, the City of New York initiated what they have described as an effective mode of neighborhood based policing. Localizing or neighborizing police patrolling is very much in line with out theme of starting redevelopment activities at the neighborhood level. Although local police are traditionally associated with "brutality" and unnecessary abuse and contempt for the working poor and people of color in particular, it must be acknowledged that much of the crime in the black and latino neighborhoods is committed by blacks on blacks and/or latinos on latinos and vice versa. Accordingly, the extent to which such neighborhood patrolling reduces crime in the working poor communities should or may be construed to advance safety for the working poor and thusly empowerment. But however and whatever may be done, it is vital that neighborhood residents be involved and take leading roles in seeking and maintaining safety in their neighborhoods especially when and where their children (ages 13 through 19) may be either the victims or perpetrators. In many instances, safety in the neighborhoods may simply mean preventing crime before it happens.

Family and parental involvement calls for such preventive measures as guiding and supervising their children as well as ensuring that children behave as they should both at home and out in the streets. With a community run and controlled neighborhood school as outlined elsewhere in this chapter, we can bring the school, the parent and the juvenile system to bear on this problem and have some confidence that it will be done in the interests of both the child and community. Teachers, counselors and other school personnel will ensure that children are indeed in the classrooms during the school hours and those not in classroom are promptly reported. Guidance and supervision of children during the school hours, that is, ensuring that each child is in school and in class when and where they are supposed to be, should not be insurmountable.

The principal idea underlying this approach to neighborhood involvement in guiding our young people is predicated on the assumption that parental involvement and participation in the control and guidance of their children cannot and should never have to be substituted. In the majority of cases and times, the best solution to juvenile problems is within the family circles. It is in the overall best interests of society to involve parents (by law or persuasion) in this type of activity than to have to pay to keep these children in jail later on.

In order to minimize juvenile crime in the late afternoons and early evenings and in order to also use their time in a constructive manner, we propose that each community and neighborhood use their recreational facilities like the Y's, local schools, churches and social service agencies to plan and involve neighborhood youths in fruitful athletic, cultural and academic activities such as would help them to be and grow up as productive members of their communities. Similarly, traditional criminal justice system should be neighborized to constitute a network of neighborhood based police precincts and courts.

But if we must have some places where crime and drugs can be tolerated and sold, (for instance, we do not appear to be too upset with prostitution when it exists in other than our immediate neighborhoods), perhaps the idea of designating certain areas as "crime zones or drug colonies" may be something whose time has come in view of the fact that criminals will always exist somewhere in society although nobody may want them as neighbors. Because housing, home ownership, business and economic development have already been discussed in the previous chapters, it is not necessary to repeat them here although they constitute what is conventionally known as investment.

Housing and the empowerment of the working poor

We have devoted a whole chapter (chapter six) on housing and home ownership and their effects on the individual owner and the community or neighborhood. It is not necessary therefore for us to expend more time and space on that topic here. But it is important to make some key points for emphasis on that subject because the point of this chapter is empowerment and both housing and home ownership have their empowering attributes. In that regard, we go back to our theme of involving the working poor in their own individual and neighborhood improvement activities. Whether we are developing new housing or rehabilitating old projects for owner occupancy, the working poor (as opposed to commercial developers and the real estate community in general) should assume leading roles. Being poor and working is not being stupid. Traditional commercial and residential developers should be utilized sparingly, if at all, in new developments and renovating old housing for the working poor and low income people.

There are a number of cogent reasons for favoring the working poor. For one, our proposal discussed in chapter six for home ownership is intended to encourage and facilitate full participation of the working poor, the blacks and the latinos in the development of their homes and their communities. Two, and as we argue later in chapter seven, it is an unnecessary drain of resources and capital from the working poor neighborhoods to use out of neighborhood contractors and/or real estate developers. Three, using outsiders needlessly deprives the working poor and people of color the opportunity to either acquire construction skills or practice the skills which they may already have in their neighborhoods. Fourth, the working poor and minorities have not been able to participate fully in the free enterprise system even when good opportunities occur in their own neighborhoods. And, finally, the practice unnecessarily perpetuates dependency of the working poor.

Unlike the commercial and residential developers, the rise and involvement of the Community Development Corporations (CDC's) in the inner city neighborhoods during the last quarter of a century, appears to have started a process of reversing the decline and decay of many working poor areas. Typically, the CDC appears to succeed in owning and managing housing developments in many of the most blighted urban neighborhoods. (*Task Force Report on Community Based Development*, 9/1987:7-8; Peirce & Steinbach. 1990:17-18). In this way, CDC's have created and extended neighborhood power and influence and control over this aspect of community life. By increasing influence over housing the working poor, the neighborhood is accordingly empowered in this particular sphere of community life. Even in economic terms, the CDC manages to at least retain some rental income in the neighborhood when such property is owned and managed within the neighborhood. That is empowerment!

Economic empowerment

Chapter seven is devoted to community and neighborhood economic development. Most aspects of economic empowerment are discussed in the chapter. As was the case with the housing and home ownership component of empowerment, economic empowerment is discussed here for emphasis only. We therefore do emphasize the fact that empowering individuals and communities in all other ways is predicated on economic empowerment. When successfully and properly carried out, economic empowerment enables communities and neighborhoods to develop and maintain sources of income without which nothing else could work. Economic empowerment, then, reflects those situations where and when individuals and neighborhoods are able to reasonably influence or control the flow and availability of goods and services needed in and out of the neighborhoods. When achieved, economic empowerment also directs the flow of capital and other resources in and out of the neighborhood.

While it is considered normal for a neighborhood to seek economic assistance from all willing and able sources, it is naturally expected that the residents of the neighborhood in question must be similarly expected to take their own initiatives to help themselves. In other words, no permanent community redevelopment can come from outside the community and that involved communities and neighborhoods must take their own initiatives and provide leadership for their own home grown and nourished redevelopment. Appropriate neighborhood initiatives and entrepreneurial pursuits have been outlined and described in chapter seven and reasonable precautions have been taken to ensure that community development, whatever shape or content, is sufficiently rooted and sustainable in that community.

On more specific terms, economic empowerment of an individual or a neighborhood requires that there be a framework within which the individual working poor would own either home or business or both in their neighborhoods. For individuals and neighborhoods to realize and fruitfully pursue existing opportunities, it is necessary that there be public policies which support and encourage home and business ownership.

For empowerment to be meaningful, the proper role of government and its agencies is to create opportunities for the working poor and to feed them. When and where the government does everything for the individual, the human spirit to strive is stifled and the desire to achieve is thus reduced, if not eliminated. One cannot therefore help but admire and support the many self-help initiatives and activities that thousands of Americans undertake every year for their individual and/or community benefit.

ssence of economic empowerment

For the working poor, economic empowerment deals with acquiring goods and services in the necessary quantities and qualities more so than buying and selling stocks or managing major corporations. This is so mainly because the working poor and minority communities depend entirely on goods and services bought or brought from outside these communities. Any attempts by these communities to empower must be balanced against their near complete dependence on outside sources for their housing, food, clothing, education, police and just anything else that you may want to think of. To put this point differently, it is suggested that economic empowerment dictates that neighborhoods be able to provide these essentials of every day life to their residents. And, when this happens, a community or neighborhood can say that

79

it is economically empowered.

Empowerment and the neighborhood school

This idea of a neighborhood school being an empowering mechanism takes us back to chapter three where and when we embraced an expanded version of Donald Warren's definition of a neighborhood being of the same size as a school district. That definition encompassed the necessary operational dimensions of a neighborhood school district such as the geography and demography of a typical inner city neighborhood. So, in thinking and using the neighborhood school for empowerment purposes, we are dealing with an established community based institution. It provides an appropriate organizational framework for neighborhood redevelopment activities.

Having an operational neighborhood is one thing but empowering those who work and live there is quite another thing. Education has great potential in empowering individual community residents. But for some reasons, education does not appear to have had much of a spiller over effect in the working poor neighborhoods. In fact, a study reported in a news magazine *NorthStar News and Analysis*, Chicago: 8/89: 6) has suggested that the overwhelming majority of both black and white college graduates choose to live and work in the wealthier communities and neighborhoods than the working poor neighborhoods. Perhaps this is as much as common sense would have it. For those college graduates who came from working poor areas, their empowerment through education does not appear to benefit their original neighborhoods.

Perhaps even more crucial is education at the local level. For illustrative purposes, let us briefly consider how working poor parents could be empowered through the process of educating their children. Parental involvement in the education of children is a necessary condition to all learning. Inner city school systems are often negligent in involving poor and black parents in the education process. In any case, in empowering poor parents, the first thing that we should do is to allow these parents to choose where their children will attend school. For too long, this choice has been left in the hands of the superintendents, boards of education, teachers and their unions.

To empower working poor and minority parents and their children, we agree with the Association for Supervision and Curriculum Development that the local school system should be restructured so as to allow the maximum choice to parents and students. To this end, we suggest and outline three ways of empowering the working poor and minority parents through school restructuring. These are: school for choice, resource management and linking the neighborhood school with other community activities and programs such as home or business ownership and operation. (ASCD,1990:1). Neighborhood day care centers, primary and secondary schools, vocational schools and regional universities all have budgets and expenditures. Such budgets and expenditures could easily form the bases of and feed substantial neighborhood economic activities. These community institutions could therefore be viewed not only as learning and cultural institutions but also as economic entities and local infrastructures within the communities and neighborhoods where they are located.

The recently inaugurated school reform in Chicago ushered in a high degree of decentralization whereby each neighborhood school created a neighborhood school council composed of six parents, two non-parent community residents and two teachers. The principal of the school has a seat in the council. If this Chicago school decentralization reform were to be accompanied by a choice reform similar to Milwaukee's program, working poor parents would be accordingly empowered to make educational, economic and managerial decisions. Because the parent dominated councils will "have the authority to hire and dismiss principals, make recommendations on curriculum and books and approve budgets," (*NY Times*, 9/28/89: B13), the

81

working poor will thus influence educational expenditures which may have spiller over effects onto local economic activities. The exercise of such authority may also empower and motivate the working poor to improve their communities and neighborhoods. Electing the new school councils was said to have elicited extremely high level of participation among the working poor, black and latino neighborhoods and that of the 540 schools, only 19 (3.5%) were said to have had some problems in getting enough people to participate. *N.Y.Times*, 9/28/89: B13).

This high level of participation, allows us to suggest that when empowered, the working poor are able and willing to work and assume responsibilities to improve their living conditions. The only thing that is missing here is parents' financial ability and freedom to change from one school to another for whatever the reason. This is why we think the introduction and use of the voucher system can only improve things. If these parents had a choice, they would then have a workable mechanism to pressure the new council when and if it falters prior to the next elections.

1. The neighborhood school as a choice

In school choice, we have in mind exactly what the subheading says. We take it to be self evident that the poor and minority parents have little or no choice at all as to where their children may go to school. We think and believe that they should have the right to choose like the rest of us do. *The Association for Supervision and Curriculum Development* as made what we consider to be a convincing case for restructuring the local school system to provide choices to parents and their children. ASCD's definition and description of choice seem to associate the idea of choice with a sense of power, freedom and options. (ASCD:1990:1). The essence of choice is simply to enable parents and their children to determine which school to attend; make an input in the curriculum and contribute to other pertinent issues in the learning process. The pamphlet says school choice will transfer education decision making from the state, city, board of education and the unions to the individual parents and their children. (ASCD.1990:9).

The emphasis here is on the expectation that this newly acquired ability (through restructuring) to make choices will enhance both the sense and actuality of self reliance for the working poor and the minority parents. And, if it appears that the targeted parents are either reluctant or unable (which would be an understandable phenomenon in light of past denials) to assume the appropriate educational responsibilities, a parent education program to accompany the restructuring process should be designed and put into effect. Correspondingly, the decision making role (and power) of the board of education and the teachers' union, (these two organizations have traditionally made all kinds of educational decisions on behalf of and for African American and Latino families), should be diminished!

2. The neighborhood school as a community resource

The second approach is to restructure and manage the neighborhood school as a community resource that has economic, cultural technological and intellectual properties. The envisaged restructure and management will complement the choice structure outlined above. We wish to convey the notion that, when dissatisfied, the working poor parents thus empowered will use their freedom to choose another school for their children other than the neighborhood school(s). The choice made may mean additional financial resources to the school thus chosen. And, when a school has financial resources, it has the ability to pay its bills. School bills include salaries, maintenance, supplies, insurance, catering and cleaning. Payment of these bills would translate into jobs for neighborhood residents.

3. Neighborhood school's multiplier effect

The premise here is that local control of the neighborhood school and parental right to choose where their children will go to school will lead to (a) an improved school system and (b) a multiplier effect on the overall neighborhood outlook. A multiplier effect here is likely to be in the form of positive impacts on home and business ownership and management. A good school system will attract people from other communities and neighborhoods to relocate to or visit the neighborhood as either residents, home owners or even as businessmen and women.

4. Empowerment by skills

To a large extent, community and neighborhood empowerment depends on the available and pertinent operational skills. The absence of the necessary skills in the needed qualities and quantities almost always cripples many a community project. Even when an individual or neighborhood are empowered in all the other ways and the individual or neighborhood had skill deficiencies, neighborhood redevelopment would not be implemented and managed correctly. And if the idea is to cultivate and sustain self reliance, it is important that such operational skills be permanently domiciled in the particular neighborhoods.

Because our objective is to empower the working poor and the minorities so that they can lead in the effort to rebuild their neighborhoods, we need to recognize and accept the fact that being poor, by its very nature, completely eliminates, or at least minimizes, the chances of the working poor being both working poor and professional at the same time! That would be contradiction in meanings. For, in the so-called free enterprise system, it is not just unusual and professionally freakish to produce too many professionals who are at the same time working poor but a virtue impossibility! Professionals are men and women who undertake or undergo through a system of structured instruction and/or training which makes them qualified and classifies them as members of a particular profession for which they studied or trained such as the medical, nursing, legal or teacher's professions.

In dealing with many of the necessary operational skills, it is perhaps

84

best to attempt to attract them to relocate in the working poor neighborhoods. It, of course, goes without saying that these neighborhoods will need various types of services such as health, medical, police and so on. The real challenge for community empowerment is to ensure that those professionals who work in the working poor and minority communities (teachers, nurses, doctors, law enforcement personnel, public employees and others) can be made accountable to and by the communities they serve. Without any form of accountability, the presence of these professionals in the working poor and minority communities would not necessarily be empowering.

Religious empowerment

For those community and neighborhood residents who are religiously inclined, the local church's extra-religious programs and activities constitute another viable arena for influencing what is happening in the community and neighborhood. In many cases, the local house of worship is one place where one's social or economic status should not interfere with one's involvement and participation in the church's social and community programs. Church based programs and activities like the teenage program, the seniors or men's or women's group, the Y, the choir, missionary work, housing, homeless people, day care center, and feeding the hungry make up the bulk of what constitutes social and human services in many working poor and minority neighborhoods. Also equally empowering are such church sponsored and/or affiliated activities as voter education, voter registration, civil rights advocacy, education, job training and job referral activities. There are many and diverse community interests and activities. To the extent that community residents are involved in one or more of these church and/or religiously based activities, they have thus created and enhanced their community's influence over its affairs through such this religious affiliation.

Importance of religious organizations in community and neighborhood development has been well underscored by Peirce and Steinbach in *Corrective Capitalism* (1987) and *Enterprising Communities* (1990). Peirce and Steinbach point out that many community development corporations (CDC's) started in church basements and have continued to enjoy church support. They further point out that religious groups have brought to the CDC movement a near universal presence which penetrates nearly every "nook and cranny of American communities." (1987:65).

The power of advocacy

As used here, the term "advocacy" conveys the idea of support on behalf of the working poor and minority citizens to acquire, control and use reasonable amounts of goods and services in their own neighborhoods. The object is to make working poor and people of color full participants in the act and process of creating and distributing the goods and services they receive and consume. Although advocacy may be provided by groups or organizations at any level of society, our primary interest is in the nonprofit and voluntary community based groups whose members are primarily motivated by either self or community improvement and are not necessarily paid for their efforts. Community based advocacy groups may not be as zealous as the true believers, but they tend to be very mission oriented, believers in their objectives and confident of their abilities to achieve their goals. (Sherraden:237-239)

Advocacy for the working poor may use any one or a combination of several techniques and methods depending on the need or issue at hand. Having been politically and economically disenfranchised and exploited, poor people have turned to community and neighborhood based nonprofit advocacy groups like neighborhood and block associations, community action committees, campaigns against hunger, legal aid, citizens for fair housing and community group for social action. (Peirce & Steinbach, 1987:65-69)

More specifically, when the sanitation department fails to pick up garbage in a particular neighborhood for a couple of days (as it so often happens in the working poor areas), the neighbors thus affected should get together and form a "clean neighborhood" committee. Their affiliation with one another for this or other purposes enhances their community's influence on the administration of public policy in their neighborhood. Or, when the school system continues to fail their children, to transfer them to another school or join the PTA or form a new parent committee for quality education. (Sackrey, 1973:110-120). Carrying out the purposes of such a parents' education committee will similarly enhance their individual and neighborhood influence over local affairs. The essential point here is that those thus affected will actually do something concrete to influence things. And, that is empowerment!

The power of direct action approach

Another form of advocacy is direct action for self support or support for others. Striking is a good example of this tactic. Striking occurs when individual and group interests are either one and the same or are closely intertwined. Unlike other forms of advocacy, direct action tactics are initiated and pursued through different approaches and techniques. Indeed, the essence of the approach is in the techniques used which may include work stoppages, demonstrations, sit-ins, letter writing, telephoning and boycotting - all of which can be effective sometimes. (Worthy:259-269).

To further illustrate how actual application of direct action tactics to community empowerment may differ from the type of advocacy previously discussed, we may liken the former to a strike and the latter to a collective bargaining session between labor and management. In this regard, we hasten to add that in nearly all collective bargaining cases, strike is either actual or threatened. (Shafritz,1985:409). So, the distinction between direct action tactics approach and traditional advocacy is rather nebulous. With the possible exception of strike, the rest of tactics used by direct action activists are in fact widely used by individuals and groups who seek to rectify some type of grievance.

Leadership as the base for empowerment

Leadership is a necessary first condition for community and neighborhood empowerment. We accept Theodorson's definition of leadership as the "exercise of influence and authority." (1969:227). This exercise of influence may be, as Shafritz (1985:237) has added, formal or informal and it involves directing and coordinating the work of others. Therefore, community and neighborhood empowerment must have competent and committed leadership - a leadership that is resident in the particular neighborhood. As is normally understood, the purpose of leadership is to guide and articulate needs and aspirations of those being lead. We need leaders in starting and managing neighborhood programs or organizing neighborhoods for civic, cultural, economic or political purposes.

Resolving neighborhood disputes and conflicts

Among the many needs that the working poor have are those pertaining to resolving disputes and the ensuing conflicts. By being poor, the working poor have very limited economic and legal abilities to resolve various types of disputes and conflicts that they face in their neighborhoods. In middle class neighborhoods, most people do have both financial and legal abilities to resolve disputes and conflicts. This is obviously not the case with the working poor, who, one would expect, have more disputes and conflicts. This section therefore articulates the need for and outlines a specific mechanism for resolving some of the disputes and conflicts in the working poor neighborhoods.

For our purposes here, the concepts of dispute and conflict are intertwined in the sense that a dispute, as Harold Roberts suggests, does often lead to a conflict (Roberts, 1971:107). And because a dispute can easily lead to a conflict, or, is often one and the same thing as a conflict, we use the two terms to convey the idea of one person or social unit intentionally interfering with another individual's or social unit's pursuit of their goals. (Robey, 1982:143). In more specific terms, disputes (and ultimately conflicts) result from how we acquire and use power to discriminate, benefit, reward, deprive, punish, exclude, alienate, or do any of the other things which cause disputes and may ultimately lead to conflicts.

A similar illustration exists with respect to potential problems that may arise from sharing of and competing for limited resources. Or, for that matter, the inherent potential for disputes in having to work together (as we must in real life) and /or having to be (as we must) interdependent both as individuals and groups. In other words, there are actual and potential disputes and conflicts in and within all spheres of life. The question therefore is: with which of those disputes and conflicts can the working poor live and which ones can be resolved in order to enhance their self reliance and neighborhood viability?

Using what they do in St. Paul, MN. as a general guide, it is possible to separate those disputes which are purely personal in nature (criminal charges, family violence, divorce and cases where one of the parties refuses mediation) from those emanating from primarily the conditions of being working poor (consumer-business cases, landlord-tenant disputes, neighborhood problems, small claims, juvenile disputes, and

89

employee/employer problems). In this scenario, personal disputes would be left to the individual to handle while the disputes emanating from the condition of being poor or living in a poor neighborhood would be resolved through the envisaged mechanism. (*Dispute Resolution Center*, St. Paul, MN, undated brochure).

Operationally, we envisage the dispute/conflict resolution mechanism as having one of two generally known formats. One, it may use a management-union mediation format. Or, two, it may resemble Judge Wepner's People's Court. Either one of these formats would be empowering to the working poor in their neighborhoods.

Some de-empowering factors

In the preceding sections of this chapter, we have described a number of approaches and techniques of empowering the working poor and minority communities and neighborhoods. The number suggested is neither exhaustive nor without contradictions. The approaches and techniques presented are not without corresponding contradicting and/or negating elements. We have labelled such obstructive elements the *de-empowering factors*. We have outlined some of them below.

De-empowering factors would therefore encompass those situations and obstacles which the working poor and people of color generally encounter whenever they attempt to influence or control their educational, economic or political status. Indeed, it is unlikely that any one of the empowerment approaches suggested could ever be put into effect without encountering some serious opposition from various individuals and groups who live off the working poor. Implementing these ideas may in fact be more troublesome and complicated than one may be lead to believe.

Some of the so called de-empowering factors which most community residents are likely to encounter when they attempt to gain influence over various aspects of neighborhood life include such traditional groups and institutions as local political establishment, unions, banks and lack of pride and leadership. A brief review of each may shed some light to the point.

Likely opposition by local political establishment

Much as we argued for involvement in the local politics for empowerment, we must also acknowledge the fact that most working poor, especially when they are black and latino, have had serious difficulties getting integrated into existing political system because much of it is controlled by political "machines." Political machines are sufficiently institutionalized mechanisms intended and designed to:

> protect the power of the organization and the
> economic interests of its ultimate white leader-
> ship and business support; the machine attempts
> to prevent the formation of multiracial challenging
> coalitions through co-optation, building on and
> generating divisions among minority leaders and
> groups and establishing minority officer holders
> against whom other minority people find it difficult
> to run. (Browning,Marshall & Tabb,1990:217).

This passage is unambiguous. It puts it like it is. The practice of controlling and manipulating local political structures to favor the white and powerful neighborhoods has been (and continues) to be a widely used system of de-empowering the working poor, black and latino communities and neighborhoods. (Patterson, 1975:178-210). This form of politically induced and imposed powerlessness speaks to the reasons why we have given empowerment such a high priority in the struggle for rebuilding our inner city neighborhoods. If we cannot overcome political obstacles, redevelopment of the poor inner city neighborhoods will be difficult to bring about.

When unions impede empowerment

To the casual and partisan observer, unions have always been and still are for the little man regardless of the economic or racial status of the individual. They (unions) ceaselessly brag about how faithfully they adhere to the principles and practices of equal opportunity, racial equality and for all the other things that the working poor and minorities need. Contrary to such claims as referred to here, unions are not now and have never been entirely nondiscriminatory against color people. In a preceding section, we discussed how certain community based organizations and groups may be sources of community empowerment. In this segment and without getting into too much details, we want to caution working poor and minority communities and neighborhoods that unions - teacher and construction unions in particular - have been and continue to oppose any form of empowerment among the working poor - especially when the working poor are black or latino.

Take, for instance, the 1966-68 struggle for community school control in the Ocean Hill - Brownsville sections of Brooklyn, N. Y. which pitted the poor and powerless black and latino parents against the powerful Albert Shanker's United Federation of Teachers. (Levin, 1970:134-135; *NY Times*, 3/16/1969: 7E). Because these poor parents' needs for being involved in the education of their children ran counter to the dominating interests of the mighty and powerful, they were crashed and suppressed ruthlesslessly. It was a classic case of the powerful fighting the powerless to maintain their privileges! More recently, teacher unions in New Jersey and Wisconsin (*NY Times*,7/3/1990: 14) have not only objected to such empowering reforms as the voucher plan but have also threatened to sue to prevent any such changes which will interfere with the security of their jobs or alter the prevailing status quo.

In a similar manner and as is generally accepted, the criminal justice system (i.e. police, sheriffs, courts and prison system) has lost trust and credibility in the working poor, black and latino neighborhoods. Instead of being and functioning as a source of security and an object of trustworthiness in these communities and neighborhoods, criminal justice system has become an object of mistrust, resentment and even hatred among the poor and minority inner city neighborhoods. (Blackwell:260-263). For community empowerment to be meaningful, it will be necessary to change both the content of the justice system and the manner by and through which justice is administered in the working poor and minority neighborhoods.

Redlining negates empowerment

The problem of redlining often negates the potential empowerment of housing. It is one of those problems which working poor and minority neighborhoods have not been able to resolve. Redlining is that practice commonly used by banks, mortgage houses, savings and loan houses and insurance companies to deny mortgage and/or insurance to African Americans and Latinos in particular and the working poor in general. This practice used to be an official policy of the FHA starting in 1935 when this agency started redlining many neighborhoods by separating black and white residential areas for purposes of determining mortgage eligibility for FHA home mortgages. (Blackwell,75:151). The practice is still commonly but silently and evasively used by many banks and financial institutions to deny and avoid investing and insuring properties and vehicles in working poor and minority neighborhoods. (City Limits, 1/1990:6; *NY Times*,5/17/ 1990:A18).

But the point of these remarks is to emphasize the fact that community and neighborhood empowerment must, among other things, include ability to attract and generate capital because without it, the case for community and neighborhood redevelopment becomes untenable. Although community investment is discussed in a later chapter, it is important to add that for empowerment to succeed, we must find some way to either overcome or circumvent the practice of redlining.

Lack of community pride hinders empowerment

Although clearly intangible and not often discussed, the absence of pride in the working poor and minority communities and neighborhoods has been and continues to be very devastating to these communities. However one may look at it, there can be no avoiding the fact that if you do not like your neighborhood, it is likely that you would not want to live there. And, if you ended up living there (as many may have been compelled to by economic and political circumstances), you probably would not go out of your way to improve it. Most likely you wont be bothered with it! You are likely to go about your other business and, whenever possible, you and your fellow residents who hate their communities and neighborhoods want to get out fast.

Earlier on, we discussed some neighborhoods where residents didn't seem to care. Such neighborhoods as the transitory and anomic neighborhoods typify communities in which residents do not have pride. And as we noticed, the working poor have nowhere else to go. They cannot afford to relocate to anywhere. Their economic abilities limit them to where they now live which is certainly not a reason for them to be content and have pride in where they live. Crime and drugs are common everywhere most of the times. Garbage is also all over the place. The school buildings are often dilapidated and the learning process is marginal at its very best.

Community change does not just happen. Those who live there must seek or initiate it. If municipal services are rotten, it will take those who live there to do something about it. The process of empowering a neighborhood must therefore include creating and nurturing community pride. And as we argue in the next chapter, community pride starts with the development of roots in the community. Owning and operating some property in one's community is probably the most significant step in creating community roots and pride because they now have a stake.

Lack of local based leadership stifles empowerment

Just as community based leadership is a necessary condition for community empowerment, its absence almost guarantees that nothing is likely to happen in that neighborhood. Without leadership, there is no vision. The absence of locally based leadership cripples the hopes and aspirations of the working poor and those who have had a long history of abuse and denial as the African Americans and Latinos. A community may have all sorts of resources and skills at its disposal, but if it lacks articulate and foresighted leadership to make its case both its internal and external constituents, it is unlikely to ever develop sufficient influence over its affairs. (Walton:46-47).

Leadership helps to coordinate and sustain the pace and direction of the neighborhood redevelopment efforts. Good leaders help make the way where there may be none. Or make it easier where and when it may be difficult. Leaders help create and attract more resources. Indeed, power cannot be exercised properly without and outside institutionalized leadership. In many instances where community development corporation (CDC) exist, some communities may be somewhat empowered by and through the CDC. We would therefore want to suggest that the organizational model represented by community development movement may have created and perfected an organizational model for creating and developing community based leaders. And because these community based organizations are both philosophically and operationally closer to the working poor and the minorities than public bureaucracies, we suggest that our public policies governing public assistance as well as addressing various aspects of community and neighborhood redevelopment, should be altered to reflect and emphasize self initiative and a neighborhood based approach similar to what has been going within the CDC movement.

Planning and Implementing Community and Neighborhood Redevelopment

Introduction

This chapter outlines and discusses the process and techniques of planning and plan implementation at the neighborhood and community levels. While embracing the fundamentals of planning in general, the chapter focuses on and emphasizes planning at the neighborhood level. As a general rule, planning encompasses that process of identifying needs, establishing programmatic goals and objectives and determining the nature and amount of resources required to achieve such objectives. (Theodorson, 1969:64). Our layout and discussion of planning for the redevelopment of depressed communities and neighborhoods embraces the physical, social, economic and policy planning phases discussed later on in this chapter. We think these phases are basic to most planning endeavors for various purposes. What we do differently is that we consider some approaches and techniques of gathering data to be more suitable and useful than others. In passing though and without favor, it may be noted that we have made a point of making less use of those approaches and techniques which are either expensive or require high technology skills in data gathering. Working poor are, after all, poor people!

Planning for the redevelopment of the run down communities and neighborhoods dictates, therefore, that we begin by determining, as accurately as possible, what are the community and neighborhood needs and resources. If properly done, such a determination or survey will identify the nature and extent of needs and resources available. Such a general procedure of identifying needs and resource requirement is here equated with the traditional procedure known as needs assessment. But before discussing needs assessment and/or other aspects of planning or parts thereof, perhaps a note of caution is in order. The point is that we would want the reader to bear in mind the fact that we are dealing with poor people and that their problems are essentially problems of *want* and *inadequacy*. They are either lacking something or they have too little of something. And, one of the problems that the working poor and their neighborhoods often face in their search for resources, is that most funding sources (including the government) require the recipients of their grants to make use of some form of consultancy as a condition of the grant.

Neighborize the planning act

Because the goal is to create and maintain self-reliant communities and neighborhoods for the working poor, then planning activities and procedures should emphasize *neighborization* of the redevelopment effort and the necessary expertise to perform and maintain community and neighborhood programs and activities. The use of non-resident expertise and consultants to perform planning and its components in the working poor communities is universally expected and accepted because these skills are often not in existence in these areas. Use of experts and consultants has been a common feature of anti-poverty and community development activities and programs. But what is not ever discussed or even mentioned is the fact that it can be (and we suggest as much) disadvantageous in some important ways. First, it is expensive. And when you are dealing with poor people, it is prudent to be inexpensive. Secondly, it encourages outflow of community resources. Working poor neighborhoods cannot afford to export their limited capital. Thirdly, it denies local expertise the opportunity to grow and flourish.

We are therefore inclined to suggest at the outset that poor and minority people seeking to create livable and sustainable neighborhoods should get in the habit of using cheaper and, as much as possible, community based expertise to do their needs assessment and/or community planning. And, if the local expertise is nonexistent (as is often the case), then make its creation or development a priority of neighborhood's rebuilding efforts. Indeed, even third world countries have learned the lessons of not just acquiring any technology, but rather of acquiring what they call "appropriate technology." (Singer:1-27; Haberer:102).

Our point here is to de-emphasize unnecessary use of externally based expertise for consultancies. Like infant industries, neighborhood expertise needs some (not total) protection like certain industries need tariff sometimes. To provide the proper context for community and neighborhood redevelopment planning, we have introduced and utilized the concept and practice of needs assessment as a first step in this process to illustrate where and how to initiate community and neighborhood redevelopment.

Needs assessment

This is the traditional technique used by individuals and organizations to explore and assess needs. (Holt et al:8-10). For those communities and neighborhoods attempting or planning to undertake some form of community redevelopment, we suggest that they start with an assessment of their actual needs prior to committing any resources. As used in this book, needs assessment carries the same meaning as surveying the neighborhood or taking community inventory. In layman's terms, the question is : What do or don't we have in this neighborhood? It is important for the community to know its needs, what is or is not needed, the extent and amount of the need, and the time frame for meeting such needs. It is also necessary for a community to know the nature and the amount of resources available. When does the community need what resources and for what particular set of needs? For example, nearly all working poor communities and neighborhoods have an abundance of underutilized, unused, misused and unusable human resources. (Tabb: 106-110). Similarly, these same communities tend to have many unused vacant lots as well as abandoned vacant buildings. (Mills & Hamilton:223-227). One of the reasons why communities and neighborhoods should take inventories of their needs is that it is very useful for them to be able to determine what is needed by who, when and where.

Some approaches to needs assessment

Neighborhood needs may be determined or established by and from a variety of sources and techniques. In general, community needs can be deduced from (a) existing sources, (b) generation of new data and (c) other sources. (Holt et al:57; York:72). Among (a) the existing sources are (i) secondary data such as the US Census, (ii) trade fairs such as exhibits and promotion literature, (iii) expert judgement of knowledgeable and well informed individuals, (iv) service statistics from existing records and reports. (b) Generating new data may include (i) questionnaires formally administered to samples, (ii) public hearings (e.g. expert testimony), (iii) brainstorming, (iv) research and observations (including feasibility studies, need assessments and consultancies) and (v) community based institutions such as churches and fraternal organizations.

Use of these approaches and techniques to identify neighborhood needs may depend on time, place and the prevailing situations. Because we are dealing with the needs of the working poor and discussing how to make them more self-reliant, it is important that we avoid prescribing complicated and expensive ways of simply finding out what they need here and there. We shall therefore focus on those methods and techniques of surveying neighborhood needs which we consider to be useful, nontechnical and inexpensive. Many of the problems that afflict the poor and the minorities do not require as much high technology to diagnose as they do more common sense! Accordingly, we suggest the following approaches and sources as the affordable and effective means of surveying community needs by and for the working poor.

Community and neighborhood meetings and forums

Although community and neighborhood meetings and forums may indeed lack the accuracy and sophistication of the so called "hard data" (generally associated with questionnaires and random sampling), they do not only provide an accurate airing of the prevailing problems but do also give very realistic impressions of the community. Specifically, we have in mind the various community and neighborhood based organizations and groups which may be involved in social, economic and political activities, community and ethnic pressure groups, neighborhood and block improvement associations and groups, local churches, fraternal and patriotic societies and/or the local chamber of commerce. Some of the groups and organizations are the NAACP, Habitat for Humanity, ACLU, Urban League, ASPIRA, PUSH and the many community based nonprofit corporations which provide advocacy and support for citizen involvement in such issues as improving schools, better housing, fighting drug crimes.

We hasten to add here, however, that any one of these groups or organizations, regardless of how formal or informal it may be, may actually be involved in more than one form of the activities listed above. In fact, majority of these organizations and groups are actually involved in a multiplicity of such activities at the same time. But the point not to be missed here is that all these organizations and groups deal with the working poor and minorities and, in nearly all instances, they have some program or activity addressing or purporting to address the problem of poverty among the working poor and low income Americans. For many of them, assisting the poor is not only their mission but also their reason for being! Also, many of them do maintain permanent bases in the working poor and minority neighborhoods. In other instances, they do incorporate the working poor in the functional dynamics of their activities. It therefore seems obvious that, by virtue of their location and programs, many of these community based groups and organizations are indeed closer to the working poor (and their problems) than the once-every-10 year enumerator from the Census or the occasional academic or institutional researcher could ever hope to be. Now, this proximity to the problem, we would want to suggest, has the potential, if not the actuality, of informing us about the particular community situations more than the Gallup Poll! It is those who live with and close to the working poor and minorities who are likely to be more informed and knowledgeable about the problems of the poor. It therefore behooves those involved in identifying community and neighborhood needs and problems, to either collaborate or consult with those who live in the poor neighborhoods.

To summarize the point, the primary reason for undertaking any survey of community needs and resources is to utilize the results as the basis for structuring redevelopment programs and activities. When community based expertise is used to determine neighborhood needs as seen by and through the eyes of the working poor, it is likely to develop a more realistic picture and impression of the poor neighborhood. And as previously suggested, such an approach and source of data will be less expensive, save needed resources and certainly spare the working poor that helplessness and the confusion that sometimes accompanies what Staudt has referred to as "long and dirty research, with its huge, tedious questionnaires and uneven results conducted in the name of science with the 'tyranny of random sampling'"(p.92).

Service records

Most neighborhood based service activities have their respective organizational contexts within which they occurred. There are several ways of identifying needs from the service records. One of such ways is through expression. Needs are often expressed. And, as York points out, expressed need can best be identified through the examination of service statistics. These are the data on agency clientele. They are easily "the only true barometer of what people in need are demanding of the agency". (York:67). For instance, program waiting lists make good measures of unmet expressed needs. When these data are periodically tabulated for agency reports and other purposes, they do "constitute perhaps the least expensive source of need assessment data". (York:67)

In other words, when communities combine the use of community based know-how with proper use of similarly based sources of data, they are likely to generate not only accurate information but more importantly, a more realistic view and impression of the working poor neighborhood. We may simply have to overlook the working poor's fascination with and allure of high technology as the essential ally in the search for community development or as a tool for figuring out what is wrong in and with the poor neighborhoods.

As suggested previously, it is our view that there is not much need (let alone capacity) for high technology in the ghettos of America where the key problems include lots of people on full or partial government assistance, abandoned and vacant buildings, drugs and crime, joblessness and unemployment, youth delinquency, bad schools, inadequate health services and facilities. And the list goes on.

For such communities and neighborhoods, the local municipal or county housing office can provide the numbers of vacant buildings or the number of homeless people. The local criminal justice system units can provide information about juvenile problems. Similarly, information about various sectoral community level problems can easily be retrieved from both public and nonprofit agencies. These are inexpensive and reasonably reliable sources of community and neighborhood information on which needs assessment or any other form of neighborhood profiling can be based.

Brainstorming

Another useful and inexpensive technique for determining neighborhood needs is brainstorming which has been defined as a "creative conference for the sole purpose of producing suggestions or ideas that can serve as leads to problem solving".(Shafritz, 1985:50). We embrace this definition. Brainstorming allows expression of unpopular or unfamiliar ideas, some of which could turn out to be valuable if develope. (Hicks & Gullett:125). Operationally, it is desirable for a brainstorming session to have the following basic attributes: (a) no serious evaluation of ideas, (b) a very free flow of ideas, (c) solicit more and more ideas, and, (c) combine and improve ideas thus generated. The most fruitful organizational format for a brainstorming session is usually comprised of small groups of five to six individuals. (Hicks & Gullett: 125)

For purposes of conducting community needs assessment, the format outlined above can be operationalized at the community levels. Furthermore, a variant of traditional brainstorming has been described by Holt et al. as "well suited for needs assessment purposes". This form of brainstorming is called negative brainstorming. The focus of this variation of brainstorming is to "find faults, fault possibilities, weaknesses, lacking or unfulfilled functions" in a given community context. (Holt, et al,:98)

Poor and minority people can be counted on to speak up and identify what they have and do not have. We suspect that there is already too much of speaking up now. In fact, being 'negative', and especially in saying what you need, is the easiest thing for most of us. After this process of identifying community and neighborhood needs and resources is completed, it is up to the community leadership as well as public officials to conduct the appropriate analyses and evaluations of all the ideas thus generated. It is an effective and inexpensive method of finding out community needs and resources.

Consultancy

This is when a neighborhood temporarily retains the services of an individual or organization because of some presumed expertise. (Shafritz:84). Consulting has now become a universal professional practice in virtually all areas of human endeavor. It is often a technique of either transferring technology or using such technology where it might not otherwise have been used or available. So, one way of looking at consulting is as an equalizer.

But in our view, the purpose of retaining and using consultant expertise would be to investigate and establish community needs and resources in anticipation of and preparation for community planning. Although we have previously alluded to the rather common practice of using experts at the neighborhood level for various reasons and purposes which often include identifying and analyzing community needs and resources, we must bear in mind the fact that being a poor neighborhood automatically precludes that poor neighborhood from functioning like a middle class neighborhood where the problem of affordability may not be as acute. This is one of the reasons why we select to de-emphasize the use of hired out-of-neighborhood "expertise" in most aspects of community and neighborhood redevelopment. We believe it is economically unwise to require or even encourage poor neighborhoods to use sophisticated and expensive technical know how and tools in the same way and extent as middle class neighborhoods.

Sampling

Although there are many other methods and techniques of surveying community and neighborhood needs and resources which we have not even mentioned, we want to use this brief outline of the sampling techniques to conclude this section. As a research approach, sampling attempts to study a representative number of cases within a targeted community in order to generalize about a condition or situation in that community or neighborhood. Some of the techniques in the sampling procedure are: simple random, cluster, systematic, stratified, quota, telephone and mail sampling. (Wright,1979; Miller, 1991:60-64). Although sampling does in fact have higher rates of accuracy and reliability, it is too expensive and complicated to operationalize.

Planning for Neighborhood Development

Successful completion of needs assessment and the identification of neighborhood needs and resources available or needed, should naturally lead to planning for the particular neighborhood's redevelopment. As previously mentioned, planning is that process of establishing goals and determining the nature and amount of resources required to achieve the goals thus established.

To provide both the context and vehicle for meeting the neighborhood needs as may have been previously identified, this section summarizes various types of planning and implementation strategies needed for the redevelopment programs and projects. Contextual and operational goals and objectives should reflect the known and documented neighborhood needs and problems. But because the type of neighborhoods with which we are dealing have limited resources, it is most desirable that such neighborhood needs be prioritized in accordance with that neighborhood's abilities and resources. Prioritized needs will, in turn, serve as a guide for the neighborhood redevelopment goals, objectives, programs and activities.

A sense of progress in neighborhood redevelopment programs and activities may be detected and perhaps measured by and through the fulfillment of previously identified needs. More specifically, fulfillment of needs requires that community resources be allocated in accordance with definite and specific operational plans and procedures established during the planning phase.

Planning Approaches

According to Burchell and Sternlieb, there are four major categories of planning (1979:viii-xix). These are physical, social, economic and policy planning. For our present purposes, the four planning approaches are equally applicable to community and neighborhood redevelopment. And, in keeping with both the themes and assumptions undergirding this book, we suggest that these planning approaches be operationally linked so as to enhance planning complementarity. Although our definitions of these types of planning may at times appear to differ with those of Burchell and Sternlieb, we have retained and used their categorizations of planning.

Physical Planning

Our perception of physical planning is similar to an infrastructural policy. It encompasses the process of constructing and maintaining neighborhood facilities and services such as bridges, traffic signs and signals street lighting, maintenance, signs, cleaning, snow and refuse removal, water and sewage systems, zoning, waste collection and disposal, animal control, building inspection and maintenance, park maintenance, electric power and gas distribution, beautifying, tree planting and maintenance of same. (ICMA,1984:91). The public policy which governs the location, construction, use and maintenance of these facilities and services determines the quality of community life.

Part of being the working poor, the black and latino in urban America means living with run down infrastructures and chronically bad public services. As was noted in the chapter on neighborhoods, the anomic neighborhood is characterized by run down residential and commercial buildings, unkept streets, broken curbs and side walks, uncollected refuse on the streets, missing street and traffic lights, and the story goes on. Implementation of a community's infrastructure policy is generally influenced by many factors which include political and value dominance and orientation of policy makers and administrators. Additionally, it is influenced by the extent to which affected citizens participate in the policy making process. It is for such a reason that public policy ends up actually determining who got what and who didn't. Which section or ethnic group gets its streets cleaned or garbage collected? Who pays for the cost? Who benefits? Who defines what is the intended public good? Does the policy unify or displace the neighborhood? (Kruschkle & Jackson:114). And as we have argued in the chapter on empowerment, working poor and minority citizens must be involved at all policy stages: planning, policy making, implementation and administrative processes. And the starting point is at the neighborhood level.

Social Planning

Because we are engaged in an effort to rebuild the poor inner city neighborhoods, it is important that we also develop some mechanisms to manage and guide the social upheavals and turbulence inherent in the anomic and transitory types of neighborhoods. (Warren:62-63). Garson and Williams define social planning as the "forecasting of social policies and trends and the development of coordinated policies to change or direct social welfare and wellbeing" (1982:370). Allowing for the fact that this definition can be interpreted in different ways, our interest here is in that part of it which seeks "to change or direct social...wellbeing" of the working poor. We use the concept to mean that the ultimate goal of social planning is to change those social and related conditions which hamper the working poor and people of color.

Without having to discuss and critique welfare reforms (because we reckon that has been amply done by others), we are counting on the process of empowerment (discussed in a previous chapter), home ownership and the accompanying economic ownership and management (to be discussed in later chapters) to positively influence the behavior of the working poor and therefore impact on and guide inner city social upheavals and turbulence referred to above. Apart from the impact of ownership, the planning process and the social plan must ensure that those poor individuals who are eligible for or are receiving public assistance would also be required to work or to acquire more operational skills and/or engage in self employment activities.

Economic Planning

With regard to economic planning, there are possibly several ways by and through which economic regulation and manipulation is accomplished in the United States. But the phrase "economic planning" is generally associated with the government planned economies of the third world and the former socialist and communist countries rather than the capitalist economies which are generally based on market forces. (Chandler & Plano, 1988:58). For the purpose of this book and the community development and neighborhood effort it articulates, economic planning embraces such practices as business retention, attraction, expansion and formation. (Luke et al., 1988:33). We have discussed these aspects of economic development in chapter seven.

Contrary to what some may consider to be normal practice, community and neighborhood economic planning should begin with business and job retention. If a community is able to retain the businesses it already has, then we would suggest that an attempt be made to expand some of the existing businesses. If neither retention nor expansion or both are adequate to meet community employment needs, then the third and fourth strategies should be put in place. The latter two are business attraction and formation. The goals and objectives of economic development as set out in the neighborhood development plan should incorporate the four planning approaches outlined by Burchell and Sternlieb as well as the implementation sequence suggested here.

Policy Planning

Policy planning has been defined as that process of establishing goals, objectives, and priorities of public policy making. "The activity of policy planning requires formulators and decision makers to investigate the rationale,

110

intent, purpose, and strength of policy so that the resulting program is consistent with the intended aims." (Kruschkle & Jackson:61). And although we have retained much of this understanding and usage, we do, however, want to add two other elements.

First, and in keeping with the themes and assumptions stated in the first chapter, neighborhood residents must be included in the process of investigating the purposefulness and relevance of the policy being formulated. Secondly, policy planning, while dealing with neighborhood redevelopment, must emphasize and require linkages, not just as desirable but also as necessary attributes of enlightened public policy. The role of public policy in paving the way for empowering the working poor and sustaining community and neighborhood redevelopment efforts must be considered as especially critical. Without a supportive governmental apparatus, no form of community and neighborhood redevelopment could ever hope to succeed. The preceding remarks have framed the context for and outlined the relevant approaches to planning a linked community and neighborhood economic development.

Now, with the results of the needs assessment, established goals for neighborhood redevelopment and the resource requirements, we are in a position to specify the outstanding issues we face as a community. For example, do most working poor people work in or outside their communities or neighborhoods? How much money do they make as a neighborhood and where do they spend it! Do they own any businesses in their neighborhoods? With which banks do they do business and do the banks do business in the poor neighborhoods and communities? Detailed answers to these and the other pertinent questions raised and answered during the need assessment process will form bases for goal setting and the resource requirements for community and neighborhood development projects and activities.

Implementing Community Development

Typically, implementation is the execution of the plan or the policy. It is putting into practice what has been planned or formulated as a policy or project. Implementation follows the planning process or policy formulation and precedes the process of management. It is the link (the chain) that connects the theory or the policy to practice and the real world. (Goggin, et al.:3-26). Implementation is therefore transitional in nature and ceases to be once the plan is installed and the regular management process or the routine takes over. In a sense, implementation is terminal, in this sense. With regard to plan or program implementation, review of the following implementation sequence of community and neighborhood redevelopment efforts should also include a familiarity with Figure VIII:

> 1.　To ensure that community and neighborhood redevelopment programs and activities will be indeed linked and in conformity with the leading themes and assumptions, contribute to and enhance a coherent neighborhood life, it will be necessary to have a sound and comprehensive neighborhood plan. To avoid possible confusion, the suggested plan could be a revised version of the current borough or town plan. It does not have to be a new plan if there is one in existence. In operational terms, the plan (whether new or revised) should reflect most, if not all, community and neighborhood based ownership and operation of residential and economic establishments.
>
> 2.　Linkages and complementarities amongst community and neighborhood programs.
>
> 3.　Encourage and promote cooperation amongst community and neighborhood activities.
>
> 4.　Reflecting geographical and administrative parameters (Figure VIII), an ideal plan should encompass an entire neighborhood, or, at the very least, adjacent neighborhoods.
>
> 5.　Although plans could encompass a city, a county or a

congressional or other types of administrative districts, it is recommended that plans be restricted to neighborhoods as defined or described in chapter three.

6. When and if local political conditions are not conducive to such comprehensive and linked redevelopment, some consideration should be given to the neighborhood based nonprofit groups.

7. Neighborhood based blue and white color skill; for example, skills associated with maintenance and repairs should be resident in the neighborhood; similarly, doctors, accountants, lawyers and law enforcement personnel serving this community should also be resident.

8. Include a monetary and human capital investment and reinvestment plan by individual neighborhood residents as individual owners, public and private partnerships.

9. Partnerships may be entered into between municipal, county and state levels of government and local banks, credit unions, savings & loan and foundations.

10. Human capital investment should emphasize labor and service investment in either acquiring or rehabilitating one's residence or providing neighborhood service to a good cause.

11. Human capital investment may also be in the form of community pride which actually makes the other forms of investments possible.

As a general rule, involvement of community and neighborhood residents in the planning and implementation of community projects and programs is not just a desirable goal to be emphasized, it is a necessary condition to be required. This involvement is important because it has the distinct advantage of linking the original community need with the envisioned solution of a concrete reality as would be represented by the implemented project. Furthermore, such involvement has both empowering and motivational attributes which encourage and boost the confidence of the working poor in self reliance.

Traditionally, those who are economically and politically powerful and working hand in hand with the bureaucratic network in charge of community apparatus, have not been known for their regard or empathy for the working poor and people of color. Whatever else one may want to say, the record of community and neighborhood development planning over the past thirty years, has yielded little or nothing that has weathered the test of time! (Jencks & Peterson:460-478)

Our emphasis here is that planning and developing Black and Latino communities and neighborhoods is continuously bedevilled by economic and political power imbalances. That is, these communities cannot do what other communities do. These communities are politically and economically handled as colonies (Tabb:21; Fusfeld:28-40;). What is rather amazing is how easily this structure and the control it imposes on the poor and minority neighborhoods appears to escape everybody's notice! Until such colonial rela-tionships between the working poor and wealthier neighborhoods disappear (and no one, least of all this author, has illusions about the day it will disappear), there is not much that anyone can do to make Warren's integral and anomic neighborhoods equal. But absolute economic and political equality is not what we are seeking! We seek to empower the working poor to do for themselves in their neighborhoods what you and I, and all the other good doers, do or try to do for them.

Home Onwership:
The Bases of Neighborhoods

Introduction

> Because home ownership plays so vital a role
> in the financial well-being of American families...
> Virtually any form of home equity promotion
> should be encouraged.
>
> (Michael Sherraden)

> Home owners were more involved than respo-
> ndents who did not own homes, that is, those
> who were renters or had other living arrange-
> ments.
>
> (Norweeta Milburn & Phillip Bowman)

In this chapter, we have attempted to make a case for home ownership by that segment of Americans we identified as the working poor. Owning a home as an asset not only improves the owner's household stability but also psychologically connects such an owner to a viable and hopeful future. Ownership also stimulates the new owner to develop other assets including human capital. Furthermore, it increases individual's efficacy, social influence, political participation and enhances the welfare of the young ones. (Sherraden :295). The key point though is that home ownership constitutes the basis on which community and neighborhood redevelopment activities can be linked for maximum benefit to the residents and their communities. By converting the working poor from renters dependent on partial public assistance to home owners, we will thereby establish permanent residents as well as stakeholders with vital interests in the future of their communities and neighborhoods. Owning a home has its tangible and often intangible side effects and after effects to both the home owner and the neighborhood. It shows, among other things, that the home owner is a permanent feature of that community.

To redevelop run down and blighted neighborhoods, we need to have people who live and have a stake in their future in these communities and neighborhoods. And, as Milburn and Bowman have pointed out (Jackson:44), "residents who are home owners are physically rooted in their neighborhood". When and where this is the case, residents have a stake in their communities and can be counted on to care for both their properties and neighborhoods.

Neighborhoods, we have argued, provide the context within which to cultivate and nurture a sense of social and cultural belonging, pride and permanence as well as enhancing the neighborhood economic exchange. These important community attributes are less likely when and where residential stability as would be the case in the transitory or stepping-stone types of neighborhoods. There needs to be some form of permanence which can only be brought about by either economic or residential ownership or both. For most people, owning a home is probably the single most important investment that they are likely ever to make in their life time. In many ways, home ownership is the nearest thing to the fulfillment of the American dream. People may acquire other possessions such as boats, cars, clothes and even aircrafts, but none of these would appear to be comparable to owning a home.

But although home ownership is almost unanimously regarded as the ultimate American ideal, this apparent unanimity changes instantly when we are dealing with poor people, especially when the poor are people of color. In anticipation of the likely arguments against home ownership by the working

116

poor, we want to begin by noting two points here. One, when given the society's view of the poor, one cannot even attempt to associate the poor with ownership. Indeed, the fact of being poor is clearly incompatible with the fact of owning an asset or a home. It violates logic to be both poor and a home owner at the same time. This is a difficult argument to ignore even with good reasons. But it seems to us as though this argument has more of an appearance of logic than accuracy and validity of pure logic. It has more to do with how the society views the poor than any form of logic. We have offered another section on this topic later on in the chapter. But before dealing with this question, an overview of the history of home ownership in the US may assist us in placing things in the proper perspectives.

Some historical notes

For the most part, provision of housing in America was considered a private sector concern. And although there was no formal US housing policy committing public funds for housing until after WWII, the Homestead Act of 1862, under which pioneers were given 160 acres of land, serves as the earliest governmental attempt to facilitate ownership. Here, we only want to note the idea that this was perhaps the very first asset-based welfare policy in US history (Sherraden:191). To be sure, the government did provide housing for soldiers during WWI for a very brief period. But it took the great economic depression of the 1930's to get federal government fully involved in public housing affairs. The Housing Act of 1934 created the Federal Housing Administration (FHA) to insure home mortgages built by the private sector.

The purpose of FHA loans was for "new construction, purchase, or rehabilitation of inner city urban homes" but only a negligent percent of these loans were ever made for rehabilitation of inner city urban homes. Even though it lasted for a brief period, the 1937 housing act included a slum

117

clearing program "and created the US Housing Authority which built some 114,000" units for low income people (Palen:242-243).

By the time WWII came to an end, it was clear to most keen observers that "urban America, especially the central business districts, was headed for economically hard times"(Palen:244). And although some slum clearing was going on during this time, the basic problem was the cost of "buying [urban land], tearing down [old buildings] and rebuilding the inner city were not economically feasible for private developers." (Palen: 245). The 1949 Housing Act was passed for the purpose of providing funds for urban renewal. It contained two important elements: public and private sections. One section dealt with provision and production of public housing. The other dealt with urban redevelopment .

Commercial and financial groups were interested in urban redevelopment because it was expected to serve as the buffer against encroachment by slums. Residents of the newly rehabilitated urban housing were similarly expected to be middle class families with sufficient purchasing power. From this point of view, housing rehabilitation was not necessarily intended to benefit the poor. Be that as it may, the Housing Act of 1949 was perhaps a turning point in governmental involvement in public housing in at least one important way. It not only embraced urban redevelopment but also provided public funds to

> buy, clear, and improve the renewal site after which the ownership of the land would revert to the private sector.When the renewal area was approved, the authorities were given the power to buy properties at market prices and, in cases where the owner refused to sell, to have the property condemned and compensation paid through the government's right of domain.
> Once the city acquired all the land in the renewal area, the existing buildings were destroyed (as modified in 1954) and the land was cleared. New streets, lights and public facilities were then installed, and finally the land was sold to a private developer who agreed to build in accordance with an approved development plan.The developer paid about 30% of what it had cost the local government to purchase, clear, and improve the

land. This so-called *write-down* was the difference between what the land had cost the public and what it was sold for to the private developer. Two-thirds of the city's loss was madeup in a direct cash subsidy from the federal government. Thus, the control of the program was, and is, basically local, while most of the government funds are federal. (Palen:245).

Ideas of interest deducible from this quotation include government's right of domain to take and distribute private property, expenditure of its funds to enhance its policies and the practice of assisting citizens (including wealthy developers) to acquire property or assets. For our purposes, these ideas are useful because they suggest different methods by and through which public policy has been and continues to be used to assist citizens to own assets. The book attempts to apply these ideas to empower the working poor through accumulation of assets. What no one should do though is assume or think that such accumulation can be achieved easily. Whatever may or may not happen in the pursuit of this endeavor, politics has an important role to play in either enhancing or hindering ownership of any type of assets especially for those who have or traditionally exercise less political power. In the next section, we provide a brief outline of political impact on ownership of any assets in the US.

Politics of housing the working poor

A recent Report of the *Twentieth Century Fund Task Force on Affordable Housing* identified and recommended four strategies for housing poor and low income people. The first strategy would assist the low and moderate income families (some of whom are easily the working poor) to meet their housing needs; the second strategy would increase housing supply; the third strategy would promote tenant self-sufficiency while the fourth would support increase but equitable funding of housing as well as sound fiscal prudence. (p.11).

119

With the exception of the third strategy which acknowledges but thrashes Bush Administration's "New Paradigm" (which they have defined as "giving poor people, who are currently the objects of vast and sometimes paternalistic federal policies, greater authority over their lives"), the report does not seem to share the themes stated in our chapter one or, for that matter, our operative thesis that ownership empowers. But our reason for citing the four strategies outlined and well articulated in this report is that, by and large, they represent the mainstream support and advocacy for housing the poor. This advocacy for mainstreaming public housing for the poor in the 1990's is like a throw-back to an era goneby when government was more hospitable to the poor. Nowadays, it is almost a cliche to mention that both Reagan and Bush Administrations (though to a lesser extent in case of the latter) were not particularly hospitable to the poor (working or not).

While we are not necessarily opposed to the strategies advanced in this report, we do feel, however, that the record of public housing is clear and does speak for itself. Like the other dead-ended public assistance programs, public housing has not provided the poor (particularly that segment we have identified as 'working poor') the right to be involved and participate in that process of improving their lives. As we have argued elsewhere, there exists natural expectations for results when we do something or something is done for or to us. So, what is or should the expectation be after providing public housing for an able bodied and mentally fit person? Consider, when an eligible student is given financial assistance to attend college, society looks forward to someday when that young man or woman would be self-supporting, and, certainly, a contributing member of his/her community and neighborhood? Such then, is the expectation. What then is the expectation for publicly housing somebody?

Although both the idea and legal provisions for home ownership by the poor and low income appears to have been included in the various versions of public housing programs over the years, the emphasis of ownership by the poor has never been a significant part of public housing. (20th Century Report:42-48). Perhaps when given the economic realities of home ownership and the society's perception of the working poor and minorities, such lack of emphasis is understandable. Additional factors regarding lack of emphasis for home ownership may be related to racial discrimination against African Americans who have a high proportional representation among the working poor.

We may observe too, in passing though, that when all is said and done, public housing is a good source of local revenue, provides jobs for administrative and maintenance crews at the municipal level, and, provides working opportunities for the construction industry. Indeed, the federal government, at the behest of the construction industry, pays for the construction, rent, management and maintenance of public housing. In this sense, we are satisfied that the working poor and minorities are mostly political pawns in the politics of public housing. We therefore agree with Mills and Hamilton that "much of the political support for public housing has come from the construction industry". (Mills & Hamilton:241). And, for those who keep a keen watch over our domestic economic performance, they will have noticed that depending on how well or poorly the construction industry is doing, the federal government will either curtail or increase construction of more public housing. (Mills & Hamilton:241). Such a reaction by the federal government is generally a response to the economic needs of the middle class rather than an effort to enhance home ownership by the working poor.

FHA's homogeneous neighborhood policy

When considering all the factors which may have contributed, directly and indirectly, to the decay of inner city public and private housing, one factor appears to be singularly important. That factor is the role of government itself acting through its agencies. The federal government, through its agencies, designed and promoted residential segregation and discrimination against black potential property owners. Between 1934 and civil rights era of the mid-1960's, FHA was systematically engaged in building segregated residential neighborhoods as well as denying African Americans opportunities to own homes. The federal government, it has been said,

> insisted upon discriminatory practices as a prerequisite to government housing aid. The FHA official manuals cautioned against infiltration of inharmonious racial and national groups, a lower class of inhabitants, or the presence of incompatible racial elements in the new neighborhoods. Zoning was advocated as a device for exclusion and the use was urged of a racial covenant, prepared by FHA itself, with a space left blank for the prohibited races and religions, to be filled by the builder as occasion required. (Palen:244)

With these types of disabling governmental activities, it should not be surprising then that home ownership among the poor, the black and the latino has been almost unthinkable. And, when and if such home ownership occurred (as it surely has occurred among the well to do African Americans), it has occurred in a racially segregated framework as laid down by the FHA bureaucrats. FHA has contributed greatly to the contemporary housing and neighborhood segregation. Because of the neglect that unavoidably accompanies discriminatory practices, public housing tends to deteriorate rather quickly as is evidenced by the many abandoned inner city public housing developments. Even if not all public housing is bad or neglected, the ones that have become infested with illegal drugs where drug related violence and crime reign high (and they are many in the major urban areas) do, indeed, symbolize, perhaps more than anything else, all that is bad in and about public housing, inner city neighborhoods and communities. Our task then is to convert those occupied, vacant and/or bonded up public housing units to owner occupied units by the working poor.

Who wants to live in the ghetto?

But even before we discuss a number of other issues relating to home ownership by the working poor, there is an immediate question which must be asked and answered in order to pave the way for the other topics. The question is: knowing as we all do about life in the ghetto, who would want to live there? We do not think anybody would! But then this answer is not real. The reality is that the people who are targeted by this book live now. We can imagine and argue about the horrors of drugs and crime and express our outrange and sympathies about their poverty, but the bottom line is that they live there every day. To change and improve the quality of their lives, we may choose any of the following: to relocate them, leave them as they are, keep on talking about poverty, be sorry and helpful as usual, keep on researching and writing about the poor or propose and assist them to improve the neighborhoods where they now live. We are proposing the last option. It is in keeping with our themes stated earlier.

Our operating premise here is that the working poor (many of whom are people of color) would not only agree to live in the inner city poor neighborhoods where they now live but also that their and our options in this matter are extremely limited, to say the least. And as Harold Rose once suggested, ghetto is like a fixed feature which appears to have successfully defied all attempts to tamper with it (Rose:141). It seems to us that this is an interesting insight with which few can differ. We must therefore reckon with the existence of the ghetto and doing within it whatever we can. We believe there is much that can be done within the ghetto. Without pretending that we have completely resolved these legitimate concerns, we have proposed in the following chapters what we believe to be a more practical way of initiating sustainable change in many of these neighborhoods through a system of home and business ownership.

Living in public housing is not likely to encourage self reliance

While one cannot deny that public housing has been and continues to be essential to the working poor, it would be difficult to make a persuasive argument that it has done much more than just provide shelter to the needy individuals even as their neighborhoods keep on deteriorating. From the point of view of neighborhood redevelopment, we are unable to find evidence anywhere suggesting that public housing development for working poor families has also helped turn around inner city poor neighborhoods in the manner we have suggested in this book. In fact, we believe that if there is any evidence, it probably suggests that public housing, both as a public policy and strategy against poverty, have succeeded only in exacerbating both the degree and extent of poverty as may be exhibited by the anomic type of neighborhoods. And although people like Charles Murray are basically hostile to the working poor, they are not entirely without some redeeming points of view. The argument for greater self reliance among the working poor and people of color to own homes and businesses in their own neighborhoods would appear to be incompatible with a prolonged eligibility to and stay on public assistance.

In particular, the idea and practice of self reliance would be seriously undermined by continued dependence on that combination of public assistance and public housing for individuals who are physically and mentally able. For instance, when an individual is on public assistance, he/she also becomes eligible for subsidized public housing. From time to time, this may happen to an individual for any number of reasons. But when and if it ever becomes a regular or permanent condition, a cycle of dependence emerges. We view such dependence as having potential in diminishing a sense of self worth in the individual thus dependent. Original intentions and rationale underlying public assistance and housing are almost always honorable. But when dependence on even honorable assistance extends too long, its long term effects and consequences can be devastating to the struggle for individual self sufficiency.

Who and how many live in public housing

The impression that "most public housing projects consist of large, ugly developments that are poorly maintained and managed" with large "concentrations of minority families with undisciplined children and high crime rates" and tend to "have a negative impact on the surrounding community" (20th Century:51), is not accurate. Actual facts of the entire system of public housing in the US do not warrant such a totally negative image. According to the 20th Century Fund Report," only 27% of public housing developments are high-rise buildings, 32% are garden apartments, 16% are low-rise, walk-up apartments and 25% are single family or townhouse structures." The image of the high-rise projects as the typical public housing may not be a fair representation.

Moreover, the impression one gets from politicians and mass media commentators that most public housing tenants are "welfare-dependent single-women with children" is not accurate either. The 20th Century Fund Report adds that about "38% of public housing residents are elderly", "a small but growing percentage..." are handicapped young and middle aged single individuals", many of whom would otherwise be homeless. Even although there continues to exist a significant number of single-parent households among public housing tenants, the great majority of public housing residents are "married couples without children". Also noteworthy is the fact that "about 42% of all nonelderly households in the public housing include a wager earner" (p.52).

Two other points of interest here are, one, most residents of public housing averaged $6,539 in 1988 and that both black and white tenants of public housing had about the same annual income. Secondly, the racial and ethnic composition of public housing tenants is: white, 38%, black, 49%, latinos and other minorities, 13%. "But in large urban areas, 83% of public housing households are minority." (20th Century Fund:51-52)

Our overall aim of home ownership by the working poor would be well served by all three types of public housing (high-rise, garden apartments or town houses). That 42% of the households in public housing have at least one wage earner is also of interest because it gives a clue as to who may be a working poor. Now that we have a clue as to who lives in public housing, it would help our discussion if now develop an overview of home ownership among African Americans in general and regardless of economic status. Note that they constitute about one half of public housing tenants.

Home ownership among African Americans

If we consider how government agencies discouraged and obstructed African Americans from owning homes (Palen: 244) and then consider how easily mortgage and other lending financial institutions have and continue to routinely discriminate against African Americans to this day, we might get an idea of how difficult it is going to be for the working poor (among whom African Americans constitute a proportional majority) to become home owners. Recently, a federal regulator told a US Senate Sub-Committee that African Americans who apply for home mortgages are turned down more than twice as often as whites. (*N.Y.Times*, 5/17/90:A18). Unfortunately and as Figure IX suggests, just as race has been the governing factor for home ownership among regular blacks, it is very likely that the situation will even be worse for working poor blacks trying to own homes.

Figure IX

Home Ownership Rates vs Household on Public Assistance
by Race and Metropolitan Areas:1979

Metro Areas	Households on % Public Assit.		Homeownership % Rates		H/hold Median Income in $	
	Black	White	Black	White	Black	White
Atlanta	16.3	3.5	41.8	67.4	11,232	20,654
Baltimo	25.1	4.7	36.4	67.3	2,397	20,825
Bmnghm	18.9	5.1	52.9	72.7	9,369	17,765
Boston	25.4	7.8	23.0	55.7	11,099	19,384
Buffalo	30.2	6.2	34.2	67.1	9,181	18,067
Chicago	27.1	3.8	33.5	64.4	12,609	22,501
Clvlnd	22.6	4.2	42.7	69.5	12,068	20,532
Dallas	12.8	6.6	46.6	65.6	11,792	20,198
Detroit	27.1	6.1	52.8	76.1	13,684	22,915
Gary In.	19.8	4.2	52.9	73.8	16,342	22,901
Houston	10.8	2.4	47.2	62.7	13,775	23,054
Los Ang	23.4	7.9	39.2	52.1	12,423	19,051
Miami	15.7	8.2	44.2	57.2	11,356	16,616
Milwaukee	21.7	4.8	35.2	61.9	9,382	18,937
New York	24.1	7.4	18.4	36.9	10,979	17,969
Newark	23.2	4.5	28.3	64.9	12,402	3,208
Phildph	28.4	5.6	53.6	61.6	11,369	19,683
S Frncsco	24.0	6.3	37.6	56.1	12,631	21,085
Wash. DC	12.0	2.4	37.1	61.3	16,484	26,614

Source: McFate,K. *The Metropolitan Area Fact Book*, Joint Center for Political Studies, Washington, DC, 1988.

In theory and in practice, it is not in the nature of things for the poor and the powerless to ever discriminate against the economically and politically powerful. By being poor, black, latino and powerless, one is automatically subject to both economic and racial discrimination. Under these circumstances, home ownership becomes an impossibility. Having recognized this fundamental point, we have suggested that the way to overcome this obstacle is for the working poor to be self reliant. That is, upon being empowered, the working poor will not only do what others do to provide for themselves but, more importantly, influence the system to do what they need done. That means getting involved in ones local, state and national politics and doing and going where others go to pursue their interests.

With regard to the information provided in Figure IX, let us begin by going back to Figure III in chapter two where it was noted that, on proportional basis, there were 4 nonwhite persons living in poverty in 1979 for every one white person. Corresponding figures for 1985 were 3 nonwhites for one white. This trend has continued well into the 1990's. Together with the other data, this trend confirms what is generally accepted that if the incidence of poverty is proportionately higher among people of color, then their rate of home ownership is correspondingly lower as is indicated in Figure IX. In the 19 cities appearing on Figure IX, the average rate of home ownership among African Americans was 59.6% of that of whites. The African American household median income for the same period and in the same cities was 58.8% of their white counterparts. So, if it has been this difficult for people with presumably above poverty threshold income to own homes, how much more must it be for the working poor?

Do the poor have a right to a free home?

Although not so specifically stated, the question of the working poor owning homes raises other questions. Because they are poor, how can they afford a home while others who probably have higher incomes have not been able to buy homes? Do they, we may be permitted to wonder as the editors of *Fortune Magazine* may have wondered some thirty years ago (Editors of Fortune:97-114), whether or not the working poor have more right to a free home than you do to a free new car because you are poor? Is it not incongruent, as we argued earlier, that being poor means one is not able to provide for one's necessities? One may therefore wonder as to how you can own a home or an apartment in a highrise building if, in fact, you are poor and your rent is already subsidized - saying nothing about the other forms of public assistance to which you may be eligible? The trouble with these and similar questions is that they are loaded, wrongly framed and too narrowly focused in that the economic and social cost of maintaining the poor far exceeds that of making them economically and socially independent. Perhaps a more appropriate set of questions may start by enquiring whether society is obligated to assist the poor and if it is, should pay for the subsidized rents and/or welfare hotel bills? And, regardless of the answer to the question: is it not still a fact that tax payers continue to pay for the rent subsidies and the welfare hotel bills? (Mills & Hamilton:246-248). Considering that society still pays for the bill to house the working poor, it would seem to us that, in the present circumstances, society must make a choice as to whether to keep on paying rental subsidies and welfare hotel bills indefinitely or find another way which would lessen the public financial burden while helping the working poor to be more self dependent. (20th Century Fund Report:59). Put differently, this is to say that the public is already paying these bills. The chances of discontinuing such payments without alternative support for those who are dependent on public assistance would be minimal and unwise.

Furthermore, societal obligations are not only reserved for the much taunted working poor but also extend to the nonpoor. In this regard, Michael Sherraden has pointed out that over a period of time,

the nonpoor have successfully lodged a series of claims against the resources of the state. [T]he claims of the nonpoor, enacted into public policy in the form of nontargeted welfare benefits, comprise a total of $651.0 billion or 84% of all welfare expenditures...[Of this amount] housing makes up $48.7 billion or 7.5% of the nonpoor welfare state. (Sherraden:64-65).

Affordability: Can the working poor afford to own a home?

Because this is one question we must confront head on, let us refer back to the end of chapter two where we described a working poor family of three with an annual income of $14,990 and living in a two-bedroom apartment. We use this family as the protype of a working poor family. Let us also visualize the scenario where this family becomes the owner of the two bedroom apartment where they now live as subsidized renters. We begin by making reference to Figure XI. This figure is a modified version of one adopted from the 20th Century Fund Task Force on Affordable Housing. The reader may recall that the 1991 market rental value of the two bedroom apartment was $908 of which $359 was the family's out of pocket monthly payment and the balance of $577 was subsidy. To determine how well this family can afford to own the apartment they now rent, we have developed some scenarios. In order to follow and understand our reasoning here, reference should be made to this family's income, rental subsidy and the data on Figure XI.

In scenario one, we consider the possibility of this family buying the apartment they now rent for $31,779 which amount is the average (weighted) sale of the HUD built units and as provided in the 20th Century report. Through the local bank or other community based agencies involved in low income housing development, this family applies and gets a 30 year mortgage of $31,779 at 10% annual rate of interest and a required down payment of $841 and no closing costs. In this instance, this family would have a monthly mortgage note of $248.80 which compares very favorably to the $359 they are paying now in addition to the subsidy of $577. And, if the same mortgage was for 15 years at the same rate and with the same amount of down payment, the monthly mortgage note would be $308.35 which is still less than this family's out of pocket monthly payments of $359 for a subsidized apartment.

Figure XI
Average Sales Prices
Combined 1st and 2nd Mortgage Amount and Down Payments
for Programs with Sales

Public Housing Authority	Average Sales Price ($)	Average Down Payment ($)
Baltimore (N=28)	23,434	500
Chicago (N=14)	22,076	2,670
Denver		
Upper Lawrence (N=44)	27,300	800
Arapahoe (N=44)	37,500	0
L. A. County (N=9)	87,136	1,270
McKeesport (N=9)	21,688	3,363
Muskegon Heights (N=2)	7,550	350
Nashville (N=15)	21,177	294
Newport News (N=15)	24,213	0
Reading (N=8)	12,000	600
St.Mary's County (N=30)	12,500	1,000
Tulsa (N=1)	30,000	742
Washington,D.C. (N=23)	64,738	3,239
Wyoming (N=8)	38,153	640
Average (weighted) All Sales	31,779	841

Source: *20th Century Fund Report of the Task Force*
For Affordable Housing, New York, 1991:63
(This is an abridged adaptation of Table 4)

NOTES ON FIGURE XI: In practical terms, average sales in Figure XI do not reflect 1st and 2nd mortgages as is the case in Table 4. In nearly all cases, 2nd mortgages are forgiven after a while. Actual mortgages therefore ended up being much less than the amount we have used in our discussion. In other instances, even the down payments were given and forgiven later.

In scenario two, let us consider the most expensive units in Los Angeles County where they were selling for $87,136. In this case, the same family, now living in L. A. County and buying the unit they rent, qualifies for a 30 year mortgage of $87,136, less $1,270 down payment, at 10% annual interest. The 30 year mortgage monthly payment would be $690.05 and $855.25 if the mortgage was for 15 years. In both instances, the monthly payment is less than the $908 monthly payment paid during 1991 for the publicly subsidized apartment. The point here is that with a different public policy which emphasized ownership by the working poor, this family could easily have accumulated some equity within the prevailing subsidy system and without requiring the tax payers to pay an additional penny to what is already paid.

Scenarios three and four embrace Washington, D.C. and Chicago - the two major urban areas well known for poverty and neighborhood decay. According to Figure XI, the housing units in Washington, D.C. would sell for $64,738 while the Chicago selling price would be $22,076. Now, using the same format as in the other scenarios and respective down payments, a mortgage for the Washington D.C. units to the same family would mean a monthly note of $494.23 for 30 year and $612.54 for 15 year mortgages. Corresponding figures for Chicago units would be $155.95 and $193.30 for a 30 and 15 year mortgages respectively. Recent initiatives to convert public housing to ownership by low income people have been well summarized in one of the chapters of the 1992 20th Century Fund Report on affordable housing. In a rather comprehensive manner, the chapter broaches and examines a number of features and characteristics of the so called Public Housing Homeownership Demonstration (PHHD). Some of the points explored are the origin of the privatization of public housing in 1984, some of the reasons which prompted HUD to sell public housing, pricing policies and resale restrictions of HUD properties, how to secure and use private capital, the allure of home ownership, the desirable characteristics of the buyers, ways of determining extent of home owner satisfaction, delinquencies and defaults of this type of low income home ownership, how the nonbuyers were handled including litigations on involuntary relocations, and, finally, the major problems and constraints encountered as these HUD initiatives were pursued. (pp:57-81).

While it probably is not necessary for us to delve into all the aspects of PHHD initiatives, some of the aspects appear to support ownership of public housing by the working poor. For example, "HUD data indicate that homebuyers' satisfaction with their units was quite high [and that over] 77% of PHHD participants were satisfied [while] fewer than 10% expressed dissatisfaction." (*20th Century Report*:66). And, as Sherranden (p.295) has pointed out the positive impact of ownership on the individual person, the 20th Century Report adds that 78% of PHHD participants credited homeownership with making them feel better about themselves while another two-thirds were made to feel financially more secure by homeownership and, still, another 52% had a greater sense of control of their lives as a result of becoming home owners.

The 20th Century Report (71-80) has also provided us with the downside to the privatization of public housing. To some extent, the report enumerated a number of problems arising from the effort to convert public housing tenants to owners of where they live. One of the problems cited was that eight of the original seventeen local housing authorities never got to sell more than 15% of their housing units. Another problem was that only about one quarter of the planned public housing units were completed and sold by the deadline set by HUD. Still, another problem was the apparent inefficiency and lack of commitment of some of the local housing authorities. Other problems emanated from conflicts within some communities, flawed program designs, adverse local market conditions and inadequate buyer incomes.

Although it is not without difficulties, it appears to us that the question of affordability has been affirmatively and sufficiently answered by the foregoing. Incomes of HUD's PHHD home buyers ranged between $7,500 to $17,000. This averaged to be $12,250 which is well within income brackets sketched out in Figure I. It is therefore within reason to maintain that (with or without subsidy), the working poor can indeed afford to own and maintain homes, and, to be sure, accumulate equity like the rest of us. What is needed (and therefore what is not in place) is a new vision and a different public policy which would make this possible. Such a vision and such a public policy would have to properly focus on empowering such new home owners so that they can do for themselves what the rest of us purport to do for them.

Additional hurdles for the working poor to overcome

Being able to afford a mortgage is one thing and being able to get one is quite another thing. That being the case, a principal concern of those pursuing home ownership is how and where to secure a mortgage if HUD did not provide one. As a general practice, private real estate developers and dealers, banks, mortgage institutions and some local public officials have traditionally discriminated against African American and Latino prospective home owners even when they are middle class. One can only surmise how negatively these institutions and agencies are likely to react when dealing with the working poor. The slang terminology for this type of mortgage, financial or business loan discrimination against people of color is otherwise known as redlining.

Redlining may be traced to federal government's policies on homogeneous neighborhoods during the 1930's. But regardless of its origin, the practice is alive and well today. Nowadays, the practice is still commonly but silently and evasively utilized by many banks and financial institutions to deny or avoid investing or insuring cars and properties in many poor and minority neighborhoods. (*City Limits*, 1/1990:6; *NY Times*, 5/17/1990:A18). Now, our thrust towards community and neighborhood empowerment must include the necessary abilities to either generate or create capital. For, without

134

the necessary capital with which to finance redeveloping efforts, the case for community redevelopment becomes untenable. In the following two chapters, we have discussed both economic development and investment in the working poor and minority communities and neighborhoods. We have outlined various types and strategies of generating and creating capital. For now, let it suffice to say that for community empowerment to succeed, we must find some way to either overcome or circumvent the practice of redlining.

Another common practice, also used against the working poor and people of color, is known as *blockbusting* (Palen: 265-266; Gilliam:65-66). This practice refers to the unscrupulous efforts by white realtors to scare white home owners with the pretext that their neighborhood is fast becoming black or latino. The idea is that white home owners would get scared by the rumor or knowledge that people of color are moving into their neighborhood and that, being scared, they sell their homes at throw away prices as they flee the changing neighborhood. When and if this situation occurs, it has two effects. One, the real estate agent makes more money. Two, the incoming African American or Latino pays more for the same house. Needless to say, if this same practice has had such an effect of making it harder for the minority middle class, how much more will it prevent working poor from becoming home owners?

So, we are facing a situation of dual extremes. First, the working poor and people of color have been largely shut out of home ownership by and through the regular private sector transactions. Secondly, they have been subjects and recipients of dead-ended and virtually lifeless public housing assistance. None of these conventional modes of housing appears capable of making the working poor full participants in American home ownership. It is unlikely that either of the two approaches will make much difference in the future. Given this uncertainty and the historical inability to either house the working poor properly or improve their neighborhoods, it is necessary that we think of and develop a more viable alternative approach to local homeownership.

But before outlining proposals for home ownership and occupation by the working poor in their own neighborhoods, there are two points which should be noted. One, we accept Harold Rose's observation in the passage below that it may never be possible to change or eliminate the ghetto through any form of territorial configurations. And although this point sounds somewhat fatalistic and even deterministic, it is clearly based on historical evidence. The second point (which reflects key themes of this book) is that we must accept what we have been unwilling or unable to accept thus far that the working poor now live in the ghetto and in all likelihood will live there until the end of time! Harold Rose's apt admonition is that

> [t]he ghetto appears to be a fixed feature of urban real estate in American cities in that its disappearance is nowhere in sight. No amount of physical tampering with these configurations has reduced the extent of their territorial base. Attempts to modify the ghettos as physical entities, especially efforts designed to break them up, have met with failure, for the physical entity itself is simply an expression of a set of forces which allocate housing to black people in such a manner as to give rise to such physical entities. Thus, the removal of a segment of that entity, through urban renewal or any other programs engaged in urban redevelopment, only leads to the regeneration of additional appendages contiguous to the main body of the entity, since the basic ghetto forming process is left unaltered (Rose:140).

The Contiguous Ownership and Occupation

Concept of contiguous ownership and occupation

The analogy in chapter one and the rhetorical question as to which came first: poverty or the collapse of the inner city neighborhoods, may be appropriate here. For, if we heed Harold Rose's admonition not to tamper with the physical territorial boundaries of the ghetto and then take into consideration the presence of numerous problems in the working poor and other inner city neighborhoods, it is very difficult, if not impossible, to know or determine what to do first or where to start. It is in recognition of these difficulties that we decided to adopt the concept of *contiguous ownership and occupation*. By our definition, contiguous ownership and occupation means that home ownership and occupation initially occur and thereafter expand in a physically sequential, adjacent and continuous manner. Put in other words, this is to say that owning and occupying homes and or apartments in the redeveloped neighborhoods shall start and expand contiguously for the practical and yet instinctive reasons of security, survival and mutual interest and self enhancement. This is a fundamental aspect of this proposal. (See Table XII).

Rationale

The rationale underlying the concept of contiguous ownership, occupation and living can be illustrated in the following manner. Take two, three or more families whose economic and social circumstances are similar to those of the three-member family described near the end of chapter two. Each family's annual income falls between $9,500 and $15,000. They are similarly, though not identically, motivated in owning a home, an apartment or a condo. They live in a fairly blighted inner city neighborhood. Given their income, their chances of ever making it to the suburbs are not very good. But through the efforts of some local church, a CDC program or a Jack Kemp-type of HUD, it works out that these families end up owning rehabilitated brown stone but adjacent homes or adjacent apartments on the same floor of a highrise. It so happens that this neighborhood has its fair share of winos and junkies who sometimes like to sit up in front of any home to carry on a conversation or do some carousing or whatever they do including dropping empty bottles or helping themselves anywhere. Similar behavior by drug addicts and/or pushers

137

may occur from time to time. Judging by its appearance and what goes on in this neighborhood, it has all the characteristics of an anomic neighborhood.

Given this scenario, we feel that those families who end up as owner/occupants of the said homes or apartments will henceforth be tied together by their ownership and occupancy of contiguously situated homes or apartments. It also appears to us that, for any given potential or actual threat to these families' properties, their security will henceforth be clearly entwined. Furthermore, it appears reasonable that these families' wishes and interests in enhancing the values of their new homes would be similar. If it should occur that their properties were threatened by whosoever, one would expect that these families would cooperate in those things which protect and enhance their individual and collective interests. And as neighbors, they are likely to object to any behavior, on the part of their other neighbors or outsiders, which would appear as if it would destroy or devalue their homes or apartments. Our expectation and argument is that other similarly situated neighbors or new home owners, would behave in the same manner. It would seem to be the natural reaction.

Proposed Neighborhood Physical Setting

The proposed neighborhood physical setting corresponds to the neighborhood physical setting in Figure VIII and the residential layout in Figure XII. By sheer coincidence, our conceptualization of the residential layout and approach to the redevelopment of the blighted neighborhoods, appear to share certain features and resemblances with the Nehemiah concept. For the Nehemiah concept to work as intended and to keep prices affordable, they had to build a large number of single-family houses on cleared and unencumbered lots. In that way, enough people with real stakes in the community will be available to support the rebuilding of schools, stores and other services. (*N.Y. Times*, 8/26/90,NJ:15)

Figure XII

Contiguous Residential Layout

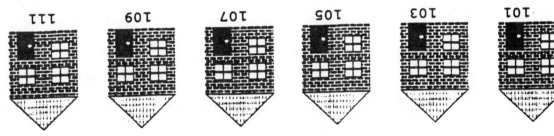

In some ways, our proposal shares in all important features of the Nehemiah Plan except on income eligibility because our income eligibility is pretty much within the prevailing poverty thresholds. We also differ substantially with the Nehemiah Plan in our advocacy for linking all social and human services assistance efforts to physical rehabilitation of particular neighborhood. Although our suggested proposal would be equally applicable to new housing development such as HUD's PHHD, our thinking is more in line with the traditional urban redevelopment or renewal preferably without the housing demolition and relocations which usually accompany the so called urban renewal (Perry:45).

And as we argue later on in this chapter, if and when our proposal would be implemented, demolition of existing housing stock would be unnecessary because redevelopment and/or rehabilitative effort would target such units. The envisaged acquisition, redevelopment and occupation of the rehabilitated homes would start and follow a numerical continuum such as house numbers 101, 102, 103, 104, 105 and or any other such clear linear sequence. This pattern of ownership and occupation would not leave any vacant spaces or buildings or apartments between any new home owners. The absence of vacant spaces would deny room for unneighborly activities. This arrangement would be utilized until the entire block would be thus redeveloped or rehabilitated, owned and occupied. The homes and blocks thus owned and occupied would constitute sound and practical bases for reclaiming and redeveloping the working poor neighborhoods. When and where this process would be followed and completed, entire neighborhoods would be characterized by homes and apartment buildings thus owned and occupied.

If, as it is likely to happen, the effort is to rehabilitate and convert abandoned apartment buildings to owner-occupied premises, the rehabilitative process should suitably start at either the ground or top floors and continue upwards or downwards as the case may be and as is deemed practical. There should not be spaces or vacant apartments between the newly occupied floor or apartment. Neither should there be vacant floors between any occupied floors. This pattern of reclaiming apartments should similarly accommodate the previously outlined sequence of contiguous ownership and occupation of the rehabilitated homes.

So, unlike some of the past and current urban renewal practices of bulldozing high rise apartment buildings (which either creates more homelessness or aggravates shortage of affordable housing), our proposal starts by fixing up wherever the working poor may live when the proposal is implemented. A Trenton, N.J. priest, Father McCormick, has demonstrated this by encouraging and requiring working poor families to contribute and invest their labor, sweat and brains in rehabilitating city owned building apartments intended for them to own and occupy (*Times* 11/1/87:NJ1). This is real sweat equity. And, if the working poor are lacking in financial abilities, they are certainly not lacking in brain and muscle power! In the same way, neighborhood redevelopment activities should be designed for and undertaken by the people who live in and know the neighborhood, its opportunities, needs and problems. People who have stakes in a community or neighborhood will do what needs to be done for their own individual benefit and that of their community as opposed to what others may do for them.

Developing community spirit, roots and involvement

Even after the working poor have owned where they live, it is still necessary that the new home owners function as a self supporting community. So, after a sufficient number of homes and apartments have been acquired and occupied in the manner and pattern we have suggested, new communities and neighborhoods (characterized by blocks and blocks of home owners who are tied together by stakes emanating from their ownership of contiguous homes) are likely to emerge. And, as we pointed out earlier in this chapter, home ownership has its personal and individual rehabilitative values. The behavior of a home owner is quickly distinguishable from that of a rent paying tenant. For one thing, home ownership is likely to elevate the owner's sense of self. For another, it is likely to motivate the new owner to take good care of what he or she has achieved and, simultaneously, may create the twin senses of inspiration and aspiration. This, in turn, should lead to futuristic exploration of other possible avenues of possible expansion. In time, the new home owner becomes the cornerstone of his/her neighborhood. Owning a home is the key to economic upgrading and the home owner is accordingly empowered. In this sense, we agree with Blackwell's point that, in America, possession of a home is usually equated with possession of power.

Also emanating from the fact and impact of owning homes, is a concern for the neighborhood, schools, normal municipal services, worries about crime and drug abuse as well as local business climate. Almost unavoidably, these new home owners will slowly but surely develop some other common interests and needs in such areas as property insurance, plumbing, roofing, garbage collection, police protection, fire, taxes and even food stores. Under these circumstances and depending on their needs and abilities, it will be easier to interest these new home owners and residents to more and possibly different ideas on how to further improve their neighborhoods including how to nurture community and neighborhood pride. Because the question of community pride is discussed in a later chapter, suffice it here to say that community pride is created and nurtured by cultural and material attachments to one's neighborhood.

Furthermore, it is to be expected that these working poor who have thus become home owners can and will now undertake certain income generating activities in both public and private sectors. For instance, with some minimal training, some of the new home owners can be trained to provide public service to those among them who need and deserve such assistance. Instead of bringing people from outside these neighborhoods, it is more economically rewarding to both the individual home owner and his or her community that the best use of community residents be made in creating and delivering public services. An additional and essential source of income for the new home owners would be in the private sector. As indicated in a later chapter, pertinent neighborhood based small businesses such as dry cleaners, hardware stores, insurance agencies, motor shops, supermarket(s) and groceries, seven eleven, restaurants, barber shops and beauty saloons, credit unions and even banks, flower shops, appliance suppliers, entertainment materials, general or specialized clothes store, lawyers and accountant firms are all possible sources of community income within the proposed neighborhood. There are any number of economic and noneconomic activities to complement home ownership that a rebuilding community could easily get into. Next chapter deals with community and neighborhood economic development and redevelopment.

Some conceptual and operational constraints

There are conceptual and operational difficulties that are inherently associated with housing the poor. We have, for instance, discussed some of the philosophical problems which may be associated with the idea of providing what may amount to free homes to the working poor. Hard as the idea may be to sell, especially when referring to individuals who are physically and mentally fit, it has a great deal of merits. From the taxpayer point of view, one may use the following arguments to sell the idea.

First, out of the $775.6 billion US government uses to subsidize Americans of all colors and economic echelons, $651.0 billion (84%) goes to the middle and property owning classes. The balance, $124.6 billion (16%), goes to support the various groups of poor Americans including the working poor. Not to be missed here is the $48.7 billion expended for tax and subsidy for the nonpoor housing compared to $16.2 billion used for housing the poor.(Sherraden:61-65). The other expenditures include direct and tax expenditures on such items as education, employment, social services, health care, income security and nutrition. Without a question, what is good for the

143

nonpoor should be good for the working poor. Secondly, even if one had to discount the huge public expenditures that are made in the various forms to keep the economically strong stronger, one would still have to reckon with the reality that, given the available choices to us as a society, the history of that portion of public assistance intended to help the less fortunate amongst us has been unfairly and inaccurately stereotyped and, perhaps more importantly, it may have negatively impacted on our minority citizens. Because of such stereotypes and the consequences emanating therefrom, public assistance has not been very successful in improving poor neighborhoods or, for that matter, in lessening the impact of persistent poverty on the working poor. We therefore believe home ownership by the working poor is not only defensible as a public policy but also as a long term approach to making most working poor more economically independent. It is economical, moral and very much in keeping with the American ideals.

If the preceding concerns addressed apparent matters of propriety (though it was really a case of twisted logic which unfairly targets the poor for getting less of what most nonpoor get), the next couple of paragraphs deal with what may appear as unfairness to working poor home owners. It will be recalled that the thrust of our proposal was that the working poor would be helped to improve the ghetto where they now live. The assumption underlying our proposal is difficult and uncomfortable in that it, in effect, asks the working poor to give up their ultimate vision and dream of a life in the suburbs in exchange for owning a home in the ghetto! Would it be fair to expect them to give up life time aspirations, invest their time, energies and money in such neighborhoods? Even if we do not have a more adequate answer to the question (and we do not), it is clear to us that there are no other realistic choices the working poor have or could ever hope to have. If one agrees with our view, then the apparent unfairness in the question would not exist. So, in the absence of any other clear choices and in the knowledge that ownership has proved to be a motivator to many people, we believe our underlying assumption that the working poor will do what others do is well founded.

Similarly troubling is the uncomfortable impression that our proposal locks up the working poor in their ghettos for ever and succeeds in keeping them out of everybody's sights. This impression could be more forceful if one or both of two other conditions were present. First, if we could show that our previous neighborhood redevelopment efforts did indeed improve the quality of life of working poor families. Point of it is that the working poor are still the working poor because things have not worked too well for them. Secondly, if one had predicted and determined with certainty when the working poor will stop being working poor, then perhaps our proposal could be accused of aborting the poor's journey to the good life in the suburbs! We obviously do not believe that either of these conditions could ever be demonstrated. That being the case, we reiterate that our underlying assumption has merit as an alternative to what we now have.

Another potentially disruptive and complicated problem implicit in our proposal is the phenomenon of freeridership. (Ackerman:35-36). To illustrate the point, let us consider what could happen within the contiguous and block by block home ownership neighborhood we have proposed. We have assumed and continue to maintain that self interest grounded in the pride and feeling of ownership will motivate the new home owner to take care of his or her property and be involved in the maintenance of the neighborhood.

Now, it could easily happen that the owner of house number 105 (in the contiguous neighborliness) does not pick up the leaves or shovel the snow or perform some of the other neighborly chores which make and keep a neighborhood attractive and clean. The cumulative effect of this type of unneighborly behavior will surely make it more difficult to maintain, beautify and clean the neighborhood.

Or, in order to keep the neighborhood safe and free of drug peddlers, the new home owners decide, with the assistance of the local police, to establish

145

a voluntary neighborhood crime watch program. For some reason, the owner of house number 107 does not volunteer either his time or money to enhance the crime watch program. Again, the net effect of house number 107's refusal to cooperate will undoubtedly create a serious problem for the other home owners. In such this setting and circumstance, it is impractical to prevent house number 107 from the benefits accruing from his neighbors' contributions.

Because free-ridership can easily turn out to be a major demotivator among the new home owners, we would suggest that there be some form of formal procedures with appropriate sanctions to accompany this home ownership. The reason for legal provisions and sanctions would be to regulate and encourage good neighborly behavior. Regular home ownership has its regulations and requirements too. Perhaps through a home owners council or the local municipal government or through some lawfully constituted agency, home owners behavior should be regulated (Lank, et al:51) especially when dealing with first time home owners who are likely to experience some difficulties associated with home ownership. Continuing education, home owners workshops and seminars are other ways for cultivating and nurturing the desired home owner behavior. Furthermore, the overseeing agency may establish some type of standards for all the home owners for the maintenance of their homes. Needless to say, inability or failure to fulfill any set conditions of ownership should disqualify that particular individual.

Summary

In view of our past inability to develop and stabilize working poor neighborhoods in the inner city areas, and, in contrast to the traditional ways of housing and subsidizing working poor, we have suggested and argued that a more meaningful and practical approach to assisting the working poor is to make them home owners. To that end, we proposed a physically contiguous and sequenced pattern of home ownership which can create and enhance common interests and mutual responsibilities among the new neighbors. The proposed system of ownership and occupation is intended to:

a) create and enhance community and neighborhood roots and involvement;

b) motivate home owners to aspire to other ventures and achievements;

c) create basis for community and neighborhood empowerment;

d) contribute and assist in the creation and distribution of public services;

e) assist and attract business and economic development;

f) form the basis for support and advocacy for better public schools;

g) form the basis for a more effective crime prevention programs;

h) form the basis for controlling drug proliferation.

Community and Neighborhood
Economic Development

Introduction

> We have suffered form an over-reliance on government. And
> it has zapped the creativeness and spirit that was so much a part
> of life for our grandparents. We must look within ourselves,
> and find a place within the capitalist system.
>
> Bobby Rush

This chapter seeks to establish some realistic ways of reviving economic life in the inner city poor communities and neighborhoods. This mission is to be accomplished by creating and suggesting some mechanisms by and through which the working poor in the inner city areas can own and manage neighborhood economic establishments. Owning and managing local businesses are linked to home ownership discussed in the previous chapter. The economically live neighborhood would thus be characterized by residents who own homes or businesses or work in these establishments. Perhaps more than any other chapter of the book, this chapter takes to heart nearly all the themes and assumptions outlined and described in chapter one.

In the themes, we argue and maintain that (a) whatever we do, it must start at the neighborhood level where the people we want to assist now live, (b) both human and physical attributes of the neighborhood should be linked and done at the same time, (c) we should acknowledge and accept that working poor are a permanent feature of our society and that ignoring them or trying to make them middle class would not be realistic, (d) the working poor, like the rest of us, should not only participate in their own uplift but also take leading role in that effort, and, finally, (e) ownership and management of both residential and business establishments should be by those who live and work in the particular neighborhoods.

So, when given these themes, the collapse of the inner city neighborhoods, the level of poverty and social chaos common in some parts of these areas, how do we or could we revive the economic life? And, when given the American transition from an industrial and postindustrial society to what has been described as technoservice society (Levine et al, 1990:433), should we then plan to re-industrialize the deindustrialized areas or should we strive to bring back the industries which either closed down or left for overseas or should we rehabilitate the run down neighborhoods and leave it at that or should we strive to bring back the middle class or, may we ask, would any of this or all of it make neighborhood redevelopment? Or, exactly what is it that should we do? (Meehan, in Bruyn & Meehan:131-137).

Because it is almost certain that there are no complete answers to the questions we have posed, we suggest, as a starting point for the search for a more practical and sustainable redevelopment of poor inner city neighborhoods, that we choose from four possible courses of actions. The first course of action would be to attempt to recreate the past American industrial majesty. Another one would be to keep on doing what we have been doing since the 1960's. The third course of action would be to develop or create something entirely different the likes of which we have not seen or known. And the fourth would be to redefine, select, combine and refocus elements of our past and present efforts to assist the working poor and rehabilitate the blighted inner city neighborhoods. But before discussing each of these possible courses of action, let us first define some of the key terms we have used in the chapter as well as structural features of a typical neighborhood economy.

Defining community and neighborhood economic redevelopment

Available literature on community and neighborhood economic development or redevelopment is not very clear as to what constitutes community and neighborhood economic development. Although the term *development* is used interchangeably with the term *redevelopment*, our preference for the term redevelopment is because it conveys a sense or feeling of *doing-it-over again*. At one time or another, many of these neighborhoods were economically viable and that we are seeking to revive that viability. This idea of doing-it-over again is also implied in such conventional terms as rehabilitation, restoration and renewal. Otherwise, much of the traditional literature appears to equate community economic redevelopment with community control and ownership, community development, business development, entrepreneurship, urban renewal and so on. (Luke, 1988; Milofsky, 1988; Tabb, 1970; Fusfeld, 1973, The American Assembly, 1969; *The Review of Black Political Economy*, Vol.10. No.1, 1979). A notable exception to this rule is Chicago's Center for Neighborhood Technology.

Our view of neighborhood economic redevelopment is a combination of Sherraden's idea that public assistance policy should "move away from support and toward growth, away from entitlement and toward empowerment" (p.190) and Fusfeld's view that we must "shift the outward flow of income, resources and people that now drain the ghetto of its development potential". (107-108). In other words, meaningful economic redevelopment in the neighborhoods means accumulating individually owned assets by those who live in the particular neighborhoods and halting the outward flow of their income. Making owners out of consumers, (although quite a departure from the current and past economic thinking as well as the prevailing public policy) (Perry:224), would be a much more empowering strategy in the long term. Our view of rebuilding the neighborhood economy is therefore pegged, as it were, on home and business ownership and management. And it also retains in the community that type of income which is either resident or is earned in the neighborhood. Accordingly, this chapter puts forth and emphasizes the ideal that neighborhood residents should own and operate as many businesses in their neighborhoods as possible and that local ownership and management would complement and sustain the practice of home ownership.

Structural attributes of an inner city poor neighborhood economy

There are many ways of looking at and describing the economic structure of the inner city poor and minority neighborhoods. One way was offered by Harold Cruse who depicted the ghetto economy as having two sides; one side is laissez-faire, free enterprise, capitalism, and, the other is welfare state and anti-poverty, (Cruse:63). While this conceptualization may be accurate, we do not find it particularly operational. For our part, we delineate four essential attributes which, we suggest, must be fully considered in any future attempt to redevelop the inner city poor areas.

The first attribute encompasses the nature and the pattern of the working opportunities (jobs) in the poor inner city areas. For a variety of reasons which include powerlessness, lack of skills, racial discrimination, motivation and opportunities, most residents of the inner city poor neighborhoods (when and if they work at all) end up holding low paying manual and menial jobs. These jobs usually pay minimum or below minimum wages. We are therefore dealing with a work force that is barely skilled, if at all. This labor force has clear implications when considering economic redevelopment in the inner city areas.

The second characteristic of the working poor neighborhood economy is related to the first one. For mainly political and economic power reasons, the higher and better paying jobs in the working poor neighborhoods are held by nonresident professionals, civil servants and craftsmen and women who generally live in the suburbs but work in the inner city areas. These job holders include teachers, police officers, municipal employees, firefighters, public housing employees, and so on and on. The economic consequences of this pattern of employment are discussed in a later section of this chapter. Suffice it here to mention that these employment patterns constitute one of the major ways through which these poor neighborhoods continue to export the little capital (income) available to them for possible for re-investment in their neighborhoods. This is the point to which Fusfeld was referring to when he urged that we halt the outward flow of income from the poor neighborhoods.

The third feature of the inner city poor neighborhood economy is that most of the working poor residents are either on full public assistance or partial subsidy of one kind or another. The problem to reckon with here, as Sherraden has argued (p:3-5) is that the current philosophy and practice of public assistance are geared to transferring income to individual pockets. And because this is only a transfer and for consumption purposes, it cannot, by its very nature, make permanent changes to the recipients. In fact, certain features of current welfare policy forbid ownership of any assets. And because this book is mainly devoted to advocacy for local neighborhood ownership and management, the reader will appreciate the importance of this attribute of the poor neighborhood economy. That is, in order to revive these poor neighborhoods' economy, we must transform income transferring into property (asset) ownership.

The fourth and final characteristic of the inner city poor neighborhood economy is consumption. Whether true or untrue, there exists an appearance

153

(or may be an actuality) of high consumption of various luxury items in the ghetto neighborhoods and less and less ownership of such key assets as land or building. (Gilliam:66-81). If one considers the fact that everybody in the poor neighborhoods eats, drinks, partakes entertainment, travels to and from and does all the other things the rest of us do, one would have concede that, even if not unusually high, there exists at least the normal consumption. The significance of the point is that the poor and the working poor do not produce or provide much of what they consume. They have to get from somebody else and this is the economic significance of this consumption because it sustains the outward flow of income from these communities. A desirable situation to which neighborhoods should strive, is either to produce reasonable amounts of what they consume or be able to (through some form of exchange) negotiate some favorable terms such as employment or re-investment from those with whom they have consumer relationship.

Taken together, these structural economic features of the poor inner city neighborhoods constitute the principal way(s) by and through which these communities lose or export capital to the suburbs. It is not that we lack understanding or appreciation of some of the critical or even immediate needs and necessities that often compel or necessitate high consumption or make any savings harder if not impossible, (saying nothing, of course, about the welfare regulations which forbid any type of ownership without penalty). Rather, when one examines the economic circumstances of the working poor, it becomes readily clear that we must seek some change in direction and that without enough dollars circulating in and within these neighborhoods to generate more dollars, the future prospects for redeveloping these neighborhoods do not look good. To redevelop these communities economically, we have made, later on in the chapter, some simple economic proposals which, first, conform to previously stated themes and, secondly, are in consonance with the above features of inner city neighborhood economy.

With the preceding as the context within which to revive neighborhood economy, we turn our attention to three key aspects of such redevelopment. The first is a summary of how our neighborhoods have fared under and within the free enterprise system. This aspect also reflects on the four courses of action to which we have repeatedly referred to as the economic structure of the poor neighborhoods. The second aspect is a brief description of ideal business or economic ventures which we consider to have reasonable chances of surviving in the inner city areas. Using the second aspect as the base, the third aspect develops what could be easily described as a practical step by step plan for neighborhood economic redevelopment.

The neighborhood economy in a free enterprise system

In a capitalist system, individuals accumulate and invest capital. By accumulating and then investing that capital, such individuals are able to influence (and often control) what goods and services are produced and where they are distributed. Both the condition of being poor and the government's policy, do not encourage (let alone permit) the working poor to own assets and/or have saving accounts exceeding certain amounts. This means that the working poor cannot accumulate capital. Under these circumstances, the working poor cannot hope to be capitalists in a capitalist society. And, without capital, it is not possible for them to invest in their neighborhoods.

Along with other factors, lack of investment keeps these neighborhoods poor. The invisible hand that Adam Smith talked about guiding and regulating the economy to everyone's benefit (Sackrey:73) has been turned and twisted around enough (by legal, economic, political and administrative practices) to deny the poor, black and latino equal participation at the economic arena. And, as Bobby Rush suggested one time, we must now look within ourselves and see if we can find a place within the capitalist system under which we live and labor. (*NY Times*, 6/3/90:22). That the free enterprise system has not dealt

OUACHITA TECHNICAL COLLEGE

fairly with the poor, black and latino is widely acknowledged. The following are a few examples.

One of the arguments that has been put forth deals with the economic condition of African Americans. This argument maintains that the views and analyses of black poverty by mainstream economists has been inconclusive and distorted in that majority of these economists fail to assess the impact of racism and fear in causing and fostering economic discrimination. Sackrey argues that institutionalized discrimination is a major impediment in controlling poverty among African Americans. It does indeed call into question the entire economic system for allowing and encouraging economic discrimination based on race to occur even when, by law and rhetoric, all of us should be granted similar opportunities to build a good life. (Sackrey:69-78). Scanning current literature on the problem of poverty (Murray, 1984, Wilson, 1987, Jencks, 1991) and granting that these authors are not economists), you are left with little doubt that there now exists a serious attempt to down play the race factor as a significant, if not the prime, factor in explaining the persistence of poverty among certain groups within the American population. Without ascribing either the cause or the origin of American poverty, *The Report of the Task Force on Community Based Development* (1987) notes that there is hardly an American city or region without an economically depressed neighborhood. The Task Force readily acknowledges that the depressed neighborhoods, whether in cities, small towns or rural settings, share a common reality: market dynamics have failed them. *The Task Force Report*:10).

In the introduction to their manual for local action for community economic development, *The Center for Urban Economic Development* at the University of Illinois (Chicago), appears to have deviated from mainstream American economic thinking on how to approach the economic redevelopment of the poor urban communities. Specifically, it appears to us as though they have reject the mainstream economic efficiency view that "the

156

benefits of an efficiently operating economy will trickle down to households and communities if the private economy is left to operate without outside intervention". They argue that local economies are greatly affected by (a) such external factors as plant closings and the resulting effect on average individual and communities and (b) key public interest decisions made by private business people regarding what is produced, who is employed and how much they get paid (pp.1-2). And, finally, the very title of *Corrective Capitalism* (1987) of a recent Ford Foundation Report on the origin and evolvement of community development corporations (CDC's) written by Peirce & Steinback, clearly suggests not only some form of failure of capitalism in the inner city areas but also some possible ways of correcting these failures.

And if the preceding remarks were not sufficiently convincing to the reader, perhaps a casual visit to the nearest inner city neighborhood will quickly bring the point home. Our view though is somewhat different in that we do not consider the existence of economically failed neighborhoods to necessarily be a failure of the entire free enterprise system. Rather, we view it as more of a failure in the application of the system than the system simply being anti-black or anti-latino. The thrust of our argument is that suitable economic activities and ventures can be gainfully pursued in, within and by home owning poor neighborhoods. Many inner city economic activities and ventures are extractive and non-lasting because they lack permanent bases. Home and business owners not only make the best bases but also the best stakeholders!

Appropriate neighborhood business ventures

Earlier on, we identified four possible courses of action open to us in the effort to economically revive our poor neighborhoods. That is, to economically revive these areas, what should we do? Try to create the past industrial status? Can it be recreated if that was desirable? Or, may we continue to do whatever it is we have been doing for the last three decades? Or, can we create something entirely new? What would it be? Or, may we do all these things? Although we do not promise adequate answers to these questions, adequate answers are found when the questions are considered in the context of the neighborhood economic characteristics also previously outlined. Adequate answers would be those which can and must use and involve the working poor in improving their lives and neighborhoods.

To be gainful and sustainable, neighborhood business ventures must be linked not just to home ownership but also to that community's needs, earnings and purchasing power as well as the other available community resources. Home owners and their families will make the primary patrons for such neighborhood establishments. Although in some ways they may have similar needs, home owners do have their unique needs that are different from those of renters. And, considering that we are dealing with the working poor, it goes without saying that their economic abilities are limited to the level of their income. Therefore, if the neighborhood has home owners or is preparing to start a home owners program, then there are certain types of business ventures that would be natural and more appropriate than others. In particular, we suggest redeveloping of a neighborhood's economic life focus on food stores, clothing stores, hardware stores, pharmacies, insurance agencies, maintenance and repair services, mom and pop groceries, laundromats, dry cleaners, restaurants, barber shops, saloons, legal and medical services, taxi service, motor repair shops, newspaper and magazine stands, movie houses, stationery and book supplies, banks and credit unions, local government activities (including police and local judicial system, fire, public works, sanitation, financial services, health, economic development, social services) and probably the most important of them all: the school system. These are, without exception, the hallmark activities and services in any neighborhood, rich, poor, black, latino or white. They constitute the base of a neighborhood's economic life. Let us, therefore, strive to revive them especially in the African American and Latino neighborhoods.

For the suitable neighborhood size and location, the reader is referred to chapter three where various aspects and types of neighborhoods including sizes and location (Figure VIII) were discussed. The size and the circumstances of an economically viable neighborhood may vary from place to place. For instance, Chicago's Center for Neighborhood Technology has described the average Chicago neighborhood as one which has a substantially bigger economy than most towns and cities in Illinois (1986:6). To illustrate the point, the Center cites a minority neighborhood with an 1985 below average household income as follows: 70,000 residents 5,600 owner occupied housing units, 22,600 renter-occupied units, 15% unemployment rate (1980), $583.3 million total household income, $5.4 monthly food bill, $36.0 million yearly household gas & electric bill (1983). Assuming that this particular neighborhood will spend its income locally and thus spur its local neighborhood economy, the Center visualized a neighborhood that has 10,000 employed residents each of whom made about $15,000 per year. These working poor neighborhood residents created $230 million in total expenditure, 16,120 total jobs, $20 million federal income tax and $5 million state and local taxes.

Based on the above account, it seems that this particular neighborhood has a great deal of economic potential to be viable. The envisaged employment and the number of jobs created appear impressive. The downside to this otherwise positive picture is in the limited number of locally owned homes. Let us therefore consider the implication of the 22,600 renter-occupied units. Let us assume, as Galliam suggested elsewhere (p.56-81), that the overwhelming majority of those units are owned by people who do not live in this particular neighborhood. If this assumption is valid, then the next assumption would be valid too that the larger portion of rental income accruing from the 22,600 renter occupied units would eventually be sent to the landlord's neighborhood bank. If we further assume that the average monthly rents for these units were $400 per unit in 1988 and that 90 percent of them were owned by nonresident landlords, simple calculation shows that an estimated $97.6 million was earned annually and exported to the landlord's neighborhood. Similarly, if we consider the food bill and allow that 99% of that food bill was incurred at one of the food chain stores (assuming $190 monthly food bill per housing unit in 1988), that would be an additional $63.7 million sent out of the poor neighborhood annually.

By most yardsticks, the people depicted in this scenario are identical to the working poor. An annual income of $15,000 is low income for a family of three in almost all the states. But in our proposal, we envisage a neighborhood whose annual average individual income varies anywhere between $9,500 and $14,999. The question we face, therefore, is not whether or not that such families exist, but rather that because they exist and do appear to somehow make do with those meager and marginal incomes of $ 9,500 and $14,999, what should we do economically to make their economic lives more adequately provided and rewarding?

Keeping capital in the working poor neighborhoods

In the immediately preceding paragraphs, we attempted to depict a typical case of how poor areas could (and usually do) export capital to other neighborhoods (usually to the suburbs). So, the first step in developing neighborhood based businesses should be to convert most, if not all, rents to both public and private housing units into mortgage payments which would thereby translate into home ownership. To the extent such ownership may lessen the number of renters, then the particular neighborhoods will have thus decreased the outward flow of needed capital. This is the first step in establishing gainful and sustainable business ventures in poor neighborhoods.

The second major step of halting the outward flow of needed capital (discussed below) is in reducing employment of out of town residents.

We do not want to suggest that accumulation of assets or savings by individuals will eliminate poverty or drugs or crime in the inner city neighborhoods. Nor do we want to suggest that poverty and other social ills will somehow disappear from everyday life because somebody owns a condo or has $5,000 in savings bank. We do, however, want to suggest, and even argue, that home ownership coupled with local ownership, management and patronization of businesses will not only reduce the expansion of the existing economic imbalances among neighborhoods - especially between suburban middle and upper income neighborhoods (which are largely white) and the inner city poor urban neighborhoods (which are largely black and latino) - but also boost individual roots in the community. As it is now, the relationship between the haves (suburbs) and havenots (inner city neighborhoods) is similar to that of a colony and the mother country where nearly all the economic benefits accrue only to the mother country! To illustrate the outward flow of income from the poor inner city areas to the surrounding suburban neighborhoods, refer to Figure XII.

Figure XII represents a construct depicting a city whose majority of employees live in the neighboring suburbs. This is a common characteristic of modern urban-suburban economic and residential relationships in US. In this illustration, the overwhelming majority employees live outside the city where they work. Even when there are local municipal ordinances requiring municipal residence for municipal employees, one is more likely to find that those who work in the poor neighborhoods like the school teachers, law enforcement personnel, health and hospital professionals, school teachers and administrators, landlords, fire fighters, businessmen and women, social and human service professionals and providers, deli and restaurant owners, other regular public employees and just about anyone who makes a reasonable income do not live there.

161

Figure XII

Conceptualizing the Outward Flow of Income
From Inner City to Suburbs (1988)

Description		Average No. Employees	Annual Salaries ($)
Total employment		2,000	26,800
Residents	500		
Nonresidents	1,500		
Teachers		1,000	29,400
Residents	200		
Nonresidents	800		
Firefighters		90	29,850
Residents	20		
Nonresidents	70		
Police		410	31,400
Residents	70		
Nonresidents	340		
Residents	790		22,075,000
Nonresidents	2,710		100,664,000
Totals		3,500	122,739,000

The economic implications of this pattern of employment and its accompanying drain of actual and potential capital are serious for the working poor neighborhoods and communities. While about 30% of city employees are residents in the illustration, only 20% of the annual salary bill remains in the city. The balance of 80% goes to the neighborhoods where non-city resident employees live. These employees' purchasing power goes to their suburban neighborhoods where they live, shop, pay taxes and patronize other business facilities. It is in this sense that one may argue that the inner city poor communities do indeed subsidize the wealthier suburban communities through this form of capital transfer. An additional point that should be noted is that the continued outflow of capital through employment of nonresidents clearly negates most benefits associated with job creation as a strategy for community economic development. When most jobs are held by nonresidents who naturally take their purchasing power where they live, it increasingly becomes harder to create jobs based on the local economy. When this phenomenon dominates a neighborhood economy, its structure becomes colonial in nature. (Blackwell, 1975; Sackrey, 1973; Tabb, 1970). Without effective control of this drain of the available capital, job creation programs cannot be viable options for community and neighborhood economic development.

The other forms of capital transfer from the inner city to the suburban communities include tax dollars which are not invested in or spent for the working poor communities, bank deposits by the working poor end up as loans or mortgages elsewhere. (Swack, in Bruyn & Meehan:79-80). Already, we have mentioned the transfer of rental income to the landlords' suburban bank. The working poor inner city neighborhoods from which these incomes may have been earned are thus denied benefits accruing from these incomes. Home and business ownership, though not a panacea, should go a long way in diminishing this form of capital flight and encouraging greater circulation of such dollars in and around the neighborhoods and communities from which they originated and thus generate some more dollars.

Job retention and creation

In many working poor neighborhoods, job creation is probably the single most important way of reviving economic redevelopment. We have already examined how jobs can be and are often used to drain capital out of the working poor inner city areas to the suburban communities. It is important, however, to avoid conveying the impression that job creation is either undesirable or useless in redeveloping neighborhood economies. To convey the importance we attach to job creation, we have approached the problem from two perspectives.

First, we have attempted to address the problem of job retention, usually referred to as business retention. Secondly, we have considered what we think is a sustainable job creation approach which in many ways resembles contemporary urban economic development. Although Luke and his colleagues have not isolated job creation as an economic development technique by itself, we fully share their views on attracting and retaining business enterprises. (Luke, et al:92-111). Their views summarize various approaches and techniques used at both state and local government levels to attract and retain businesses. If we differ with Luke and his colleagues, it is in the greater emphasis we put on involving the working poor in the process of self improvement and self-reliance. We also take it as a given that creating and retaining jobs in suburban neighborhoods is essentially different from the same process in the poor inner city neighborhoods.

For our purposes, job retention has two meanings. One, it means to preserve or to hold on to existing jobs in the neighborhood. In other words, to use a variety of appropriate means, as suggested by Luke and his colleagues, to ensure such jobs or their sources stay in the intended neighborhoods. The other meaning is that it defeats the purpose to preserve jobs in the community only to have them taken over by people who are not residents of the intended community. This latter point is especially true in contemporary urban America where the Enterprise Zones have been hailed as the savior of the inner city poor neighborhoods. Even after almost a decade of Enterprise Zones, one does not find much evidence suggesting that the jobs generated by the and through these Zones go to the working poor. (Hansen, in Green:10-22). Anyway, both meanings emphasize the primacy of creating and preserving jobs for community residents.

Figure XIII

Conceptualizing Employment Patterns
in the Inner City Poor Neighborhoods

Quant.	Description	est/jobs	est/av./sal. ($)
6	Police Stations/units	136	30,900
3	Fire Brigades	44	28,300
	Govt. All pub. empl.	1,500	26,400
3	Public High Schools	110	32,000
6	Public Primary Schools	200	32,000
16	Day Care Centers	180	19,800
3	Supermarkets	220	21,000
3	Banks	85	22,000
5	Savings & Loan Hses	55	21,200
3	Credit Unions	45	22,500
20	Churches	120	17,500
15	Saloons	60	30,000
10	Barbershops	50	35,000
10	Ins./Real Est.Agncs	30	45,000
5	Mom & Pop/Groceries	15	25,000
10	Drug Stores/Pharmacy	55	20,000
10	Gen. Maintenance Co.	70	15,500
4	Landscapers	8	20,000
5	Roofers	15	25,000
15	Plumbers	45	25,000
8	Painters	16	28,500
15	Clothing/Wear outlets	120	20,000
3	General Stores	50	18,500
3	Shoe Stores	15	20,000
20	Gas Stations	60	20,000
5	Car Shops	20	22,000
3	Car Dealerships	65	27,500
5	Hardware stores	10	19,500
5	Restaurants	75	25,500
15	Deli/Cof./Nwsppr	75	20,000
25	Cab / Bus Drivers	30	28,000
	Working Elsewhere	1,000	25,500
	Miscellaneous	500	25,000
Totals		5,006	127,936,100

As for job creation, we think of it as adding more jobs than already exist in the community. Job creation means using different ways to either actually develop new jobs which did not exist before the effort was made or to attract outside jobs into one's community. But the key point to bear in mind though is that creating jobs is meaningless without job retention. Indeed, effective job retention is the best argument for job creation. The jobs shown on Figure XIII are the type of jobs which are found in most working poor neighborhoods and communities. They are mostly performed by nonresidents who moved out of that neighborhood when blacks or latinos moved in but continued to hold on to the jobs they had prior to their emigration to the suburbs. These are not high technology jobs. They are the type of jobs that most neighborhood residents can perform with minimal education or can be learned on the job.

But the mechanics of transferring these jobs to the community and neighborhood residents is likely to be a difficult, if not an impossible, task. Like anyone else, the incumbents should be expected to up still resistance to any attempt to take their jobs away from them simply because they changed their residences. It would probably be unwise to pursue such a course of action while trying revive a neighborhood's economy. A long term solution for this problem may encompass some change in the laws governing residential and working relationships, zoning, inducing those who work in the community to live in it by improving the quality of life in the community (and avoiding any form of giveaways that the poor city can ill afford) and perhaps more importantly, putting in place a future recruitment strategy which will enhance the principle of working where one lives.

Starting businesses in working poor neighborhoods

Introduction

To put the following discussion in the proper context, starting a business in the poor neighborhoods should take into account the (a) five themes developed earlier, (b) questions raised on what may or may not be done in the effort to economically redevelop poor areas and (c) structural features of neighborhood economies. Starting a business in poor neighborhoods must consider these points. While discussing the structural features of the poor neighborhood economy, we mentioned that perhaps the most obvious business opportunity in most working poor neighborhoods is consumption. Poor people are consumers everywhere and every time. They do not produce what they consume. It is the condition of being poor. However, if organized and selectively conducted, consumption is a real source of economic power and influence. But as argued in the chapter four, the poor are rarely, if ever, organized. Consider, for example, the potential for economic power and influence when given the estimated annual African American consumer expenditure of $300 billions in 1991. Even if this amount was still less by $100 billions, it is still an awesome amount. Two to three hundred billion dollars at the disposal of any body or group, ought to sustain and energize anyone's economic initiatives.

To ensure that the poor, black and latino inner city neighborhoods benefit proportionately from the economic and service activities based and performed in their communities and neighborhoods (just as the suburban middle class benefit from economic and service activities based and performed in their communities), the following suggested procedural steps to economic redevelopment should be taken and considered together with those similar steps outlined and described in the last chapter. If there is an appearance or actual repetition between this section of this chapter and the last chapter, it is intended for emphasis. And although it is obviously possible for a neighborhood to start implementing these steps at any point, we recommend that implementation follow the same sequence as appears here.

1. Safety

Safety is a pre-requisite for starting and staying in business in the inner city neighborhoods. The first step, therefore, is to ensure that community residents and their properties are safe from violence which is so common in these neighborhoods. It is the starting point in neighborhood economic redevelopment. Safety simply means protection from crime and criminals in and around the homes and neighborhoods for the home and business owners, apartment building owners and their tenants, the children, customers and visitors. Providing community and neighborhood safety may be done in different approaches and techniques. These may include the traditional use of alarms, group monitoring and patrolling, guards and police, pressuring civic officials to clean up drugs and prostitution, running workshops on self security procedures and techniques, and finally following and joining forces with other home owners and business people in those activities that may enhance mutual safety.

Under Police Commissioner Lee Brown, New York City has recently initiated neighborhood based policing. By 1991, all the city's 75 precincts had neighborhood management teams made up of police supervisors and civilians (community board district managers, members of the precinct community councils and other residents) who met regularly to identify and solve neighborhood problems. (*N.Y. Times*, 5/17/92:35). This approach is an additional method of promoting neighborhood safety. Even though we recognize the value of policing at the neighborhood levels, we still would want to strengthen neighborhood safety by linking such neighborhood policing to other neighborhood institutions and activities as the neighborhood school, home and business owners' associations, churches and youth groups.

2. Cleanliness and physical attraction

Over the years, we have visited and patronized small business establishments in the poor inner city neighborhoods. The establishments have included delis, groceries, insurance agencies, barber shops and saloons, car repair shops, gasoline stations, banks, supermarkets, clubs and bars. And with few exceptions here and there, we cannot say that many of them were either clean or well kept. To be sure, many of them had one or more of the following characteristics: untidy, unattractive, dirty, poor or indifference in customer relations, poor quality of merchandise, more expensive and lacking in variety of consumables.

Our premise here is that the working poor, like their middle class counterparts, would like to visit and patronize clean, attractive and well kept eating or shopping or entertainment places because such visits and patronage would reflect well on them as individuals and patrons. We therefore propose that after safety, the next major consideration in establishing a business in the depressed areas should be given to clean-liness and physical attraction. In this sense, cleanliness includes both the premises and merchandise. For instance, walls, floors, shelves, lights, decorations and all the other parts of the premises should be painted, washed, dusted or appropriately cleaned at least once or twice a day. It would also include the quality and cost of merchandise; how fresh and packaged the merchandise is and also how well the merchandise is arranged and displayed.

It is not enough to just make your place of business clean and attractive. In order to be and stay clean and attractive, the business person must require that his/her customers maintain acceptable standards of behavior. For instance, it is not in the interest of the business establishment to allow teenagers and other undesirables (as are found in the ghetto) to hang around the premises after they have been served. This is the responsibility of the business person and not that of the landlord or the local police. If need be, the business person should seek cooperation of the neighboring businesses or work out some arrangement with the local police to provide the necessary security or crowd control. The responsibility to keep the place clean and free of the undesirable elements belongs to the business owner.

It is also our view that to keep the place of business clean and attractive, does not require a loan from the local bank or a grant from SBA. Nor does it require that the establishment be in the suburbs. More than anything else, it requires the business person make full use of his/her blood and sweat - the real human capital.

3. Engage in that type of business which is likely to succeed in your neighborhood

In the preceding section on what we consider to be natural and appropriate business ventures for the poor inner city home or business owners, we listed the types of economic endeavors in which the working poor have at least reasonable competitive advantage. Similarly, the conceptualized employment patterns depicted in Figure XIII show different occupational activities that are performed within the poor inner city neighborhoods. None of these appears to be beyond the abilities of the ordinary person. We are, in fact, persuaded that even in this age of high technology, there is no adequate substitute for common sense. High technology is no longer "high" in the context of the South Bronxes of America. What is or could be "high" in the poor inner city neighborhoods is what can and will work there. Big time 'property developers' and their high finance and high technology approaches are at least partially responsible for some of the mess and damage that one encounters in the poor inner city neighborhoods. Although one would want to avoid the imagery (if not the substance) of the third world countries where technology is usually sorted out ahead of time in order to determine whether or not the particular technology is usable and useful, (appropriate technology), (Singer:1-10; (Williams & Gibson:9-17), it is important for South Bronx, Central L. A., Chicago's South Side and other working neighborhoods to

170

consider how practical and beneficial is high technology in their communities and neighborhoods where the basic problem is lack or shortage of necessities of life.

The working poor who are likely to be less educated, may be excused for being too mesmerized by the promises of high technology without ever realizing that, at the very best, high technology can only be marginally applicable to their immediate situations. In a perceptive observation, Susan Hansen has noted that

> Advanced technology industries in which U.S. enjoys comparative advantage are unlikely to employ the long term unemployed: educationally and socially disadvantaged minorities, functional illiterates, the handicapped, high school dropouts, or many of the older people laid off from manufacturing industries. (Green:20).

It perhaps bears repeating that we often forget or ignore the fact that the most stable and enduring economic activities in many neighborhoods, regardless of income, continue to be food stores, clothing stores, hardware stores, pharmacies, insurance agencies, maintenance and repair services, mom and pop groceries, dry cleaners, restaurants, barber shops, saloons, legal and medical services, taxi service, motor repair shops, newspaper and magazine stands, movie houses, stationery and book supplies, banks and credit unions, local government activities (including police and local judicial system, fire, public works, sanitation, financial services, health, economic development, social services) and probably the most important of them all: the school system. These are, without exception, the hallmark activities and services in any neighborhood, rich, poor, black, latino or white. They constitute the base of a neighborhood's economic life.

4. Cultivate and engage in mutually supportive business and neighborhood activities

Here are several things that all working poor neighborhood businesses can do for their own individual and collective benefit, mutual advancement and survival:

(a) Pool common and/or like resources

When and if two grocers are located in the same neighborhood and do sell greens from South Carolina or Georgia, it is suggested that they coordinate their purchases or jointly secure their supplies from the same supplier with whom they can negotiate for fairer prices. This principle has the same applicability to similar situations where supplies of the various products and commodities may be both competitively and cooperatively acquired. Although it could be more convenient to have such suppliers formally organized by either product or line of consumption, it need not always be that way. It is the responsibility of the individual businesses to stay competitive by finding or developing ways of lowering their operating costs which in turn will encourage and attract neighborhood and community patrons. Similarly, it would be cheaper for the would-be supplier to have customers in the same vicinity as that may reduce transportation and supplies expenses.

(b) Patronize your neighborhood businesses

When you have a business luncheon, seminar, workshop, or vehicle servicing, business supplies, home and business repairs, catering, laundromat, banking and entertainment, you should make a point of always using neighborhood based services and facilities. The working poor people in general, and black people in particular, are especially prone to going outside their own communities and neighborhoods to patronize services and facilities in the suburbs while some of such services and facilities (although not necessarily of the same quality) can be easily obtained in their own communities. We suspect that this is due, at least in part, to the fact that the working poor and people of color in particular do not have pride in their own neighborhoods, and, as such tend to prefer to go downtown or out of town or the Hilton or the Sheraton which **is always** miles away from where they live and usually will cost a bundle!

Patronizing downtown and/or out-of-town facilities is duplicated in numerous ways by and through which the working poor spend their income in other communities and neighborhoods. If there are no suitable meeting facilities in the poor neighborhoods, an attempt should be made to develop some or at least clean up and decorate the neighborhood school gymnasium for the particular purpose and end up benefiting a community based caterer who will almost certainly never have a chance to cater at either the Hilton or Sheraton!

Any serious efforts to attract out-of neighborhood customers to patronize the newly established businesses must be preceded by residents of the particular area patronizing their neighborhood business establishments. Neighborhood residents must demonstrate their pride in their own communities. Charity begins at home! So long as community people do not patronize their neighborhood businesses, there would never be a good reason start any business venture in that neighborhood. (Butler: 275). Neighborhood economic establishments should never be based on the assumed or actual support from nonresidents. The subject of community pride is broached again in a later chapter.

(c) Hire your neighbors

To the neighborhood based and owned businesses, the practice of employing neighborhood residents is in their very best interest both as business people and members of that community. Employees would be, in this case, also the neighbors and customers. It becomes easy to count on them in matters of their neighborhoods and places of their work because they live and work in their neighborhood. This is how you cultivate and nurture community and neighborhood roots and community pride. It is the way these neighbors can become stakeholders in their communities and neighborhoods. For the business person, it would not be enough to just hope and pray that their employees, who would also be neighborhood residents, would spend their income within this neighborhood. It would be necessary to do some of the things we have already suggested to attract and sustain their involvement in their neighborhoods. If and when this is done, it will then enhance both the individual and neighborhood economic empowerment.

(d) Organize or join neighborhood groups or associations

For the neighborhood based business to survive and expand, it will be necessary to establish mutual groups and associations to provide the necessary advocacy. Self-supporting groups serve many functions including arranging for and demanding safety within commercial areas, liaising between the larger and bigger markets on one hand and the smaller neighborhood businesses, conducting business related research, providing information on financing and refinancing, cultivating and promoting conducive business climate including strengthening the groups' commercial, legal and political muscles as well as fighting crime and drugs in the neighborhood. (Peirce & Steinbach,1990:22-34).

The suggested block and neighborhood associations should be in addition to the traditional Chambers of Commerce chapters and the Private Business Councils. The point is that every neighborhood based business should have membership to as many community groups and organizations as possible. Ideally, these organizations should be made up of the neighborhood's business people who, by virtue of their location and business pursuits, are likely to be uniquely attuned to the circumstances and the needs of the working poor neighborhood. As much as anyone else, these business people have a stake in the community.

(e) Worker cooperative and/or employee buyouts will help

As a strategy for redeveloping neighborhood economy, worker cooperatives and employee buyouts must be distinguished from the block and neighborhood groups and associations described above in section 4(d). This distinction is in emphasis and substance. The groups proposed under 4(d) are multifaceted in that they may engage in things legal, economic, political and social at the same time while pursuing neighborhood economic development. They are community action in nature.

In worker cooperatives and buyouts, when done properly, there is either ownership or rights the exercise of which may lead to influencing what happens. Because cooperatives and buyouts can and do facilitate ownership, the idea here is to envision how the working poor could be empowered through ownership. (Henderson & Ledebur:97-100; UIC Center for Urban Econ. Dev.:17-18). Some of the economic activities pursued cooperatively are indeed similar or identical to those pursued by the community development corporations. Also, traditional worker or producer or consumer cooperatives are nothing new. They represent a philosophical outlook on the distribution of goods and services. Employee buyouts represent a more recent reaction to the industrial collapse manifested in plant closures and resulting in huge losses of jobs. But it must also be acknowledged that there exists a great deal of economic common ground between the traditional and recent cooperatives, employee buyouts and community development corporations. Indeed, the least we should do is point out those ideas and practices which are currently in use in some of the working poor neighborhoods.

Although worker cooperatives and employee buyouts may differ in origin or how they were started, we have used the two phrases to depict the same situation, that is, companies in which workers (employed or self-employed) elect their boards on a one-person, one-vote basis and "share the profits based on their percentage of wages earned or hours worked". (Bruyn and Meehan:65-78). In *Beyond the Market and the State*, Turner has described several types of worker cooperatives which have been used as strategies for community and neighborhood redevelopment.

In addition to a brief history of cooperatives, Turner has provided case studies of (a) a workers' owned sewing cooperative in North Carolina, (b) a furniture manufacturing company in Puerto Rico-Desarrollos Metalarte, (c) Rapturous Foods-a food store in Roxbury Mass, (d) The Seymour Specialty Wire Company, Connecticut, (e) Cooperative Home Care Associates of New York City, (f) Inner City Supermarkets and Pace in Philadelphia, (g) Agricultural Worker Cooperatives in Florida, (h) Southwest Detroit Construction Cooperative, (i) Jobs for People in Cincinnati and (j) SCRUB in NYC. An apparent key feature of these cooperatives is that they all address basic human needs which know no economic or social class or race. (Bruyn & Meehan:64-78).

A typical employee ownership has been defined by the National Center for Employee Ownership as "a plan in which most of a company's employees own at least some stock in their company, even if they cannot vote it, and even if they cannot sell it till they leave the company or retire." (UIC Center for Econ. Dev.:15). Allowing for some variation, we may group employee ownership into two general types. The first type is the employee stock ownership plan (ESOP) which may or may not include worker control but into "which employers make stock contribution to their employees in order to receive tax benefits. "This plan has been described as essentially an employee-benefit plan. The second type is very similar, both in structure and purpose, to the worker cooperative which was previously described. (Ibid,p.15)

As a strategy for starting neighborhood based businesses, worker cooperatives and employee ownership plans appear to have great potential in sustaining neighborhood redevelopment. They do involve and encourage many community residents to have interest in a community based venture and therefore a stake in the fate of their community. These same workers and employees become either actual or potential home owners. Some advantages

176

of worker cooperatives and other forms of employee ownerships include :

    (1) securing sources of initial and/or operating capital,

    (2) borrowing and then re-loaning to members,

    (3) starting and sustaining credit unions for members and their families,

    (4) facilitating acquisition of appropriate sources of supplies,

    (5) expanding on ownership participation by recruiting more members,

    (6) providing the necessary technical and managerial assistance in running such ventures, and,

    (7) ability to command the power and clout of a group in dealing with both internal and external environment. (UIC Center for Urban Economic Development:14).

Community and Neighborhood Investment

Perspectives in community and neighborhood development

For our purposes, the idea of community or neighborhood investment is intended to convey the general use and application of different resources (monetary, physical, human etc.) to generate individual and community wealth. Wealth, as described elsewhere, refers to "the value of one's total possessions and rights to property". (Rosenberg:472). And, because working poor individuals do not own much of anything, they cannot accumulate any possessions which situation explains why they are not wealthy. Thus, community and neighborhood investment as envisaged here seeks to create and increase ownership of homes and businesses by the working poor in the neighborhoods where they live. As such, it increases that community's wealth which, in turn, lays the foundation for reviving that particular neighborhood's economic life. Like home and business ownership, the purpose of community investment is to create wealth among the working poor and thus make them economically self reliant. Put differently, this is to say that community and neighborhood investment, as conceptualized and used here, refers to the application of human, monetary and physical resources to spur and increase a neighborhood's ability and effort to provide goods and services necessary for

179

the decent livelihood of its residents. It thus means

> more than simply investing money in a particular
> geographical place. Community investment involves a
> commitment to addressing social issues as well; that is,
> recognizing that the allocation of capital in the
> community requires a commitment to meeting the needs
> of those people and groups who have typically been
> ignored by the traditional capital markets.(Swack in
> Bruyn & Meehan:79)

One of the key points we made in the preceding chapter is that community and neighborhood economic redevelopment must start by halting the prevailing outflow of capital (see Figure XII) from the poor inner city neighborhoods to the wealthy suburbs in the form of wages, rents and fees earned by suburbanites who work or own properties in the poor neighborhoods. (Swack, in Bruyn & Meehan::79-80) One cannot hope to make a convincing case for investing in a community or neighborhood which is not able, for whatever the reason, to retain much, if not all, of its residents' earnings. Both home and business ownership require an investment strategy which is community and neighborhood based and oriented. Such a strategy must also take to heart and sustain the basic assumptions we made in the first chapter. In particular, that strategy must view investment as a participatory process based and operating at the community and neighborhood levels. And, instead of attempting to transform the working poor people into middle class people, as some people have suggested (Bartik:209), we take the position that it is more practical and useful to improve both the people and their physical settings by investing where they live and have stakes.

Our broad conceptualization of investment is deliberately intended to encompass nonmonetary types and sources of investment. Our reasoning here is that the working poor (and society as a whole) are caught up in a no-win situation. Conventionally, investment is generally restricted to money and/or things monetary. This restriction seriously curtails the ability of traditional investment to deal with and adequately address the problems of the inner city neighborhoods. When you consider the fact that poor communities and neighborhoods are poor precisely because they do not have money to invest or are unable to attract and retain traditional investment, it becomes clear that as long as these depressed communities and neighborhoods keep on relying on monetary investment as the way by which they expect to redevelop depressed areas, it probably will never be accomplished!

Without either discarding or diminishing the role of traditional investment, we suggest that, for the working poor to be directly involved in their own uplifting, traditional investment should be suitably complemented by human capital and sweat equity. The working poor should be able to provide this latter form of capital. In any given year, from coast to coast and north to south, millions of Americans volunteer their time, energies and services to benefit themselves, the poor, the elderly and young. More concretely, the Habitat for Humanity (Atlanta) or the Better Community Housing of Trenton Inc. (Trenton, N.J.) are excellent examples of sweat equity. That is, prospective owners or occupants are required to actually put in manhours of pure labor and sweat in the rehabilitation or the construction of the apartment or house they hope to buy or to occupy.

Types and sources of traditional community and neighborhood investment

Among the various types and sources of community and neighborhood investment, we have interest in three or four of them. First, there is **public investment** which forms the bases of all community and neighborhood social and economic life. Public investment puts public dollars into public works and community infrastructure on which the rest of community life depends. Part of the reason why inner city neighborhoods have become poor and depressed is because public investment has not done what it should do. Public spending, for whatever purpose, is politically derived. Politicians and other public officials appear to cherish opening and groundbreaking ceremonies for public projects. They yield political dividend. It is because of such political considerations that government is more inclined toward capital spending than routine maintenance of local infrastructure. (Savas:29-30). Therefore, if working poor communities and neighborhoods want to be treated equally in infrastructural maintenance and delivery of other services, it would be necessary for them to be politically empowered as suggested in chapter four. It is as much a consequence and a trait of poverty as it is a condition of powerlessness for the working poor neighborhoods to be short changed in public services and maintenance. Political empower is a pre-requisite for attracting public investment.

The second type and source of community investment is the private sector investment. By private sector, we have in mind that nongovernmental portion of our economy which is made up of profit-making and privately owned and operated economic entities. Although this is potentially the most suitable source and type of community investment, it has proved, over the years, to be the least reliable in working with and assisting the working poor. The key point here is that the working poor have not been very welcome in the private sector. Further explanation of these remarks is provided in a subsequent section.

The third type and source of community investment is the nonprofit (also referred to as **independent** and **third**) sector of the economy. Conceptually, this sector represents those human efforts which neither the public nor the private sector appears to be equipped to carry them out properly. The sector also appears to bridge the public and private sectors by providing what Gies and his colleagues have described as "mediating structures" standing between individuals in their private lives and such megastructures as government bureaucracies. In other words, nonprofit organizations and agencies bridge those gaps which occur because of the marketplace failure and government limitations. (Gies et al, 1990:ix). For various reasons some of which we hope to explore later on, the nonprofit sector, much more than the other sectors, has taken to heart the cause of the working poor.

Any serious consideration of the these types and sources of investments for economic redevelopment of the poor neighborhoods must determine how each one of them can be counted on by the working poor. With the exception of the nonprofit sector, the other two sectors (and notwithstanding Enterprise Zone efforts) have clearly avoided investing in the working poor and minority communities and neighborhoods. Indeed, within the recent past, we have all witnessed what amounts to an exodus of both public and private capital out of the poor inner city areas. In light of the foregoing, it would appear prudent to look beyond (as we have done) these traditional types and sources of capital in the hope of delineating what the working poor individual can and should do for him/herself within the total effort of improving his/her living conditions.

1. Public investment

We construe redevelopment of infrastructure in the poor neighborhoods to constitute the essence of public investment. A neighborhood's physical structure and network, that is, streets, street lights and signs, sewer and drainage, highways, bridges, tunnels, waterways and the prevailing system of public utilities make up a neighborhood's life network. In nearly all meaningful ways, a community's infrastructure not only determines but pretty much shapes that community's life. Although limited to mixed-use realty development, a compre-hensive discussion of the importance of public investment can be found in a Mixed-Use Development Handbook by the Urban Land Institute. (pp.123-143.)

Redeveloping and maintaining neighborhood's infrastructures is a

183

public responsibility which requires appropriation and expenditure of public funds. It is in this sense that the construction and maintenance of a neighborhood's physical setting constitutes community investment. A community or neighborhood which needs and seeks this investment must be able to influence those public policies which guide the appropriation and allocation of public dollars. Put differently, this is to say that the ability of a neighborhood to attract public dollars is generally proportional to its ability (power) to influence state and local public policies including zoning ordinances. When examined from this point of view, it is not surprising that working poor and minority communities across the nation have not had as much success with this type of public investment as they should. The reason for this is in politics. Public sector decisions are fundamentally political and with the poor, the black and latinos being politically powerless, or nearly so, it has been rather easy for state and local politicians and public officials to ignore their needs for infrastructural development and maintenance. Poor and minority communities are dirty and unkept precisely because nobody picks up the garbage on timely basis. Streets are rarely repaired or cleaned. Both public and privately owned apartment buildings are generally unkept and somewhat dilapidated. Crime prevention and law enforcement services are inadequate and when they exist, there exists a great deal of racially motivated police brutality. These factors, among others, clearly discourage both neighborhood resident and prospective outside investors.

The underlying assumption here is that community and neighborhood residents who are stakeholders will more than likely put pressure on public officials to do the necessary physical rehabilitation. We are satisfied that when and if guided and driven by self-interest in the preservation of what they own, home and business owners can be counted on to take greater interest in civic affairs including voting and attending public meetings. Most public officials do pay attention to voters. And because they have something at stake, the working poor voters are likely to act and behave in the same manner as their middle class counterparts when it comes to defending what they own. Public investment is, therefore, one type of investment that no neighborhood can and should do without. The only requirement is that those who need and seek it must be politically and civically involved.

2. Private investment

Although the American economy makes the best case for what private capital can do in creating, distributing and consuming goods and services, it is unfortunately not a major player in the economic life of America's poor inner city neighborhoods. This fact is especially underscored by the economic traits of the inner city economy already delineated in the preceding chapter. It was in that chapter that we noted that the inner city poor neighborhood economy is characterized by low paying menial jobs at or near minimum wages, high proportion of better paying jobs being occupied by nonresidents, most residents are either on partial or full public assistance, and, lastly, (apparent or actual) high consumption. Even though we have already touched on the role of the free enterprise system in the neighborhood economy, perhaps it bears repeating that there ought to be some way by and through which the working poor can participate and contribute to the economies of their neighborhoods.

With the deindustrialization of urban America (Green:7) and the ensuing relocation of many plants, we do not expect our major corporations (many of which have already relocated to overseas places) to turn around and invest in the working poor and minority neighborhoods although these same poor people are often among the best consumers of the products made by these companies. To counterbalance this corporate behavior, working poor and minority community consumers should engage in selective buying and consumption of the products made by the companies which invest in their neighborhoods. Selective buying and consumption is a fairly used tactic to exert pressure.

185

Following this idea of using consumer dollars to exert pressure, let us illustrate our discussion with a case of a supermarket store which does profitable business in an inner city poor neighborhood. Community residents may want to suggest to the store owners to invest in their neighborhood. The suggestion may be in the form of a food processing or packaging plant. If store owners care and are sufficiently informed, they would realize that their business in this particular store depends entirely on these neighborhood consumers. If the company's response to this suggestion is in the negative, then the particular neighborhood may opt for selective buying and/or consumption. In the event the chain store pulls out (as it may well do), then this community will have an opportunity to select one or more of the options presented in chapter seven. But if the response is positive, it would be prudent to ensure that those working in the new plant are neighborhood residents who would also be home owners.

Assuming that the company agreed to relocate one of its plants to this neighborhood, then the sequence of these events would be crucial in ensuring that, first, there was some investment and secondly, the use of neighborhood residents as workers in the new plant would have the effect of checking the outflow of capital. Within this same scenario, the food store chain store may reduce its transport expenses because the supply depot thus relocated would be closer to the supermarket. Our emphasis is on the idea that it is not in the interests of this community to agree to any arrangement which may result in further outflow of its residents' capital. So, instead of allowing themselves to be ignored or frustrated by potential or actual investors, the working poor should make full use of their consumer dollars to bargain or negotiate for better economic relationships.

3. The nonprofit investment

As was mentioned previously, the nonprofit sector mediates between the individual on one hand and public and private megastructures such as governments and corporations on the other. In this context, mediation means that when and where the marketplace has failed and the government is not able or structured to correct the problem, these new organizations - the nonprofits - step in to do what is usually regarded as public good. Gies and his colleagues characterize the nonprofit sector "as the most capitalistic of our economic responses (because it reacts) to marketplace failure by filling economic voids with volunteer time and charitable contributions".(p:xxiii). Thus, when the marketplace stopped or withdrew its investment in the poor neighborhoods and government continued to display chronic inability in adequately reviving neighborhood economic life, the nonprofits came in. In other words, when the banks, insurance companies and other private sources of investment did not invest in or withdrew their investment from the inner city poor neighborhoods and the government, for whatever reason, was unable to do any better, various philanthropic and religious groups and individuals stepped in.

As to whether or not investment by the nonprofits has made much difference, we suspect that there would be differences of opinion. What some may perhaps agree is that nonprofit agencies have distinguishable records in developing and managing housing, assisting the development of small businesses, organizing and coordinating other groups to provide assistance, entering into coalition and partnerships with others to develop or manage projects, providing human and social services, advocacy for neighborhood needs, employment opportunities and functioning as a conduit for resources from external sources into the neighborhoods. (Clay, in HUD & Howard Univ. Institute, 1985:22). But with specific reference to the working poor neighbor-hoods, we are now sufficiently persuaded that the nonprofit sector remains by far the bigger investor or the principal channel through which the other sectors invest in these neighborhoods.

Investment in the working poor neighborhood has largely been made by religious, health, educational, housing, economic, sports and youth institutions. These organizations and institutions (sometimes with the cooperation of local government agencies) have done far more in creating and generating economic development projects, producing and delivering human services than either the government or the private sector. Their investment of time, effort and resources are, in the real sense, the mainstay of much of the investment endeavors one finds in the working poor neighborhoods. With a few exceptions here and there, most social service agencies and providers in many poor communities and neighborhoods throughout the country depend on the nonprofits.

While credit for these investments belongs to all segments of the nonprofit sector, a special mention of the religious groups is in order. As suggested elsewhere, (Peirce & Steinbach, 1987:65; 1990:56-57), religious organizations have especially distinguished themselves in the development of housing, economic development, health and social services to the working poor neighborhoods. In fact, most of the successful and innovative community development projects have been initiated, funded, sponsored, supervised or simply affiliated with one or the other religious groups or organizations. For instance, most day care centers in the working poor communities and neighborhoods are similarly affiliated with or located in some church building. Other nonprofit investment activities and projects may include sponsoring small loans to community residents or church members, arranging for property and personal insurance, education, sponsoring and funding work programs, job training and worker cooperatives.

Although clearly implied in the preceding remarks, it is important that we specifically acknowledge the emergence and phenomenal growth of nonprofit's community development corporations (CDC's). These are the community and neighborhood based legal entities created by religious and charitable organizations (and at times by government) to investment in neighborhood projects and carry out other redevelopment activities. Citing other sources, the *UIC Center for Urban Economic Development* suggests that there were 8,000 formally organized community based groups involved in the various aspects of community development during the early 1980's. Reporting on the results of a survey conducted by the *Christian Science Monitor* about 1980, they suggested that one out of three of all Americans living in cities of 50,000 and over had participated in a neighborhood improvement effort or protest. Fifty percent of those who were interviewed indicated that they would get involved in the future. (Community Econ. Dev. Strat., 1987:6).

A more recent study of community based development in America done by Peirce and Steinbach (1990) for the *Council for Community-Based Development* indicated that the total number of the community based organizations involved in economic and noneconomic community issues and problems could be as high as 9,000 and in all 50 states. Geographically, these nonprofits were distributed as follows: northeast - 35%; central states - 26%; southern states - 22%; and the west had 17%. Almost 67% of them operated in the urban areas and 87% are involved in housing production, management and/or advocacy (Peirce & Steinbach, 1990:16-17). Other activities included building and rehabilitating shopping centers, neighborhood shopping strips and industrial parks, economic development, cooperatives and social services.

Even without refined measurements, it seems clear that the growth of CDC's is sufficiently illustrative of the important role that the nonprofit sector now plays in assisting the working poor. On basis of this discussion, we can conclude that the nonprofits have, in fact, responded more affirmatively and vigorously in answering the call for investment in poor neighborhoods than the other two sectors of the economy. Another conclusion we find plausible is that the organizational model represented by the CDC's - and especially the fact that they are community and neighborhood based and encourage participation by neighborhood residents - is in complete accord with at least three of our themes for this book. In some instances, these CDC's have not only used but also improved on our next subheading - that the working poor are not and cannot be so poor as not to be able to to significantly contribute to their own uplifting.

Self Help Can Be An Effective Approach to Community Investment

1. Broadening the concept and practice of neighborhood investment

One of the basic themes stated in chapter one was that self help is a necessary condition for meaningful redevelopment of the working poor neighborhoods. This section discusses self help as an investment. In order to understand and use self help as an investment, we need to broaden the concept and practice of investment to encompass more than monetary investment. There are other things and ways that people (and certainly the working poor) can and should use to create assets and improve where they live. Traditional conceptualization of investment has put the working poor people in a no-win situation. The point of it is that if one takes investment as Rosenberg defines it as the "use of money for purpose of making more money" (p.234) and then consider the fact that working poor people do not have and/or apparently cannot get money which is what is conventionally referred to as investment, it becomes very clear that the working poor are in a no-win situation. It is in recognition of this predicament that we make a case for nonmonetary supplemental investment. That is, using those things that one can and should do to create assets and also help improve one's neighborhood. For the working poor to continue to wait for and depend on the traditional capital to flow into their communities, it must be realized such waiting and dependence are clearly indefinite. Thus far, it has not happened and, from all indications, it is not likely to in the near future. This is one of the reasons why we must think of other ways or combinations of such ways which needy people can use to either initiate or enhance ownership of assets. The following are some of the things and/or ways the working poor could do and/or use to help themselves and/or enhance whatever opportunities are available to them: safety, credit unions, rotational loans, education, entrepreneurship and "sweat

190

equity."

2. Community and neighborhood safety

Although we do not normally associate neighborhood safety - that is, personal and property safety - with the idea or the practice of investment, we believe it is very much in order to do so when dealing with the inner city neighborhoods where violence is out of control. Lack or absence of safety in these areas has so effectively determined what can and cannot happen that, it is not possible to pursue neighborhood redevelopment without first controlling crime. We therefore subscribe to and accordingly advance the notion that community and neighborhood safety is a form of investment itself which in this case precedes other types of investment. Because no prospective investor would want to invest their money or energies in high crime areas, personal and property safety must be taken as priority considerations when planning for community investment.

Echoing similar sentiments, a recent editorial of the New York Times entitled "to restore New York City" recited drug related crime, flight of manufacturing jobs, bad school system, crumbling housing, aids and such other urban ills, suggested that the starting point is to reclaim the streets because "to give priority to so many problems is to give priority to none. The most urgent, the heart of civility and of urban life, is the street. Safe streets are fundamental." (*NY Times*, 12/30/1990:10E)

Now, if the streets are not safe, the neighborhood cannot be safe. And because it is a generally accepted fact by the working poor, the African American and the Latinos that they cannot depend on the local police department to defend them, we are thinking in terms of what the working poor and the minorities can do for themselves and not necessarily what the regular law enforcement forces could do. We embrace the idea that safety is something that working poor people can and should be able to provide for

191

themselves and their communities. And, just as we must think of and pursue alternative forms of community investment because we cannot count on the traditional sources to invest in the poor communities, we must similarly look beyond the failed and often abusive local police in search of alternative ways of providing safety for the poor, the black and the latino neighborhoods. So, what exactly can or should the working poor do? Here, too, it would be very useful if we just quit pursuing the impossible and spend a little time pursuing the possible.

The possible in this case starts with empowerment as suggested in chapter four. Empowerment should lead to involvement in the known and proved neighborhood activities such as visible crime watch, business and neighborhood patrolling, installing home and business security devices, working with churches, school system, community and youth agencies and coordinating these activities with the local law enforcement system. None of these activities requires anything that most working poor do not have or cannot do. And, considering that most urban neighborhood crimes are comprised of drug related shootings, burglary, theft and muggings and are committed by young boys, it is not impossible for an interested neighborhood to zero in on every boy in the neighborhood. Besides, even the most violent amongst the neighborhood drug peddlers will not long withstand a determined community pressure against their illicit trade. This is something we all can learn from the Nation of Islam.

So, when all is said and done, we maintain that most people (especially when they are home and business owners) are likely to object to and resist strenuously any attempt, even by their own children, to turn their homes or apartments into crack houses. Therefore, the extent to which crime control in the poor neighborhoods enhances personal and property safety, is, in our view, another form of investment. In this sense, crime deterrence is built in and around ownership.

3. Sweat equity

A second type of nonmonetary and nontraditional community investment is what the Habitat for Humanity calls "sweat equity." This is the input created when men and women invest their labor and talents to create, repair, maintain and beautify their homes, businesses and neighborhoods. It is using what Estelle James has described as "volunteer labor" (James: 168-170) for self or other people's benefit. It is an investment that every able bodied and mentally fit working poor person can and should be expected to make to improve his or her living conditions. It does not require a college education or a middle class income to use a hammer or clean one's front or back yard. Thus, when we contribute labor and know-how to rehabilitate an apartment building where we may end up owning a condo or supervise an after school youth program in the neighborhood, we are, in a real sense, investing in our community. There is an individual and community benefit in our investment.

To illustrate the point, let us briefly note how sweat equity has been measured by Atlanta's Habitat for Humanity (GA) and the Better Community Homes of Trenton (N.J.). Recent attention and popularity of sweat equity have emanated from the efforts of the former President Jimmy Carter's attempt to provide decent housing for and to needy families through the Habitat for Humanity. As is commonly known, the Habitat for Humanity builds homes for sale or renter-purchase arrangement for the poor and needy families. But our specific interest here is in the 300 hours of 'sweat equity' on Habitat projects that a Habitat homeowner must put in before they can move into their new home. This 300 hours of labor and sweat is followed by more hours spent on training and involvement with community and neighborhood activities. (Fact sheet for buyer applicants, PHH:12/91). A similar form of "sweat equity" has been in use by the Better Community Housing of Trenton (N.J.) where

every prospective homeowner has to agree to donate one day a

193

month of voluntary labor for 10 years covered by a mortgage.....
This is in addition to 50 hours of volunteer labor on the homes
of others and 100 hours of work on the home that they
themselves hope to buy. (*N.Y.Times*, New Jersey Weekly,
11/1/1987:1)

Better Community Housing also requires these new homeowners to train and acquire additional skills with which to help themselves and others, too. To reemphasize the point, it is truly a disservice to keep on impressing on the working poor that there is nothing they can do for themselves and their communities because they receive public assistance or do not have bank accounts or college degrees. Besides creating assets, sweat equity manifests the kind of community and neighborhood pride and involvement that we should admire. This is the type of investment only people can make, require no cash or stock and help themselves and their neighborhoods!

4. Neighborhood credit unions

Michael Swack has described a credit union as a "cooperative, nonprofit corporation created by and for people affiliated by common bond, for the purpose of promoting thrift among its members and of loaning funds to its members at reasonable interest rates." (Bruyn & Meehan:90). Although chartered and regulated by both state and federal governments as banks and S & L are, credit unions are membership institutions controlled by members who own shares and who have a common bond of work or residence. Among the various types of credit unions, our interest is in what Swack calls a community development credit union or CDCU (Bruyn & Meehan:90) because this type of credit union is not only an off-spring of the community development corporation (CDC) movement discussed in chapters two and seven but also because they are generally restricted to serving poor people who cannot get loans or other facilities from the banks.

Now, for effective use of neighborhood credit unions as an alternative source of community investment, it is our view that such community based credit unions have potential of being the most reliable source of investment capital for the working poor and their communities. As we see it, the problem would not be one of being unable to establish credit unions because there are many detailed guides on how to do it. (NCUA, 12/89:1-9). Neither would the problem be one of a lack of members and/or share buyers. The main problem is likely to be one of an insufficient number of (social and economic) supporting institutions in the poor neighborhoods. The absence of such institutions is likely to invite social and economic chaos which, in their turn, may stifle or hinder prospective investment endeavors in the working poor neighborhoods. Earlier on, we referred to this same phenomenon as being present and/or contributing to what we have described as the breakdown of the traditional neighborhoods.

While acknowledging that working poor communities and neighborhoods may not have functioning social and economic institutions (see `anomic' neighborhood in chapter four), we must also recognize that the church and certain fraternal organizations are generally strong and vibrant institutions in these neighborhoods. We therefore propose that community and neighborhood churches, fraternities and sororities be used as the institutional bases on which to build and develop systems of community development credit unions. In other words, members of such neighborhood churches can and should be encouraged and assisted to form their own credit union within the framework of their church. The church, in this instance, would be the sponsoring agency while the church members would suitably control their credit union. Under normal circumstances, the pastor may be a member but not one of those involved in any management roles so as to avoid any appearance of conflict of interest.

Similarly, those fraternities and sororities with strong presence and commitment in the working poor communities should be encouraged and assisted where and when necessary to establish credit unions for their members and their families. In the same manner, home owners, business owners, neighborhood school employees, public and private housing residents and others who may be similarly situated, are all groups who are somehow tied to one another and who should be encouraged and assisted to form their own credit unions.

With regard to size and capitalization of a credit union, the NCUA does not require any minimum number of members but it does suggest a preferable number of 500 potential members (NCUA,12/89:1-5). When we examined NCUA's Region I roster of New Jersey credit unions, we found out that 1 out of 8 credit unions in New Jersey had fewer than 200 members in 1989 and in some cases, membership was less than 40. Their assets ranged from a high of almost $ 210 million to a low of barely $12,000 and with no fewer than 15 of the 394 New Jersey credit unions having assets of $ 50,000 or less. (NCUA,12/89, Region 1: New Jersey).

Now, one of the possible inferences that can be drawn from these figures is that by forming a church or neighborhood credit union, the working poor would be encouraged to make some savings or keep those funds within their neighborhoods and thus curtail the outflow of capital from their neighborhoods to the suburbs. A second inference is that neighborhood residents will have places in their own communities to make financial transactions. Instead of the extortionist check cashing joints one sees in and around the poor neighborhoods, there will be formal financial establishments. A third inference is that these credit unions could financially enable working poor neighborhoods to invest in those activities and ventures which would create, improve and maintain affordable neighborhood economic viability and standards.

For further illustration, let us take two adjacent public housing developments with a population of 4,000 people. There are a total of 996 units in both developments. On basis of neighborhood and economic status, residents of these developments can establish a credit union with a potential membership of 1,000 but only 100 are initially interested and able to participate. The average individual member share is about $ 500 and a total group's share of $50,000. Besides the advantages mentioned above, the members of this credit union will have two additional advantages. For one, they can take small business loans of no more than their share ($500) and use it to start a home based business in telephone answering service, lawn mowing, plumbing, painting, janitorial chores, grocery and a host of other similar home based enterprises for primary and/or supplemental income. For another, they can all agree to manage their credit union and thus create an additional venue for skill development. In other words, those members who may end up managing the affairs of the credit union could easily gain and develop more skills.

Other possible types and sources of investment

1. Syndication

Community based syndication is another possible source of community investment. We use the term 'syndication' to mean a group of investors joining together for purposes of investing in acquiring or developing real estate properties. (The Urban Land Institute:122). As a general rule, syndications may involve huge sums of money from outside sources which, of course, the working poor do not have. We pointed out in the previous chapter how incomes earned in the poor neighborhoods are routinely sent out of the poor communities. Because syndications will generally involve outside investment, we are cautious in even suggesting syndications as alternative sources of community investment. To the extent possible syndicate investing should be community based because the traditional syndications, that is, those formed by and for big financiers are either for tax shelter or profit making. Syndications, by their very nature, are extractive, that is, they encourage the outflow of neighborhood income and resources to the investors' community. This, as we have continuously argued, is precisely the problem that has bedeviled the working poor communities for so long in their efforts to attract and retain viable businesses in their areas.

2. Rotational business loans

Although functionally similar to the neighborhood credit unions, establishing a system of community based and restricted rotational business loans could serve unique and particular purposes (of assisting non-credit union members to secure small loans) or be a supplemental source of community investment to the neighborhood credit union. Funds for these types of loans may be raised from public and private sources as in the cases of public/private partnerships that now appear in many urban and poor neighborhoods. It is further suggested that such loans be restricted so that only residents of the particular poor neighborhood or community could be eligible and that once taken, the loans must be used within this particular neighborhood or community.

A final form of community investment tends to combine one or more of the preceding types and sources of community investment. This occurs when big employers or tax payers want or are compelled to close down their operations for whatever the reason. (Hansen, in Green:7-22). This phenomenon is commonly known as the `plant closing' or simply as the `closing down'. When this occurs, several approaches may be used to save the plant and/or the jobs or the local tax base. One, the workers may get together and decide to buy off the company. A second scenario is one in which a community based group may be formed to acquire the company. A third scenario is when the local government arranges for the continuation of the company through some form of local incentives including tax deferment refinancing and/or loan arrangements. The fourth scenario is when a combination of any of the above approaches is utilized to keep the plant or company operating.

Long Term Community and Neighborhood Investment

1. Investing in people

By investing in the people, we mean developing the human capacity through education and training to perform general and/or specific tasks as may be deemed necessary under the prevailing conditions. When dealing with the working poor, it would not be enough to invest in the education and training of the adults. An even more determined effort must be made to invest in the young ones who will be future citizens. Indeed, we would want to suggest that education is probably the single most important and enduring investment that a community could ever make for its future. When thus educated and trained, residents of particular neighborhoods will be equipped to secure, provide or negotiate for most of their basic needs.

Besides using one's education and/or training to secure suitable employment and thus way demonstrating the usefulness of education, we can even use a much simpler test of how useful and attractive education can be to any family. Take, for example, what happens when families want to relocate from one city to another or from one state to another. One of the first things that they check on is the quality of the education system. In other words, how good is the school system?

We may also view education as an investment in the future of a community. In fact, this is clearly the purpose of education. For, if a community, for whatever reason, does not take the necessary trouble to invest in the education of its young people who will be its future residents and leaders, that community is certain to experience difficulties trying to be viable in any endeavor. Regardless of how it is done or who does it, certain attributes of a result-oriented education ought to remain constant. For

199

instance, there ought to be a sustained flow of students (who are academically functional at respective grades) from lower primary grades to university and professional levels. Beyond that, respective communities and neighborhoods should make the necessary effort to ensure that some of those students who go on to professional schools will somehow be brought back to utilize their skills in some way which benefits them as individuals while at the same time enhances community's social and economic viability. We view it as desirable that communities and neighborhoods from which students come should be attractive and rewarding enough to college educated young people to want to live and work there.

Along with their inability to attract and retain traditional investment, working poor communities and neighborhoods are further handicapped by a similar inability to attract and retain their young ones who finish college and/or professional school. Testifying to this inability, a study reported in the *NorthStar News and Analysis* of Chicago (8/89:6), suggested that only an average of 7% of college graduates who lived in the poorest suburbs while an average of 56% of college graduates lived in the 15 richest suburbs. For example, in Bell Gardens, Ca.,a predominantly black suburb with a per capita income of $5,337, only 2.4% of its residents are college graduates compared to 77.5% of residents of Kenilworth, a suburb of Chicago, being college graduates and with per capita income of $61,950. (*North Star*:6). Granting that these two instances do not constitute sufficient evidence on which to base any argument, we are nevertheless constrained to refer back to our earlier arguments in chapter seven (see Figures XII & XIII) that the general trend in local employment patterns is that people from out-of-town (often the economically or educationally better off communities) tend to hold the better paying jobs in the poor neighborhoods while the working poor themselves tend to spend their consumer dollars out of their communities. This predicament truly diminishes (and possibly eliminates) working poor neighborhoods' capacities to make both short and long term community investment.

2. Education facilities as a community investment

Following the preceding remarks, it is suggested that the local school system
 should be so restructured and managed as to reflect and directly benefit the neighborhoods and communities where it is located. Or, to put it in another way, this is to say that although various school facilities may be physically located in the working poor neighborhoods, they do not often function as integral parts of the particular working poor neighborhood. They are generally fenced, locked and chained until 7 a.m. the following morning. One may therefore be forgiven for viewing them as somewhat irrelevant institutional facilities to the social, cultural and economic life of the particular neighborhood. Our idea here is that in additional to the curricular instructional mission to which these facilities are dedicated, they should also serve as sources of economic, social and cultural vitality of the neighborhood where they are located. This view retains the necessary compatibility with our linkage theme.

3. Community entrepreneur-investors

To cultivate and sustain the spirit of self help and independence, working poor neighborhoods need some type of mechanism (preferably internal) to both ignite and sustain a spiral of self renewal. It is a way for spurring community growth from within. That, left to itself, the particular neighborhood will not slid back into urban decay and chaos. Such a way or mechanism, we believe, may be found in developing neighborhood based entrepreneurs. In pure economic terms, an entrepreneur would be one engaged in breaking new economic or business grounds as opposed to one who is involved in routine management. (Ackerman:162). Entrepreneurship may therefore be described as an attitude, a state of mind or mental predisposition generally characterized by such qualities as creativeness, imaginative, persistence, perseverance, determination and, if you will, stubbornness to pursue and achieve particular goals. (Ackerman: 165-168). The thrust here is to eventually get community people who will use their resources or seek external resources to invest and even re-invest in their neighborhoods to enhance both their individual and community economic benefits.

What working poor communities and neighborhoods should do to ensure a reasonable and sustainable level of self renewal is to cultivate and disseminate the desired entrepreneurial qualities and skills especially among the younger members of their community who have interest and roots in the neighborhood. This could easily be carried through neighborhood based courses, seminars and workshops. To be more precise, an attempt should be made to create an organizational support mechanism. Here, we want to suggest a neighborhood based agency, call it the "neighborhood support circle" [NSC]. This organizational unit would be composed of actual and potential neighborhood entrepreneurs who would thus constitute themselves into a mutually supportive group of peers. Among other things, the NSC would recruit and screen its prospective members, participate in developing neighborhood enterprises and link them to one another or to some major corporate associates; solicit and sponsor small initial loans and/or credit lines for NSC members.

As long as the goal remains to rebuild and sustain a self supporting neighborhood, the NSC should avoid making financial grants to its members. We do make a point of differentiating "loans" from "grants". NSC members may, however, be eligible for revolving loans of $1,000 for specific periods after which the amount of the loan may be increased to a maximum of $10,000. No NSC related loan may be refinanced and/or exceed $10,000. Operationally, the envisaged NSC workshop and brainstorming training sessions could be scheduled in both day and evening hours. Evening and weekend schedules being intended for the benefit of those participants who work elsewhere during the regular day hours. Day time schedules, on the other hand, would be for the benefit of those who are either unemployed or on public assistance. Other operational modalities of these training sessions may include meeting facilities in the community; recording and/or video-taping of workshop and brainstorming proceedings, administrative assistants and professionally qualified workshop leaders and/or facilitators.

Communication for Neighborhood Redevelopment

Nature and meaning of communication in the U.S.

The purpose of this chapter is to suggest a community based support and promotion mechanism for the home and business ownership as well as the community economic development and investment discussed in chapters six, seven and eight. To accomplish this objective, this chapter examines how the prevailing communication media (a) influences our perception, (b) has been and continues to be used against the interests of the working poor in general and specifically against people of color and (c) how those thus disadvantaged could and must use what is available to them to influence or at the very least, minimize the destructiveness that is often wrought on them as people and as communities. The chapter concludes by specifying concrete measures that communities and neighborhoods could and should take to cultivate and reinforce neighborhood's good image and pride.

Because we do not believe that it is desirable or practical to continue to seek the physical relocation of the working poor to some other place other than where they now live, we suggest, as an alternative, that we cultivate and

205

promote a sense of neighborhood belonging to and pride in their present neighborhoods. Owning a home or a business is not enough. Ownership still needs certain intangibilities to concretize, boost and sustain that reality of owning and belonging. This positive role is what the communication media could have done for the working poor neighborhoods. Instead, what the media has done and done very well is to destroy that feeling of belonging. The negatives and hatred created and fostered by the media about and of people of color (who constitute the proportional majority of the working poor) have caused irreparable alienation of the individual working poor from his or her neighborhood. Our underlying premise is therefore that if and when residents of particular neighborhood do not have positive images and impressions of their neighborhood, they are not likely to be motivated to rebuild or maintain the quality of where they live. This, we believe, is the case in that neighborhood Donald Warren described as anomic.

But before we discuss how the prevailing system of communication influences our perception, let us first define what we mean by communication. It has been defined as the process of transforming "information, ideas, attitudes or emotions from one person or group to another or others primarily through symbols" (Theodorson & Theodorson,1969:62). It also refers to a special type of information patterning which is expressed in symbolic forms. And, as others have suggested, for communication to take place between two individuals or groups, there must be (a) a symbolic system shared by the people involved and (b) shared associations between such symbols and their referents. (Myers & Myers:15, Donnelly et al:422). For purposes of this book, the terms "communication" and "media" are used interchangeably and may be construed to mean the same thing. That is, to collect, organize and transmit information on and about the working poor and people of color to various users and interested parties. More specifically, our interest in communication focuses on the use and control of what Walton has described as the "opinion-shaping apparatus". That is, how and what these apparatus are used; who uses them, where and when are they used and for what purpose were they used. The specific apparatus we have in mind have been enumerated elsewhere as encompassing radio, newspapers, magazines, television, news conferences, meetings, public service announcements, newsletters, annual reports, public hearings, slide shows, movies, photos, brochures, flyers, direct mailings, outdoor advertisements, posters, workshops, speaking bureaus, workshops, door-to-door visits and special events. (ICMA:1984:294).

Media's influence on perception

We agree with Walton that those who use and control opinion-shaping apparatus tend to determine truth and reality in a community and that those who are powerless (as working poor are) have little or no choice but to accept that truth and reality as presented to them by those who have power. (Walton:72). The working poor and people of color look at truth and reality not only as defined by the white controlled media but also as they themselves understand it and/or would like it to be. There seems to be a two-sidedness here. This apparent dualism brings to mind Du Bois's observation of 100 years ago that there was a two-ness among black people in America. (Du Bois,1903).

Now, the media (or whatever may be the prevailing system of communicating), through what Hanes Walton has described as the opinion-shaping apparatus, gives neighborhood residents certain information and impressions of themselves and/or their community. These impressions, in turn, create certain images of people, groups, communities and individuals. And whether or not these images are negative or positive, they constitute the foundation of an individual's perception of oneself and one's environmental circumstances. And, without making this a lengthy discussion of how images affect our understanding, we may, in passing, take note of what Kenneth

Boulding has delineated as the ten functions of images. One function of images says something about our individual place within particular environment. That is, how the individual perceives himself in relation to the physical setting. Another function of an image is temporal in that it relates to history and man's place in that history. With specific reference to the working poor, their history has not been particularly positive and as such it may not be supportive of what they may endeavor to achieve.

Then there is the relational image which translates our individual and collective world into systems of regularities. This system of orderliness produces, as it were, the personal image which says something about individual roles in society and organization. The next three types of images deal with one's value orientation and emotional attributes a well as various levels of memory. The last two types of images depict degrees of certainty or uncertainty among individuals and how our own perception corresponds to outside reality. That is, how well and far are our images are shared by others or whether they are simply peculiar to us as individuals? (Boulding, 1978: 47-48)

And, as Richard Normann (p.72) has pointed out, this mental model (image), whether held by an individual or a group,

> may be a good or bad representation of reality, but whatever it may be, it is always significant because it guides behavior. True or false, useful or not useful, clear or hazy - we act (or choose not to act) according to our own perception of reality. If the image is not an exact equivalent of reality, it is at least a social reality.

This is why, as Normann continues to argue, images are not only powerful tools for exerting influence but they are also awesome instruments of communication. We therefore suspect it would be difficult to convince a nonresident to move into a particular neighborhood if those who live in that particular neighborhood not think that it is a good neighborhood. If you know that no one else would ever want to live where you live, you, too, would probably not want to live there. Or, to borrow once again from Normann, if you cannot sell your product or service to your staff or workers, you cannot sell it to the customers out there! (Normann:78).

As we may have already implied, the reason for communication in and within a community is threefold. One, it is important to inform others about what is happening in the particular community or neighborhood. Two, there is usually a need to attract outsiders as visitors, business groups, professional groups, new residents and prospective investors. Three, there is always an intangible need and value to boost the image, pride, self perception and confidence of the community in itself and its residents. If indeed this is what the media should be doing, then our argument is that the white controlled media has not done this with and for African Americans and their communities and that the mainstream media has treated African Americans and Latinos and their neighborhoods with shameless bias and distortion. In our view, the moral authority and credibility of white-controlled media with specific reference to its treatment of the African Americans, are way below those of our nation's worst used-car dealer!

Negative portrayal discourages neighborhood redevelopment

As Walton has observed, the perennial problem confronting people of color "is that (they) cannot stop one sphere of society from creating its picture of reality (which in the majority of cases is anti-black and/or distortion thereof...) (Walton:72). People of color, for a variety of reasons, have not been able to control or influence "information patterning" and "packaging" about themselves as individuals, groups, communities or neighborhoods. An objective examination of the reporting on and about life and events in the African American and Latino neighborhoods will quickly show that it is all about murder, drugs, aids, welfare, poverty and arrests of young boys. In this regard, one can easily agree with Hazel Wright that mass media has been "used as a weapon of destruction against our people, destruction of the most vicious and insidious nature because the attack is directed against our first and final citadel for survival - our minds". (Black World:2/73:31). And, twenty years later, a New York Times story discussing relations between two Chicago neighborhoods, one black and one white (and where the white neighbor insists that "I don't want to be too close to them"), mentions that although many whites acknowledge that they never had personal experience with blacks, their negative impressions of blacks were based on television reports and on stories they have heard. (N.Y Times 6/ 21/92:1).

It has to sicken you to have to be repeatedly reminded every time you pick up a newspaper or turn on the television or the radio that your neighborhood is undesirable because of crime, drugs and all the other evils of urban America, and, by some twisted logic of ethnic background or the color of your skin, you are somehow associated with or that you welcome these crimes and urban evils. With this type of depiction, it is very unlikely that anybody would want to live or be associated with that type of a neighborhood. This negative depiction of mostly African American and Latino communities has successfully frightened both the working poor themselves (who live and must continue to live there) as well as their suburban neighbors. (Black World:12/73:24). In fact, it does not seem possible that we can even persuade or require those police officers, human and health service providers, sanitation workers and many others who make their living working in these neighborhoods to agree to live where they work.

Apart from making community and neighborhood redevelopment very difficult (if not impossible) to achieve and without denying or diminishing both the magnitude and gravity of the inner city problems, negative reporting and portrayal of poor blacks and latinos make them actually resent not only their neighborhoods but also the fact that they do live there. When asked what things he liked best about living in an inner city neighborhood, one of several respondents to a questionnaire responded:

> I want to get the hell out of here. Now you're gonna ask me
> why. Well, personally speaking, I do not like the neighborhood
> and I don't like the house and I want to live in a better
> neighbor-hood. (Black World: 11/75:21)

It is one thing to deal with the physical rehabilitation of a neighborhood and quite another to have to deal with people's attitudes, alienation, self doubt and hatred. To summarize, it is imperative that the working poor and people of color who have been and continue to be negatively portrayed and stereotyped by the mainstream media find ways (as suggested later on in this chapter) to either negate the undesirable depictions or plainly stop such media exploits. But before exploring such ways of controlling or influencing these opinion-shaping apparatus, let us first indicate how communities and neighborhoods can use media to enhance redevelopment efforts.

How media can support neighborhood redevelopment

In mainstream America, media is a more supportive and constructive tool. It depicts people positively and allows them to express and display their personalities, talents, achievements and avoids unnecessary put downs, enhances exchanges in community and neighborhood information and influences neighbors' value and behavioral orientation. For media to be sufficiently supportive of working poor efforts to rebuild their neighborhoods, it must:

> (a) accentuate the positive in informing and relating to both
>   residents and nonresidents about the various events taking
>   place in the working poor neighborhoods,
>
> (b) let others know the good things and benefits of living in that

particular neighborhood,

(c) attract appropriate types of businesses and professions to the neighborhood,

(d) correct some of the prevailing negative images and stereotypes of the working poor and people of color portrayed by the media,

(e) promote community/neighborhood cultural and artistic identity, and

(f) control or reduce the amount of bias in the media against African Americans and Latinos.

As it is now, the general tendency in various types of media is to convey or display neighborhood 'livableness' through the use of material possession and physical appearance. For example, if residents appear to be wealthy, drive nice and expensive cars, have expensive and well kept lawns, streets are clean and garbage is picked up regularly, most of us become satisfied that such a neighborhood is a good one. It is not often that you hear people enquiring about the quality of residents as human beings and neighbors unless, of course, such neighbors are Black or Puerto Ricans in which case objection is voiced to their presence. Mass media's fascination with racial and ethnic issues and stereotypes quite often set aside concerns with the quality of residents as human beings. It appears to us that most people look for the material and physical evidence to declare a community suitable or good.

Given that our interest is in the working poor and minority residents of the inner city neighborhoods who do not own homes or big cars to symbolize the material and the physical appearance we suggested above, our discussion here turns to the human dimensions that we believe enhance the role of communication in supporting neighborhood redevelopment. We are especially keyed to certain psychological dimensions which weigh heavily in individual decision-making as to where to live or send children to school. The perception of a neighborhood is very important in how individual residents feel about themselves and their circumstances in life. The idea that one lives in a good community or neighborhood is likely to have some positive effects on the individual's ego and self-perception.

In addition to the preceding, we also view a useful neighborhood system of communicating to be one in which educates neighborhood residents, creates and maintains positive neighborhood atmosphere, involves residents in their neighborhood's affairs, and, maintains and supports neighborhood businesses. Generally speaking and as previously suggested in chapter seven, the working poor in general and the African Americans in particular, are notorious for not patronizing their neighborhood's businesses. We believe this is so because they do not think well of their neighbors, neighborhoods, goods and services rendered, and, because they generally do not have anything at stake in their neighborhoods.(Banks and Grambs:1972:77-80). This is so, we believe, because they do not think well of their neighbors, neighborhoods, goods and services rendered, and, because they generally do not have at stake in these neighborhoods. (Banks & Grambs:1972:77-80). We take this phenomenon to be a psychological predisposition born of ages of mental disorientation, negative reporting and distortion by media. Again, and as variously suggested, the intention is to minimize or change some of these feelings of never being depicted positively in one's local media, or, for that matter, never being able to control or influence what is said about you or where you live.

Influencing these opinion-shaping apparatus is something that the working poor can and must do. It is not necessary for residents of any neighborhood to be wealthy or middle class to make their neighborhood a good and attractive place for them and their loved ones. It is necessary however for residents of this or other any neighborhood to care of their neighborhood. And, for this to happen, two things are necessary. One, residents must be what John Bryson calls stakeholders. (Bryson: 33). That is, community residents must have a stake in their neighborhood. Here, having a stake in one's community is construed to mean controlling or owning or being able to influence a portion of it. Two, a serious effort must be made to foster a conducive climate, through the local mass media, to make both owners and residents proud of their neighborhood. When these two conditions are in place, one should expect neighborhood residents to do those things which make and keep communities and neighborhoods viable.

Three effective ways of influencing the media

Bobby Rush was once quoted by N.Y. Times advising his mainly poor and working poor constituents that we "must look within ourselves, and find a place within the capitalistic system." (6/3/90:22). Unconventional as it may be to think and urge the working poor to be and play the roles of capitalists, we believe it is not only possible and desirable but probably the only way they could ever be on their economic feet. Agreeing with Rush, we suggest that the working poor must look for their place within the capitalistic system under which they and the rest of us live. The working poor in general, and people of color in particular, may use any of the approaches discussed below to clearly exert their influence on the media. But in nearly all cases and circumstances where and in which pressure is to be exerted (see chapter four), the key element is community and neighborhood leadership. Leadership provides articulation and communication of a neighborhood's fortunes and misfortunes to internal and external constituents. It uses communication to help sort out and target neighborhood's issues as need may dictate.

Although there are potentially many ways and techniques of exerting pressure on the various media institutions, we have focused on three otherwise traditional approaches. These are economic, political and legal and, thirdly, direct action which often includes the other two.

1. The economic approach

Except in comparison to the middle and upper classes as shown in Figure I, we do not accept the idea that the working poor do not have any economic power solely because they are working poor. They do have some relative economic power like the rest of us do. We consider those consumer dollars available to them and at their disposal to constitute a significant source of economic influence. Let us cite two cases here. One, the aggregate annual food bill for the 5.8 American million families whose annual income was between $10,000 and $14,999 in 1988 (Census Bureau,1988:12) at a modest $65 per week would amount to $19.6 billions. Even as we grant the fact that working poor people do not live in one or adjacent neighborhoods and that they are scattered all over the country, there are enough concentrations in many urban neighborhoods to support the point. This was the point we attempted to make while considering the appropriate size of a viable neighborhood in chapter four. It would defy simple logic to argue that these $19 billions (regardless of how one may want to slice them) bear no economic significance.

Our second case comes from New York City's East Harlem where

> residents and business had more than $220 million on deposit in seven banks with branches in the neighborhood (in 1989), but the banks awarded a total of only 15 mortgages to owners of houses and apartment buildings in the area...the 15 mortgages granted by the seven banks (during the same year) were worth a total of $2.4 million, or about 1 percent of the value of the deposits in the seven branches. (*NY Times*,11/4/1990:44)

As the quotation clearly indicates, this is a neighborhood which can deposit over $220 million in local banks but cannot get mortgages from those same banks. It is a situation that seems to defy normal standards of logic. What the situation does say though is that East Harlem, notwithstanding doomsday accounts of poverty in the media, does have economic power. Perhaps the real problem in East Harlem is not so much lack of economic wherewithal as it probably is lack of neighborhood based leadership which could communicate and articulate this problem to this particular community.

So, even with the necessary leadership, how can and/or should the working poor influence the media economically? Perhaps the more pragmatic economic approach should be twofolded. There are two impulses here. The first one is to reduce the amount, intensity and degree of negative or unfavorable portrayal of the working poor in general and people of color in particular in the local media. And the second would be to control the same type and degrees of unfavorable depiction of minority neighborhoods and their residents. For our purposes, both ideas of "reduction" and "control" are operationally linked. If there is any distinction between the two ideas, it is one of degree and not substance. Operationally, reduction and control of amount and degree of unfavorableness are intended to employ similar tactics to bring about the desired changes. To bring about the necessary economic pressure to bear on the major electronic or print media, we suggest two main approaches, namely, selective buying and economic boycotts. Both of these approaches are as traditional and capitalistic as capitalism itself. They constitute a case of consumers voting with their own dollars. They choose and select what and where to buy.

In America, most economic threats are taken very seriously by those who would lose if boycotts or selective buying were put into effect. Both selective buying and boycott could do serious damage to a company's profit margin if carried out in systematic and sustained manner. In practical terms, selective buying and boycotting are likely to overlap. While the idea of boycotting may be more absolute than selective buying, both terms do mean the prospective consumers are not patronizing some goods and/or the services of a particular company or establishment.

To illustrate the point, let us examine an instance in the advertisement of a product or service. If a certain community or neighborhood feels that it has been slighted or negatively portrayed by a local tv channel C or radio station R or the newspaper N, the thing to do is to approach various advertisers (food, clothing, furniture, automobiles, electronic equipments and systems, etc) whose products are advertised in the particular media outlet and let them know that as consumers of their product or service, you object to their use of a particular media outlet and that you will not buy any products advertised by and through that particular outlet.

Legitimacy of your objection to what private companies can do with their products would be based on the fact that you are a consumer of their products or services or that, being a consumer, you have expendable dollars at your disposal. The idea here, of course, is to persuade the manufacturer or the advertiser to stop patronizing the particular media outlet. If the persuasion or threat is successful, then the concerned manufacturer would, in turn, inform the offending media outlet that the patronage of their advertising services would be discontinued because the manufacturer's customers object to features of the outlet. Because such neighborhood residents would be using their purchasing power to enhance their interest, the tactic would be in keeping with other practices within the free enterprise system.

2. The political approach

In many ways, exerting political pressure on the media is similar to exerting economic pressure. In both cases, it is necessary to have effective neighborhood based leadership to assist in defining and articulating issues of community concern. As suggested earlier, for the working poor to be politically influential, they must not only be registered voters but also politically organized, affiliated and involved. Another way of influencing media is for the working poor to ally themselves with officials at the municipal, county, state and federal levels of government. It is normally in the political interests of local leaders to be known, seen and affiliated with highly publicized issues.

Neighborhood based groups and organizations such as the churches,

217

fraternal and advocacy groups are important and politically influential. Quite often, if not all the times, community and neighborhood leadership in the working poor and minority areas, comes from the religious community, fraternal organizations, the various advocacy groups and professional groups. So, to ensure a more accurate and balanced reporting on and portrayal of the working poor and their communities, it would be useful if most of the community and neighborhood groups and agencies got involved. Greater involvement can be achieved through coalitions and quasi-federations of various community groups. But in nearly all cases, committed neighborhood based leadership will be a necessary condition.

3. Direct and legal campaigns

Communities and neighborhoods can and do campaign for and against various organizations and issues as it befits their individual or group concerns. Campaigns may include demonstrations, picketing, letter writing, telephoning and boycotting. Depending on the type of media transgression in question, some of the campaigns may be spin-offs and/or continuation of the economic and political strategies discussed above. Although the most common action taken against media transgressions has been legal, it probably would not be in the interests of the working poor to opt for this venue because of their limited resources to mount a legal campaign. Other segments of society have taken legal actions against one type of media outlet or another for a variety of reasons. But when all is said and done, it seems to us that most corporate media outlets have had more experience dealing with or defending against legal actions than they had dealing with economic boycotts and selective buying of the goods and services they help promote. And as we have emphasized throughout this chapter, effective leadership at the neighborhood level would be required to guide and articulate neighborhood efforts to influence the media.

Inter and intra community communication

It is important to add here that we do not visualize media in purely conflicting and controversial terms. There are times and situations when the existing system of communication builds bridges between and among communities and neighborhoods by providing commercial, social and cultural information within and outside its boundaries. And, as it has been argued elsewhere, working poor and minority neighborhoods cannot be expected to be self sufficient in either producing or acquiring goods and services that they may need. It helps to know where certain goods and services come from. Good communication system helps empowered communities and neighborhoods to develop the necessary capabilities to acquire reasonable amounts of goods and services that they may need for their survival. It is through such abilities, that the working poor communities people would create things with which to develop reciprocal relationship with their neighboring communities and neighborhoods. Reciprocal relationship may be commercial or professional. In this sense, communication within and outside any neighborhood is not only essential but also beneficial.

How else can one influence neighborhood image?

In the preceding section, we discussed how working poor communities and neighborhoods can try to limit or control the negative reporting by the mainstream media. In essence, this was an attempt to stop what somebody else does. It was not an attempt at what one can do to shape or remake the neighborhood image. This section seeks to identify and utilize those opportunities which exist within the traditional media as it relates to, depicts and treats the working poor, the African Americans and Latinos to remake, improve or simply create the kind of neighborhood image residents would

219

want. The following then is an outline of a series of inexpensive programs and activities that any neighborhood could use to help create its desired image and thus improve its economic attractiveness. More specifically, we have outlined and described a series of neighborhood and community festivals and fairs to involve and attract the entire community spectrum of plain neighborhood residents, home and business owners and managers.

Neighborhood and Community Festivals and Fairs

The purpose of these festivals and fairs would be to communicate to both neighborhood residents and nonresidents. And the intent of communication is to (1) promote and improve the image of the particular neighborhood, (2) make residents of the neighborhood aware, interested in and proud of their neighborhood by involving them in planning and staging entertainment, cultural and commercial activities of their interest, (3) attract and persuade neighboring communities and residents to visit and partake of the neighborhood's cultural, artistic, ethnic foods and commercial exhibitions, (4) provide opportunities for the local businesses and service agencies to display and promote their merchandise.

1. The Venue

The neighborhood, as previously defined, is intended to serve as the operational arena for the events and activities associated with the suggested festivals and fairs. Both the timing and content of these fairs may be achieved through a series of annual or biannual cultural, food, artistic, educational and commercial weekend events scheduled and planned to accomplish the agreed objectives, or at least some aspects of such objectives.

2. The arts, ethnic dances and matching bands

This could be the premier annual or biannual event coming as it would during holidays. Specifically, there could be fine and performing arts for both display and commercial, professional and amateur dancers, ethnic dancers and matching bands from various neighborhoods, fraternal groups and organizations as well as groups and organizations from neighboring community schools. Also, this would be an occasion when restaurants and enterprising residents could prepare and market their ethnic specialty foods.

3. Education and science fair

Although the event itself may be planned for one of the holidays, the fair could be conceived as an annual event for students, their parents and teachers. It may be divided into two divisions. One division would focus on primary schools especially grades 5 through 8. The other division would focus on secondary schools, grades 9 through 12. Envisaged activities would be educational and cultural and could include children participating and displaying their educational talents and achievements in spelling, math and science competition, scientific projects and demonstrations. Among other benefits, such fairs could cultivate and promote academic excellence and pride through school and individual competition.

4. Neighborhood / community week / month

Community week or month may be bi-annual or seasonal. It would be a time when communities or neighborhoods may want to show or exhibit their success and achievement in home maintenance, neighborhood enterprise, drugs and crime fighting, service delivery to the needy and deserving, after school programming and activities and other neighborhood based activities. Any neighborhood may have as many activities as they may want. They may want to have as many as one or five or even seven events. Hopefully, some of the activities would use available community based institutions such as churches, schools and other community based arenas.

5. Winter/summer children games

These should be some of the existing organized leagues, PAL, school based or church based games and other athletic activities where sporting competition would be mixed with some learning activities; sports events may include football, baseball, hockey, chess, tennis, or even affiliating with or seeking a sporting relationship with coaches of organized high school and college based sports.

6. Independence and other holiday celebrations

The idea here is to have a standing neighborhood committee which would be like a clearing house for requests and proposals for additional celebrations and/or events for whatever the purpose or occasion. Such a committee may also organize and stage some demonstrations and fireworks for independence and other national holiday celebrations.

7. Neighborhood festival market

This activity can take place at the same time as some of the events described above. It may also be a good idea to designate Memorial Weekend as the time when local businesses can sponsor sales promotion of their merchandise. This may be done by a company or companies sponsoring floats, dance troupes, high school/college bands to draw people into the commercial sections of the neighborhood. Floats and other events may start from one side of the city to the other. Competitions should include private, public and nonprofit organizations and agencies.

8. Recognition

Make a request or solicitation from the business community to fund certain appropriate and rotational recognition awards for excellence in each of the competing activities. Some possible names of such awards may be: Governor's Trophy for excellence in (i) leadership (ii) community service (iii) education. There could be three such awards/trophies for winner numbers 1,2,3. These trophies could be awarded annually and in a rotating manner so that there will be one trophy for which to compete. Expectation is that these competitions would create a community or neighborhood or school effort (similar to a team) in terms of excelling spirit.

9. Organization and coordination

It is suggested that the neighborhood leadership create either private or nonprofit entity to plan and initiate festivals, fairs and other desired activities with the aim of promoting neighborhood image as well as its commercial and cultural life. Now, if the entity thus created is a business venture, it would be expected to function like any other profit venture driven and sustained by the profit motive. This venue would have the advantage that those involved would clearly have stake in what happens or does not happen.

On the other hand, if the entity decided on turns out to be nonprofit, it should perhaps be made up of across section of people from the neighborhood. Some of the individuals could be volunteers and others appointed to serve fixed terms of, may be, three to four years. Preferably, the chair of such an agency would always be one of the volunteers for the simple reason that volunteers tend to be more committed. Both the organizational structure and management of such an agency would be similar to those of typical nonprofit agencies and organizations: mission statement, board and an administrative team headed by an executive director or CEO. The one requirement though that would be suitable would be that those involved in business and/or volunteer efforts must be residents of the particular neighborhood.

How Social and Human Services Can Make the Working Poor Less Dependent

Nature and reason for social and human services

We use the concept of 'human service' to mean the content of any program which is designed to solve or ameliorate undesirable social condition. (York:15). From this meaning, we have extrapolated an equivalent meaning for the phrase 'social service'. The idea here is to have the two phrases not only complement each other but also to embrace society's social phenomenon. In other words, we construe the term 'human' to be more applicable to the *individual* situation while the term *social* is intended to connote a societal phenomenon which, problematic or not, entraps the individual as a member of society. As a phenomenon, the situation may be comparable to an economic depression which affects most everybody in society whereas a worker who is unemployed, though a member of society, is individually affected. But in both cases, society still has a problem. And as was noted in the chapter on neighborhoods that there exists an unavoidable relationship between the individual and his/her physical setting, so, too, we visualize a natural linkage between the individual and societal situations whereby the individual problem

225

becomes a societal problem and vice versa. We have therefore used these two concepts to convey the same meanings.

In general, contemporary functions performed by and within social and human services encompass such areas as day care centers, unemployment insurance, social security, medicare and medicaid to dependent children, training, physical and mental health, youth and juvenile services criminal justice system and culture and arts. (Weiner,1982:146-149). In many ways, these are personal services which are often intimately related to the physical and mental well being of the recipient. (Cleary at el:216). So, the point and purpose of this chapter is therefore to make a case for using these services as bridges (and a temporary support mechanism for the working poor during the transitional period) from dependency to self reliance. The chapter may thus be succinctly summarized by that old saying that it is better to teach somebody how to fish than to give him a fish! We urge and argue that human and social services should be understood and practiced as a society's mechanism for transforming the working poor from their currently unstable social and economic conditions on to more stabilized economic and social conditions - as would be the case (and, of course, without both the substance and ornaments of middle class wealth) from *anomic* to *integral* neighborhoods. For both conceptual and operational purposes, we suggest that for the working poor men and women of America, eligibility and consumption of social and human services be regarded as temporary measures in the same vein as unemployment benefits expire after a specified period.

Recent efforts to link welfare to work

Although traditional public assistance (welfare and the related services) has not done a very good job of helping individuals to be more self reliant, a number of attempts (though inadequate and, in our view, wrongheaded) have been made during the past decade or so. The idea and practice of linking welfare to work or job training have been around for sometime and even imple-mented in a number of states. Detailed and other useful summaries of these so-called workfare programs and/or their variations are provided in Levitan, 1990, Levitan & Shapiro, 1987 and Rodgers, 1988.

For purposes of this book, we have interest in two groups of social and human services programs. The first group is the so-called means-tested cash programs such as AFDC, supplemental security income (SSI) and unemployment compensation. The second is the in-kind benefits programs such as food stamps, housing assistance, medicaid and social security. And although it is not necessarily the case, some of the individuals targeted by government for workfare or training may be the same type of individuals we have targeted as either the working poor or prospective working poor. Some recent attempts to link public assistance to work and/or training include Reagan Administration's GROW, Massachusetts Employment and Training (ET), California's GAIN, New Jersey's REACH and several others around the nation. (Levitan:108-118)

To show how inconsequential some of these social service reform initiatives have been, one need only look at their life spans. In the majority of cases, their life spans have been limited to the tenure of the particular administration which initiated them. It is therefore quite difficult, if not impossible, to determine how effective and sustainable they have been or could have been. And even though available data is rather sketchy, there are indications here and there suggesting that these attempts to link welfare to work or job training have been neither successful nor sustainable. Take, for instance, the case of New Jersey's REACH program which targeted and required all able-bodied welfare recipients with children two years or older to take steps to support their families. To ensure that this require-ment was adhered to, the State of New Jersey provided day care, transportation, job training and placement. The state also agreed to extend medical coverage for an additional year after the recipient is placed in a job.(Star Ledger,6/2/1987:21). Initially, the Reach program was accompa-nied by a series of criticisms which pointed at some of its perceived shortcomings including lack of specificity, an absence of a full complement of benefits guarding against any type of revolving door behavior on the part of the working poor and the lack of a job creating mechanism. (Star Ledger, 6/2/87:21). Contrary to the program's projected ability to reduce welfare dependence, and the initial claims of success, there were increases of 6.2%, 3.8% and 8.8% in AFDC caseloads, general welfare assistance and food stamps respectively in New Jersey for the period between June 1989 and June 1990. When translated into public expenditure, these increases in welfare amounted to a budgetary increase of about 5% for the same period. (The Record, 11/30/90: A3). And, even if we grant (as we indeed do) that these newspaper accounts are not wholly conclusive, it is our view that they do suggest that some of these recent efforts to link welfare to work and/or training, at least in the case of New Jersey, do not appear to have evolved as viable and sustainable alternatives to welfare itself. For, to be viable and sustainable, such pilot programs should not only be replicable but more importantly those participating in them should be seen and known to assume and shoulder increasing burdens of their livelihoods.

Perhaps even more disquieting is the impression one gets after examining some of our past human and social service reform initiatives. As suggested earlier (chapter two), the war on poverty has been mostly waged by and through providing human and social services to the needy and working poor. The issues and difficulties involved in changing and/or trying to change social and economic conditions of the working poor through income transfer have been rather self defeating. Indeed, the history of anti-poverty programs and activities is long, documented and truly inglorious!

A good illustration of the haphazard nature of social service piloting may be found in a study conducted by David Greenburg and Philip Robbins in which they reviewed twenty years of national funded search for possible solutions to the problem of poverty. Their review, consisting of 35 social experiments and encompassing almost 120,000 families, is very instructive. Some of the research experiments reviewed focused on testing the feasibilities of new public policy initiatives in such areas as replacing welfare programs with non-categorical negative income tax programs, national housing allowance for the low income and poor people, national health insurance and manpower development. Subsequent research, also reviewed in the same study, seemed to focus on improving existing policies and initiatives. (Aiken and Kehrer, 1985:20-22)

Our summary of the study yields a number of somewhat discouraging points. First, we construe the study to suggest that none of the major social reform proposals initiated between 1968 and 1975 were ever adopted or implemented as social service policies. And, based on that record, the authors seemed to speculate that implementation of future social policy initiatives may similarly encounter difficulties stemming from the prevailing conservative political climate. The authors also suggested that many tested social reform proposals were generally victimized by time lags. That is, testing processes take too long to be of much operational value when completed. Other problems were encountered when communicating to and convincing policy makers and practitioners to implement the tested social service reform proposals because of certain political considerations. (Aiken & Kehrer:24-28).

Although somewhat superfacial, the preceding remarks are intended to suggest that in the absence of practical and sustainable alternatives to business-as-usual social service programming, and in the presence of an ever-expanding poverty-based bureaucracy (that is, a bureaucracy whose sole reason for being is to service the poor), a persuasive impression is thus created and often given by the current public policies and modes of generating and delivering human and social services that these services constitute an end unto themselves and that the working poor are, after all, better off under the prevailing system. Such an impression as suggested here, would precisely be what we are arguing against. Public assistance, we have maintained, should be transitional and temporary for everyone except the old, young and the handicapped. And, in order for this to happen, current modes of creating and delivering human and social services must be restructured in a manner that complements and supports community and neighborhood redevelopment efforts.

In operational terms, the idea is to make neighborhoods the bases from which human and social services will be delivered. As the operational base, the neighborhood will thus render more meaning to the anticipated linkages between provision and consumption of social services on the one hand and self improvement activities on the other hand. More specifically, the use of neighborhoods as the places where residents can go for social and human services, would be likely to promote a more cohesive linkage and management of self improvement activities and programs. It is at the neighborhood level that the need and requirements of public assistance to the working poor can best be determined, delivered and monitored.

Restructuring service delivery

We began this chapter by embracing the precept that teaching a person how to fish is better and ultimately more beneficial than giving him or her the fish. We also scanned some contemporary national and state efforts to reform the current system of public assistance. Additionally, we summarized and embraced conclusions based on the study conducted by Greenberg and Robins which seemed to suggest that many of our past social services reform experiments were not implemented. And, as implied, some of the reform proposals were not politically palatable, others were overtaken by time and still others were not accepted by both policy makers and practitioners.

Without making too much of this idea that both policy makers and practitioners have been less receptive to reform proposals, there are two important points that perhaps should be noted. One, however one may want to look at it, those who work in providing and/or delivering social and human services have their jobs to protect like the rest of us. What is more important, one may be permitted to ask, reforming the social service system and thus risk losing one's job or protecting that job? Well, we suspect that most working people will protect their jobs first. But it should be remembered that protecting jobs is not necessa-rily in the interests of the service recipients. As Jackie Pope seems to suggest, the welfare bureaucracy would easily protect their jobs at the expense of welfare recipients. (Pope:73-74). The second point is that, for whatever the reason, there appears to be a great deal of faith (among these policy makers and the welfare bureaucrats) that the welfare recipient or client is indeed better off on welfare in the long run than being required to deal with the uncertainties and risks of being self dependent.

These remarks are intended to encourage and suggest changes in the organizational structures and public policies governing and regulating the production and delivery of human and social services. The idea and the ideal is to make these services more empowering to the working poor. Because of bureaucratic inertia, lack of challenges and alternatives, we suspect it has something to do with the nature of public efforts to progressively turn stale as time goes on. Acknowledging such tendencies in the public sector, Richard Normann adds that many

> potential service ideas are neglected in the public sector.
> A good childcare service would quite likely do far better
> by acting as a "broker" between families, helping them to
> make the right linkages, than by building daycare centers
> and employing expensive personnel. (Normann,1988:28).

This is one of the reasons why we tend to agree with those who argue that (see chapter two) the current system of public assistance has in many ways failed those it was intended to serve. The changes we have proposed here are intended to preserve as much of the original intent and philosophy as possible. We seek to relocate and link key service outlets to where the working poor live in order to enhance access; involve residents in service delivery, coordination and self-improving activities; and, limit the period anyone can be eligible to and receive these services.

Neighborization of social and human services

To neighborize human and social services means to physically relocate them to the neighborhoods and communities where the working poor people actually live. Instead of the main office downtown, there should be service outlets or centers located in neighborhoods and staffed by neighborhood residents. Such centers will complement neighborhood schools and conflict resolution centers discussed and outlined in both chapters four and eleven (especially in coordinating juvenile and truant transgressions of teenagers and young adults), enhance the meaning and relevance of a neighborhood's sense of being, belonging and ownership of what goes on in their community. It should also go a long way in improving the quality and quantity of the services thus delivered.

But perhaps more importantly, such physical relocation to the neighborhoods is very much in accord with the basic themes stated and outlined in chapter one. We outlined and specified the importance of neighborhoods being not just the places where we should start but also the level at which the working poor can make real contribution in the effort to rebuild where they live. Neighborhoods are the basic units of a society. Moreover, relocating social services to the neighborhoods where the working poor live naturally makes them more accessible. Being accessible and less bureaucratic has its virtues. It reduces levels of alienation from which working poor people suffer and facilitates the process of monitoring of who gets what service and for how long (in particular because we have suggested that there be a limit of how long a person can receive public assistance). One would also anticipate that proximity to the consumer will enhance both efficiency and effectiveness in service thus provided. And, lastly, because of the number of dollars that a relocation of service outlets is likely to bring to the neighborhoods (that is, through employment and income transfer programs) it should invigorate economic life in and around the neighborhoods.

Involving neighborhood residents

In the preceding section, an attempt was made to map out the physical relocation of social service outlets to the neighborhoods where the working poor live. In this section, we suggest how the working poor could and should be involved in the delivery and use of those services to which they are eligible. To involve the working poor properly in the delivery of the services for which they may be eligible, it would be necessary to review those public policies which govern service staffing and delivery. We suggest a review of service delivery with the intention of transferring both the administration and delivery to the neighborhoods. Because we are actually suggesting a situation in which the working poor would progressively assume certain responsibilities in the delivery of social services in their neighborhoods, it would be important therefore that we plan for their appropriate training. Once trained, neighborhood residents would ultimately replace the career welfare bureaucrats and other nonresident care providers now holding these positions. Unlike career welfare bureaucrats, the working poor thus trained would themselves be replaced by other similarly trained neighborhood residents. So that social and human service management and delivery positions would not become permanently held positions. Just as we have suggested that the working poor be limited as to how long they can be eligible and receive social and human services, so, too, those who deliver such services should be similarly limited. In this context, service delivery, as an occupational function, would be as transitional as its recipients are transitional. Concomitantly, the idea and the practice of training and re-training of the working poor (partially or fully on public assistance) should be a continuous feature of our public policy governing and regulating eligibility and use of public assistance. This training and re-training of and from the ranks of public assistance recipients should ensure the long term supply of trainable personnel to run the system even as they themselves continue to be replaced by those they have trained.

Now, apart from the economic and empowering value inherent in the proposed training and employment of ex-welfare recipients, there would also be a reduction in the welfare rolls and therefore savings to taxpayers. And, finally, it bears additional emphasis that both agency employees (the trained working poor) and their clients (those still under partial assistance) should be notified that the nature of administering and delivering human and social services is not a permanent occupation just as eligibility to such services itself canot be a permanent condition of one's life. For those who are of age and physically and mentally fit, there ought not to be permanent jobs or permanent clients in the public assistance agencies.

Spill-over from the neighborization of social services

In addition to the foregoing, there are other potential (if not actual) benefits we would expect to follow the transfer of service agencies from downtown to the neighborhoods. For one thing and because of the role that human and social services play in the lives of the working poor, it is very likely that such a move would strengthen both the process and substance of neighborhood planning. It would, as previously implied, enhance and facilitate the linkage of human and social services with and to other neighborhood redevelopment activities. The significance of such spill-over may not be evident in the beginning but later years may show its nature and degree of complementarity.

Another advantage of the suggested transfer of social services to the neighborhoods is the potential to enhance accountability and sensitivity in how service is delivered to the clients and how the clients, in turn, use the service. Indeed, there has always been a great deal of uneasiness (if not hostility) between those who administer and deliver social services and those who use it. There have always been racial, economic and social dynamics which tend not only to castigate the recipients of these services but also differentiate service providers and administrators and yet both groups live off the taxpayers.

In her book, *Biting the Hand That Feeds Them*, Jackie Pope has actually delineated many instances of hostilities and distrust between the largely middle class welfare bureaucracy and their largely African American and Latino clients. (Pope:86-126). Those who produce and deliver social services have rarely, if ever, been accountable and sensitive to the plight and other circumstances of the working poor. For our purposes in this book, to be accountable and sensitive would be to ensure, for instance, that a training program for prospective home owners would indeed inculcate fundamental skills of a home owner. Or that, the person thus trained or re-trained can either employ him/herself or market their skills elsewhere.

Although it is not generally acknowledged or discussed for that matter, it is our view that just as there exists a need to reduce welfare rolls, there is perhaps even a greater need to reduce the middle class designed and dominated welfare bureaucracy who not only live off the poor (in the name of providing for the poor) but who, we believe, may have been an obstacle to welfare reform (because they had to protect their jobs). It is out of such a motive that we select to construe Jackie Pope's chapter on "Organized Recipients Begin Challenging Social Institutions" to mean that the middle class professionals who administer and deliver welfare services are not known for their contributions to the national search for more workable and sustainable alternatives to the current system over which they preside. Elucidating on this problem, Pope points out that,

> Members (of the Welfare Rights Organization) were learning how and why they and other Americans were often victimized by the political and welfare processes. A sense of who gained from these systems was also acquired. NAC's strength lay in its ability to involve everyone in the group's activities promote a sense of belonging, and instill confidence into its members. They discovered that the local directors were administering each welfare office as a fiefdom, that policies varied from center to center, and that laws were ignored or enforced at each director's discretion. (Pope:69).

To recapitulate the chapter, the suggested relocation of public assistance services to the neighborhoods and communities where the working poor live, is intended to empower the poor inner city neighborhoods by involving community residents in what happens to them and their neighborhoods; by having some way for the working poor to get off the welfare rolls; and also having the effect of lessening taxpayers' burden of having to keep on paying staggering salaries and wages to the current welfare bureaucracy.

The ABC's for Rebuilding Working Poor Communities and Neighborhoods

Key steps in rebuilding working poor neighborhoods

This last chapter brings together chapters and parts of chapters to form what we consider to be the basic steps in rebuilding working poor neighborhoods. Drawing from previous chapters, this chapter emphasizes the steps we consider essential in redeveloping depressed areas without necessarily summarizing the book. These basic steps are, by design, described in general terms and are intended to constitute what we consider to be the absolute minimum that a poor community or neighborhood must do if it ever hopes to rebuild itself. In the main, these are common sense based strategies. They do not constitute new inventions. They are pieces and parcels of what exists already. Their claims and abilities to initiate and sustain neighborhood redevelopment are based on linking home and business ownership by the working poor to other neighborhood rebuilding and social service programs. And, when it is time to put these basic steps into effect, care must be taken to consider the prevailing conditions in the particular communities and neighborhoods and make the necessary and desired changes to adjust them to local circumstances at the place and time of implementation.

For instance, affordable housing is only one aspect of neighborhood redevelopment. Training the unemployed and underemployed is another aspect of the neighborhood redevelopment. Economic development is another. The list goes on to include fighting crime, creating jobs, social services, drug abuse and others. As a general rule and part of the reason why we do not have workable solutions, these phases of neighborhood activities and programs are neither conceptually nor operationally linked. And, unless and until these different phases of community and neighborhood rebuilding programs and activities are conceptually and functionally linked and thus given uniform operational life, community and neighborhood redevelopment is not likely to be sustainable.

Although we have identified and selected a number of functional strategies for redeveloping blighted neighborhoods, we hasten to add that we do not believe that there exists a specific number of particular and immutable strategies or steps which alone and exclusively solve problems of the working poor and their neighborhoods. We do not believe that there exists such a formula or formulae for community and neighborhood redevelopment. What we do believe though (and have so suggested), is that it is both possible and desirable to identify and develop some basic things on which reasonable people could agree on as constituting the necessary steps in redeveloping our poor neighborhoods.

Guided by the notion that common sense is a widely shared characteristic, we have suggested, outlined and discussed a number of basic operational strategies in this chapter. With the probable exception of a few, we suspect each one of them has been discussed, analyzed and paraded around, partially or wholly, by scholars, practitioners, politicians and community activists over the last thirty years or so.

But before we enumerate these common sense based strategies, let us establish what we deem to be the common grounds for most, if not all, of the

238

working poor communities and neighborhoods. As a general proposition, there are very few cities, towns and communities in United States which have not had or experienced some need for any one or a combination of the following: high crime rates, drug abuse, welfare, bad school system, affordable housing and homelessness, economic development, job training, waste disposal, juvenile delinquency and truancy, unemployment, job creation, public services, public and private partnerships, government responsiveness and citizen participation. If these then are the common problems and situations to be addressed, our task is to conceptually and operationally link all those programs and activities addressing problems of a particular neighborhood at the same time.

For some unclear reasons, it does not appear to us that there has been much common sense put in the implementation of the various programs and activities intended for rebuilding working poor communities. We have in mind the sights and images of all the South Bronxes of America and how they could be turned around into habitable neighborhoods. For such a purpose and as suggested previously, the following 13 are put forth.

Safety

The first basic step is safety for people and their property. It is the starting point in rebuilding our inner city communities and neighborhoods. Safety means protection against crime and criminals in and around the homes and neighborhoods for the home owners, apartment building owners and their tenants, children, neighborhood business owner and his/her premises and certainly the visitors and patrons. Although our intention here is not to rank these steps in any particular order of preference, we suspect that the need for safety takes precedence over other things. To provide appropriate community and neighborhood safety, there are any number of ways that one could use.

These may include the traditional police patrolling, use of alarms, neighborhood monitoring and patrolling, security firms, pressuring civic officials to clean up drugs and prostitution, running workshops on self security measures that individuals could take, and finally following and joining forces with other home owners or business people in those activities which enhance mutual safety.

Reflecting on the basic themes outlined in chapter one, safety must also be based in and around the neighborhoods. Community residents must not only be involved in more ways than crime watch but also in specifically working with and influencing the other neighborhood agencies and institutions whose purpose it is to provide and enhance safety. This is the reason for empowerment. It is unlikely that safety would ever be achieved in the black and latino poor neighborhoods as long as its agents (the police, prosecutors, judges and others) do not live where they work. As it is now, whatever there is now which may qualify as safety, is imposed from outside the community. This imposition, we submit, has been the basic problem in the working poor black and latino neighborhoods because, as pointed out elsewhere, the working poor have not made full use of the political and economic power and influence available to them. Available sources of power and influence were discussed in chapter four.

Like in the other aspects of rebuilding the poor communities and neighborhoods, those who live there must be involved; assume leading roles in doing and coordinating those activities and programs which create, enhance and sustain safety; and link such activities to other neighborhood institutions and activities as the neighborhood school, home and business owners associations, the criminal justice system and youth groups.

Power and empowerment

The second basic step deals with power and empowerment. This is a subject for which we devoted a whole chapter. It is a subject that cannot be emphasized enough. Without power or some form of influence, nothing will ever happen. Working poor neighborhoods, like other neighborhoods, have the responsibility to themselves - to ensure that they have the necessary economic and political abilities to influence their local economy, local government, public services, schools, crime fighting and so on. One cannot emphasize enough the absolute need for the working poor people to fully participate in the local affairs of their communities. Redevelopment of communities and neighborhoods would be meaningless and unsustainable without some neighborhood based power.

In America, power is invested in social, economic, political, legal and cultural institutions. It is acquired and practiced in, within and through these institutions. To exercise power, one must be informed and involved in his/her community and neighborhood affairs. More specifically, power is invested in:

(a) voting and one does not need a job to vote; as a matter
of fact, one can create a job by voting his or her interests);

(b) individual economic behavior and prevailing economic
institutions;

(c) public forums: attending and participating in political and other
public meetings, appearing and serving in community and other
public forums and councils (for example, serving in a police
advisory board may influence police behavior in the community,
or serving in a neighborhood social service planning council
determines the allocation and expenditure of millions of dollars);

(d) education: being an involved and active both parent or
guardian or a PTA member may encourage students, influence

and/or help determine school budget or the quality of education.

The list is endless. But the key point here is that not even a Marshall Plan for the working poor neighborhoods or the legalization of drugs (as some have urged) can accomplish as much as citizens being actively involved in their neighborhood affairs. It is the best way to create jobs, improve schools, fight racism and discrimination, fight crime, create, own and support local businesses. It is all there waiting for the working poor, the Black and the Latino to make full use of it. If empowered as suggested in chapter four, the working poor, as active voters, would be very difficult, if not impossible, to ignore.

Before leaving this section, we would want to remind the reader that the preceding comments are not intended to gloss over or ignore the many real problems that the working poor, black and latino people face everyday and everywhere. For one, American society's negative and racist attitudes towards the poor, female and people of color is well documented. But this observation, valid as it may be, is really besides the point because what must be done is insist that poor and people of color must do a better job of taking full advantage of every opportunity available to them and do for themselves what other Americans, with similar opportunities, do for themselves and their respective communities and neighborhoods. It is taking one's responsibility for oneself!

Neighborhood schools

The third basic step in rebuilding neighborhoods is to improve and maintain good public schools. Because they are economically poor, working poor families, perhaps more than anyone else, do indeed need good schools. By good schools we mean schools where children learn and are disciplined;

where schools are drug and crime free; where the external and internal condition of the schools are conducive to learning and where the physical appearance of the schools are as attractive as the neighborhoods where they are located. Good schools are essential to a good neighborhood. In fact, even if a community did all the other things right and did not have good schools, it would not be considered a good community in which to raise a family.

But the public education system in the inner city working poor communities and neighborhoods has been and continues to be as bad as it can ever get. And, with the possible exception of public school teachers, their unions and administrators (all of whom make a living off the public school system), it is an education system that has few other defenders or admirers. We therefore suggest that without negating or maligning any useful lessons from past educational reforms and changes thus far achieved, it is high time that we should think of and try something else. Education achievement of the working poor and specifically that of the African American and Latino children has been deteriorating for a long time. In that case and in view of the fact that we cannot find much else going for the current system of public education, we think the recent development in Chicago and Milwaukee public school systems somewhat encouraging.

Among the possible solutions and something that we think most school systems in the inner cities should attempt is a combination of the Chicago type of school decentralization (which structurally creates neighborhood schools with mandated parental involvement with specified powers) and expanded Milwaukee type of publicly funded choice system. We suggest expanding this program because the initial piloting program is too limited. Milwaukee's approach is often referred to as the voucher system. However it is done and whatever one may call it, the key to educational achievement is in parental involvement and control over the education of their children. If parents cannot or would not get involved, for whatever reason, society owes to itself and the children to legally require parents to perform specified functions in support of the education of their children. In our judgement, there is not now and should not be an adequate substitute for parental involvement in and control of the education of their children. And, as implied above, the problem of teacher bureaucracy and their unions is parallel to that of the other publicly based bureaucracies living off the working poor in such areas as welfare, housing and law enforcement.

Sparklingly clean and shining

Our fourth basic step is to make and keep homes, apartments, streets, business premises, and the general neighborhood vicinity clean. Let us say, *sparklingly clean and shining*! Part of the reason why communities and neighborhoods are and have been neglected (as is the case in anomic type of neighborhoods) is because of pure and plain lack of community and neighborhood pride. Lack of pride is often because the neighborhood is dirty and filthy. It is dirty and filthy because it is not cleaned often enough. Thus, the cycle becomes vicious: lack of pride begets neglect and neglect begets lack of pride! It seems to us that the physical appearance and cleanliness of buildings, streets and the general neighborhood do appeal to one's eye sight and contribute to how positively and/or negatively its residents think about it. By physical cleanliness, we have in mind the absence of dirt in and around the house or apartment; well kept homes and apartments; clean business premises with no graffiti or shoddy goods and supplies on the shelves; clean and well paved and lighted streets; street signs, garbage cans and side walk are clear and pleasing to the eye.

Now, the purpose of neighborhood redevelopment is to make that neighborhood more attractive to both its current residents as well as outsiders. If and when a neighborhood is not attractive to those who live there, it would be unlikely that such a neighborhood would be attractive to outsiders. It has everything to do with self and neighborhood pride. In other words, those who have pride in their communities and do behave and communicate with pride about their communities and neighborhoods, may become infectious to their neighbors and outsiders as well. When people like and are proud of their neighborhoods, they like to keep them clean and beautiful. And they like to live, shop and even invest there. Finally, it needs to be emphasized that a community or neighborhood does not have to be wealthy or middle class in order to be clean.

We must be more realistic and practical

The fifth basic step is that redeveloping poor inner city neighborhoods and/or assisting the working poor to be on their social and economic feet must be both realistic and practical. Those who assist the working poor to rebuild their communities (public officials, philanthropists, advocates and others) on one hand and the working poor themselves on the other hand, need to be more realistic and practical about what can and cannot be achieved in redeveloping the inner city poor neighborhoods. We view the prevailing approach to working with and assisting the working poor as especially disabling because it appears to shield them from the known and unknown hazards of life. That is, as long as someone provides for their needs, the working poor need not assume such responsibilities for their lives. And, without impugning the motives of numerous charities or discouraging assistance to those who are less fortunate among us, and further, without denying the pride and fulfillment that accompanies giving, we are compelled to concede that perhaps in too many instances, the working poor have had little or no say in what they get or how they get it. Perhaps the old saying that "beggars should not choose" still holds! Take, for instance, what occurs when and where appropriate housing authorities decide to demolish old high rise apartment buildings and replace them with new public housing. In too many instances, this type of decision leads to the displacement of many who live in the old high rise.

To be realistic, is, first, to acknowledge that we represent the middle class family as the ideal family and the suburban neighborhood where the middle class family lives is often cast and viewed as the ideal community and neighborhood. Poor neighborhoods may aspire to some attributes of the suburbs but they cannot be suburbs themselves. Secondly, being realistic is to acknowledge and accept that it is neither practical nor desirable to attempt to improve an individual's personal situation without improving his/her full partici-pation. Nor should it ever be done without improving the physical setting of the individual at the same time. Accepting these realities may help us accept the fact that it is easier and more practical to assist the working poor to improve themselves and their present neighborhoods than make them middle class. It is similarly unpalatable to pretend that the working poor and their neighborhoods are one day going to become like the middle class and their suburbs.

Either because of the dominance of the middle class values, power and material possessions or because of the powerlessness and poverty of the working poor and minorities or both, it seems as though the working poor always desire and seek to become or recreate or replicate the middle class model. There is nothing wrong with such an ambition as an ideal to be pursued. In fact, this is an ideal we support. The problem though arises when we assume, as we often do, that the only suitable neighborhood for the working poor is that which is like or similar to the suburban middle class neighborhood. Pursuing this thinking, as too many of us do, ignores the fact that the condition of being poor, by its very nature, precludes replication of suburban middle class neighborhoods in or within the inner city depressed areas. This is a fundamental conflict which is hard, if not impossible, to resolve as long as the working poor remain economically working poor.

The other factor which seems to mould inner city rebuilding efforts after the suburban neighborhood model appears to be embedded in the nature of power relations between the poor inner city and suburban neighborhoods. The question of power and influence was discussed in a previous section of this chapter. Now, when one examines the actual structure and practice of community and neighborhood redevelopment activities in the working poor and minority areas, the middle class ideal appears to disappear. In practice, redevelopment of the working poor neighborhoods is not participatory or empowering. It tends to be charitable, economically extractive and politically disenfranchising. Furthermore, most of the municipal employees who work in the working poor neighborhoods are often middle class people themselves who, by the very nature of what they do, must have vested interests in maintaining the status quo. This inner city reality makes the suburban neighborhood model impractical for the working poor neighborhoods. Consequently, much of what is done in the name of fighting poverty or community development makes little or no impact. It also tends to have very little effect making and keeping the working poor neighborhoods clean, crime free or, simply, livable places. The idea that people do not or cannot have safe, clean and livable communities and neighborhoods because they happen to be in the inner city or poor or minorities is a reprehensible distortion of reality. People make communities and neighborhoods regardless of their economic or political status.

Programmatic simplicity

The sixth community and neighborhood basic step is programmatic simplicity. Community and neighborhood programs and projects, whether they are small business ventures, day care centers, rehabilitating apartment buildings, government chores and functions including maintenance of infrastructures or private initiative, need not be so complicated as to preclude simple understanding by the working poor who may either have to implement such initiatives or be the beneficiaries thereof. These types of community based chores should always aim at making the maximum use of neighborhood residents to either implement or maintain them.

When one considers the nature and condition of the working poor neighborhoods, it is difficult to find any activity or program that actually requires high technology skills to operate. It is in this sense that we consider simplicity to be a virtue. But because so much is conceived and developed by and depends on the research scientists, experts and specialists, poverty theoreticians, academics, bureaucrats and technocrats and many well-wishers and good-doers from the nonprofit sector, the working poor and people of color have simply been reduced to a non-thinking and dependent bunch waiting to be told what to do or are given what they needed. In other words, the working poor, black and latino people have been encouraged and supported to be dependent on everyone else except themselves.

We do, however, hasten to acknowledge that involving the working poor and minorities in the redevelopment of their communities and neighborhoods may end up being more difficult than otherwise implied here. To overcome some of the likely difficulties, we have suggested a number of ways to empower them, home and business ownership and management. Over the years, our academicians and public policy makers have prescribed one solution after another for the South Bronxes of America and from all indications, it seems to have failed. As suggested above, part of the problem has been and continues to be that most working poor people have been taught and encouraged to think that their individual and community problems are not only beyond their abilities to solve but also that someone else will solve the problem(s) for them.

Our inner city educational and training activities should emphasize empowerment of the working poor in their neighborhoods and in the manner suggested in chapter four. For example, those positions and tasks listed on Figure XIII are more labor intensive than high technological or capital intensive. Neighborhood residents can and should be trained to hold most, if not all, of these positions. And if there develops a need for more or different types of skills, educational and training programs may be instituted and utilized to satisfy such needs. No neighborhood redevelopment programs and activities should be so structurally advanced as to exclude full participation by the working poor. Finally, we want to conclude this section by re-emphasizing the view that in redeveloping working poor communities and neighborhoods, simplicity of the programs and activities to be carried out should be accorded high priority.

Convert public housing to owner occupied

The seventh basic step is to sponsor, encourage and where possible require, conversion of existing public housing stock to owner occupied. The purpose here is to motivate the working poor through home ownership and self help to be more self reliant. This may be done in one of two ways.

First, the housing authority (at the appropriate level), being the landlord and mortgager of such public housing should, through its bureaucratic machinery, design and facilitate a realistic conversion of existing public housing stock to owner occupied. For those who seek real change, individual ownership of existing public housing ought to be a more preferable mode of assisting the working poor than the prevailing indeterminate and dead-end-going-no-where system of subsidized occupancy of publicly owned and operated housing for the working poor.

The second way is to immediately halt the usual, casual and often misguided policies of demolishing bonded or run down high rise apartment buildings. Destroying existing housing in the working poor neighborhoods for redevelopment or other purposes is most unwise, self-defeating, stupid and down right wasteful! There are so many working poor and homeless people who could fix up such apartments for themselves with minimal or no cost to the tax payers. Instead of demolition, housing authorities across the land should borrow a thing or two from Atlanta's Habitat for Humanity or Trenton's Better Community Housing or other similarly engaged community based groups and learn how to turn what amounts to waste to empowering tools for home ownership and self reliance.

To summarize the point, first, arrange an orderly conversion of existing public housing to owner occupied housing. Second, halt the demolition of the existing run down public housing. Clear any encumbrances including tax obligations and arrange for a selective owner-fix-it takeovers of the apartments and town houses. This process will benefit the working poor, their communities and neighborhoods.

Neighborhood entrepreneurship and training

Entrepreneurship and job training make up our eighth basic step. We take entrepreneurship as a way of or a mechanism for generating new ideas and projects for community and neighborhood redevelopment. Like anything else, rebuilding our depressed communities will require new and/or different inputs and approaches in order to improve things. The idea is not just to improve what is available in the working poor areas but more importantly to come up with different social and economic activities and programs to help revitalize life in these neighborhoods. Entrepreneurship is considered to be a good source of ideas and innovation.

Apart from the entrepreneurial attitude which the working poor need to cultivate and have, there is a real need for developing and training community people in those ways and skills which enhance the rebuilding of the neighborhood. And without having to limit such training to a particular field, it would be desirable to emphasize and insist on neighborhood based training with a view to reorienting individuals thus trained to create and/or develop community and neighborhood employment. Thus far, the tradition in both education and training has been to train the working poor for work outside their communities and neighborhoods. One possible problem with such training is that it fails to encourage internal growth and economic stability. Neighborhoods, too, do need both creative thinking and acting (entrepreneurship) as well as regular operational skills. And, without both (as we suspect is the case now), working poor and their neighborhoods are almost certain to remain stuck where they are.

Accessibility

The ninth basic step is about accessibility. That is, for commercial, residential and service purposes, it is desirable that all parts of the neighborhood be accessible to residents and visitors. As discussed in chapter one, an important attribute for rebuilding working poor communities is to neighborize various programs, activities and facilities associated with the rebuilding effort. Economic and political intercourse and enhancement require safe, dependable and clean means of transportation to and from the various neighborhood facilities and establishments. Good and attractive transportation system may even attract visitors to such a neighborhood. How accessible such a community or neighborhood is may give it competitive advantage in certain things especially when compared to neighboring areas.

Consumables

The tenth basic step deals with the quality of the consumable goods and services available in working poor neighborhoods. One of the common complaints that one hears about goods and services provided by the working poor and minority business establishments is that the quality is generally poor. Another is that these goods are expensive. Now, whether this is true or not, it is really immaterial. The real problem here is one of perception to the effect that the quality of goods and services is poor and that they are expensive. It seems to us as though such perception is fairly widespread. And if that is the case, then the thing to do is to insist that the quality of goods and services offered in these neighborhoods be praise worthy and competitive in price. To improve the quality of goods and services, an effort should be made to use appropriate neighborhood training workshops and seminars in such matters and topics as how or where to get quality goods, merchandising and display designs, merchandising and promotion, buying and patronizing local sources of goods and services. Well designed and conducted workshops may also go along way in changing those social or cultural circumstances which breed such perceptions and realities. By 'quality of consumables' we mean that, for instance, the fish available at the corner grocery or the neighboring mini-supermarket is fresh; that the meat is fresh and unstained; that milk is stocked and accurately dated; that there are no roaches and other insects; that the customer is made to feel welcome; that the behavior of the customer is acceptable; and the list goes on.

Civic involvement

The eleventh basic step reemphasizes the absolute need for the working poor (as residents, home and business owners) to participate fully in all types of community and neighborhood affairs. Participation means attending and contributing to such neighborhood activities as school board meetings, township or city council meetings, local planning board, zoning, crime watch and local policing, school activities, garbage collection and other forums at which neighborhood issues are discussed and decisions made. Additionally, there are other voluntary and nonvoluntary community forums and organizations that address such matters as school improvement, neighborhood beautification, drug and crime fighting, youth and senior activities - all of which require participation.

Neighborhood waste disposal

Although our interest here in this twelfth basic step is on waste disposal, it is necessary that we start with the broad problem of environment protection. On the matter of water and air pollution, working poor and minority neighborhoods are on common grounds with the middle class. Every body needs and uses clean air and water. So, on these broad issues, the working poor should simply join forces with others who share same or similar concerns on environmental protection. But regarding how regular waste disposal is carried out, the working poor and minority communities and neighborhoods have an additional problem of uncollected garbage or, at least, not regularly collected. At other times, dump sites with toxic and other dangerous materials are located in or near minority communities. This basic step may, however, be easily complemented (or even preempted) by the other basic steps dealing with the cleanliness and safety of the neighborhoods and communities. Our point though is that it is not sufficient to implement all the other steps outlined and discussed in this chapter without giving careful attention to both environmental protection in general as well as ensuring that neighborhood garbage and other waste are properly and promptly collected and disposed of.

Neighborhood centers for disputes and conflicts resolution

Our last basic step introduces neighborhood centers for resolving various types of disputes and conflicts common in the working poor neighborhoods. The idea here is that the more dependent the working poor are the more the disputes and conflicts they have. And, conversely, the more they resolve disputes and conflicts, the more self reliant they become and, indeed, the fewer the disputes and conflicts they will have thereafter. (Dana:5). As suggested in chapter four, the suggested disputes and conflicts resolution centers would attempt to resolve disputes and conflicts arising from consumer related matters including small money claims or property damage, tenant-landlord relations, unneighborly behavior including juvenile problems as well as employer/employee relations.

The proposed centers would empower the working poor by providing an inexpensive and prompt dispute resolution through a neighborhood based forum similar to Judge Wepner's People's Court or a labor-management type of mediation. It would also be empowering because the people involved would in fact have a choice right in their community as to how they would want their problems handled. This constitutes real justice for the working poor who are so often shafted by the present law enforcement system.

References

Aiken, Linda H and Kehrer, eds., *Evaluation Studies Review Annual*, Vol.10: Beverly Hills, Sage, 1985

Banks, James A. and Crambs, Jean D., *Black Self-Concept*, New York: McGraw-Hill, 1972

Banovetz, James M., ed., *Small Cities and Counties: A Guide to Managing Services*, Washington, D.C: IMCA, 1984

Bartik, Timothy J., *Who Benefits From State and Local Economic Development Policies?* Kalamazoo, MI.: W.E. Upjohn Institute for Employment Research, 1991

Blackwell, James E., The Black Community: Diversity and Unity, New York: Dodd, Mead & Company, 1975

Browning, Rufus P. et al, Racial Politics in American Cities New York: Longman, 1990

Bruyn, Severyn T. and Meehan, James, *Beyond the Market and the State: New Directions in Community Development*, Philadelphia: Temple University Press, 1987

Bryson, John M., *Strategic Planning for Public and Nonprofit Organizations*, San Francisco: Jossey-Bass, 1988

Burchell, Robert W. and Sternlieb, George, eds., *Planning Theory in the 1980's*, Piscataway, NJ: The Center for Urban Policy Research, 1978

Butler, John Sibley, *Entrepreneurship and Self-Help Among Black Americans*, Albany, N.Y.: SUNNY Press, 1991

Boulding, Kenneth E., *The Image: Knowledge in Life and Society*, Ann Arbor: University of Michigan Press, 1956

Brinkerhoff,, Robert O. and Dressler, Dennis E., *Productivity Measurement: A Guide for Managers and Evaluators*, Newbury Park, CA: Sage, 1990

Chandler, Ralph C. and Plano, Jack C., *The Public Administration Dictionary*, Santa Barbara: ABC-Clio, 1988

Cleary, Robert E., Henry Nicholas L. and Associates, *Managing Public Programs*, San Francisco: Jossey-Bass, 1989

Critchlow, Donald T. and Hawley, Ellis W., *Poverty and Public Policy in Modern America*, Chicago: Dorsey Press, 1989

Cruse, Harold, *The Crisis of the Negro Intellectual*, New York: William Morrow & Co., 1967

Dana, Daniel, *Talk It Out! Four Steps in Managing People Problems in Your Organization*, Amherst, MA: Human Resource Development Press, 1990

Donnelly, James H., Jr. et al, *Fundamentals of Management*, 7th ed., Homewood, Illinois: Richard D. Irwin, 1990

DuBois, W.E.B., *An ABC of Color*, New York: International Publishers, 1963

Editors of Fortune, *The Exploding Metropolis*, New York: Doubleday, 1958

Elliot, Jeffrey M. and Ali, Sheik R., *The State and Local Government Political Dictionary*, Santa Barbara: ABC-Clio, 1988

Fusfeld, Daniel R., *The Basic Economics of the Urban Racial Crisis*, New York: Holt, Rinehart and Winston, 1973

Gattiker, Urs E., *Technology Management in Organizations*, Newbury Park, CA: Sage, 1990

Geis, David L. et al, *The Nonprofit Organization*, Pacific Grove, CA: Brooks/Cole Publishing Co., 1990

Gilliam, Reginald Earl, *Black Political Development*, Port Washington, N.Y.: Dunnellen Publishing Co., 1975

Goggin, Malcolm L., et al., *Implementation Theory and Practice*, Glenview, Illinois: Scott, Foresman/Little Brown, 1990

Gordon, Leonard, *A City in Racial Crisis*, William C. Brown Co. Publishers, 1971

Haberer, Joseph, ed., *Science and Technology Policy*, Lexington, MA: D.C. Heath and Co., 1977

Hansen, Susan B., "Comparing Enterprise Zones to Other Economic Development Techniques," in Roy E. Green, ed., *Enterprise Zones*, Newbury Park, CA: Sage, 1991

Harrington, Michael, *The Other America*, New York: Macmillan, 1962

Hawley, Amos H. and Rock, Vincent P., *Segregation in Residential Areas*, Washington, D.C.: National Academy of Sciences, 1973

Henderson, William L. and Ledebur, Larry C., *Economic Disparity: Problems and Strategies for Black America*, New York: The Free Press, 1970

Hicks, Herbert G., and Gullett, C. Ray, *Management*, 4th ed., New York: McGraw-Hill, 1981

Holt, K. et al, *Need Assessment: A Key User-Oriented Product Innovation*, New York: John Wiley & Sons, 1984

Hrebiniak, Lawrence G. and Joyce, William F., *Implementing Strategy*, New York: Macmillan Publishing Co., 1984

Jackson, James S. ed. *Life in Black America*, Newbury Park, CA: Sage, 1991

James, Estellle, ed., *Nonprofit Sector in International Perspective*, New York: Oxford University Press, 1989

Jencks, Christopher and Peterson, Paul E., *The Urban Underclass*, Washington, D.C.: The Brookings Institution, 1991

Kruschke, Earl R. and Jackson, Byron M., *The Public Policy Dictionary*, Santa Barbara, CA: ABC-Clio, 1987

Lank, Edith et al, *Essentials of New Jersey Real Estate*, Chicago: Real Estate Education Company, 1992

Levin, Henry M., ed., *Community Control of Schools*, New York: Simon and Schuster, 1970

Levine, Charles H. et al, *Public Administration*, Glenview, Illinois: Scott, Foresman/Little, Brown Higher Educ., 1990

Levitan, Sar A. and Shapiro, Isaac, *Working but Poor*, Baltimore: JHUP, 1987

, *Programs in Aid of the Poor*, 6th Ed., Baltimore: JHUP, 1990

Luke, Jeffrey S. et al, *Managing Economic Development*, San Francisco: Jossey-Bass, 1988

Magat, Richard, ed., *Philanthropic Giving*, New York; Oxford University Press, 1989

McFate, Katherine, ed., *The Metropolitan Area Fact Book*, Washington, DC: JCPS, 1988

Mieszkowski, Peter and Straszheim, Mahlon, *Current Issues in Urban Economics*, Baltimore: JHUP, 1979

Milburn, Norweeta G. and Bowman, Phillip J., "Neighborhood Life," in James S. Jackson, ed., *Life in Black America*, Newbury Park, CA: Sage, 1991

Miller, Delbert C., *A Handbook of Research Design and Social Measurement*, 5th ed., Newbury Park, CA: Sage, 1991

Mills, Edwin S. and Hamilton, Bruce W. *Urban Economics*, 4th ed., Boston: Scott, Foresman and Co., 1989

Milofsky, Carl, ed., *Community Organizations: Studies in Resource Mobilization and Exchange*, New York: Oxford University Press, 1988

Mishel, Lawrence and Frankel, David M., *The State of Working America*, 1990-91, ed. Armonk, New York: M.E. Sharpe, 1991

Moynihan, Daniel Patrick, *The Negro Family: The Case for National Action*, Washington, DC: Department of Labor, 1965

Murray, Charles A. *Losing Ground: An American Social Policy 1950-1980*, New

York: Basic Books, 1984

Myers, Michelle Tolela and Gail E., *Managing By Communication*, New York: McGraw-Hill, 1982

National Academy of Engineering, *People and Technology in the Workplace*, Washington, D.C.: National Academy Press, 1991

Osofsky, Gilbert, *Harlem: The Making of a Ghetto*, New York: Harper and Row, 1968

Palen, John J., *The Urban World*, New York: McGraw-Hill, 1975

Patterson, Ernest, *Black City Plitics*, New York: Dodd, Mead & Co., 1975

Perry, Stewart E., *Communities On The Way*, Albany, New York: SUNY Press, 1987

Pope, Jackie, *Biting the Hand That Feeds Them*, New York: Praeger,1989

Roberts, Harold S., *Roberts' Dictionary of Industrial Relations*, rev. ed., Washington, D.C: Bureau of National Affairs, 1971

Robey, Daniel, *Designing Organizations: A Macro Perspective*, Homewood, Illinois: Richard D. Irwin, 1982

Rodgers, Harrell R. Jr., *Poor Women, Poor Families*, rev. ed., Armonk, NY: M.E. Sharpe, 1990

, ed., *Beyond Welfare*, Armonk, N.Y: M.E. Sharpe, 1988

Rose-Ackerman, Susan, *The Economics of Nonprofit Institutions*, New York: Oxford University Press, 1986

Rose, Harold, *The Black Ghetto: A Spatial Behavioral Perspective*, New York: McGraw-Hill, 1971

Rosenberg, Jerry M., *Dictionary of Business and Management*, New York: John Wiley & Sons, 1978

Ruchelman, Leonard I., *A Workbook in Program Design for Public Managers*, Albany: Suny Press, 1985.

Sackrey, Charles, *The Political Economy of Urban Poverty*, New York: W. W.

Norton & Co., 1973

Savas, E. S., *Privatization: The Key to Better Government*, Chatham, N.J: Chatham House Publishers, 1987

Shafritz, Jay M., *The Facts on File Dictionary of Personnel Management and Labor Relations*, 2nd ed. New York: The Facts On File, 1985

Sherraden, Michael, *Assets and the Poor*, Armonk, New York: M.E. Sharpe, 1991

Singer, Hans, *Technologies for Basic Needs*, Geneva: ILO, 1977

Sowell, Thomas, *Markets and Minorities*, New York: Basic Books, 1981

, *Civil Rights: Rhetorical or Reality*, New York: Morrow, 1984

Staudt, Kathleen, *Managing Development: State, Society and International Contexts*, Newbury Park, CA: Sage, 1991

Straus, Robert, "The Problem of Conceptualizing Poverty," in Weaver, Thomas and Magid, Alvin, eds., *Poverty: New Interdisciplinary Perspectives*, San Franscico: Chandler Publishing Co. 1969

Sylvia, Ronald D., et al, *Program Planning and Evaluation for the Public Manager*, Prospect Heights, IL: Waveland Press, 1985

Tabb, William K., *The Political Economy of the Black Ghetto*, New York: W. W. Norton & Co., 1970

Task Force on Econ. Growth and Opport., *The Concept of Poverty*, Washington, D.C.: Chamber of Commerce of the U. S., 1965.

Theodorson, George and Achilles, *A Modern Dictionary of Sociology*, New York: Barnes and Noble, 1969

The Twentieth Century Fund, *More Housing, More Fairly*, New York: 20th Century Fund Press, 1991

The Urban Land Institute, *Mixed-Use Development Handbook*, Washington, D.C.: The Urban Land Institute, 1987

Tobin, Gary A., ed., *The Changing Structure of the City*, Beverly Hills: Sage Publications, 1979

Trotta, Maurice S., *Handling Grievances*, Washington, D.C: The Bureau of National Affairs, 1976

Wadley, David, *Restructuring the Regions:Analysis, Policy Model and Prognosis*, Paris: OECD, 1986

Walton, Hanes, Jr., *Black Politics*, New York: J.B. Lippincott Co., 1972

      , *Invisible Politics: Black Political Behavior*, Albany, New York: SUNY Press, 1985

Warren, Donald I., *Black Neighborhoods : An Assessment of Community Power*, Ann Arbor: Michigan University Press, 1975

Weaver, Thomas and Magid, Alvin, ed., *Poverty: New Interdisciplinary Perspectives*, San Franscico: Chandler Publishing Co. 1969

Weiner, Myron E. *Human Services Management*, Homewood, IL: The Dorsey Press, 1982

Whyte, William H., Jr. *The Organizational Man*, New York: Doubleday, 1956

Williams, Frederick and Gibson, David V., eds., *Technology Transfer*, Newbury Park, CA: Sage, 1990

Wilson, William Julius, *The Truly Disadvantaged: The Inner City, The Underclass, and Public Policy*, Chicago: The University of Chicago Press, 1987.

Worthy, William, *The Rape of Our Neighborhoods*, New York: William Morrow & Co., 1976

York, Reginald O., *Human Service Planning: Concepts, Tools and Methods*, Chapel Hill: The University of North Carolina Press, 1982

Public Documents

National Credit Union Administration, *Chartering and Field of Membership Manual*, Washington, D.C.: NCUA, 1989

US Department Of Commerce, Bureau of Census, *Poverty in the US 1988*, Washington, DC: Government Printer, 8/1988.

US Department of Commerce, Bureau of Census, *Poverty in the US 1990*, Washington, D.C.: Government Printer, 1991

US Department of Commerce and Housing Urban Department, *American Housing Servey for the United States 1987*, Washington, D.C: US Government Printing Office, 1989

US HUD, Office of Community Planning and Development, *Report to Congress on Community Development Programs*, 1989, Washington,D.C.: US Government Printer, 4/1989

Federal Reserve System, *Federal Financial Institutions Examination Council Press Release*, 10/21/1991

The City of Akron, Ohio, Goals for Greater Akron Committee: 1973-90, Akron Ohio: Dept of Planning and Urban Development, 1992

A Brief History of Citizen Participation in Birmingham: 1972-1988, Department of Community Development, 1991

Citizen Participation Plan 8/1980: Birmingham, Alabama, Department of Community Development, 1991

City of St. Paul, undated pamphlets and brochures on: *Block Clubs Help Neighbors Help Neighbors, Community Councils, Community Organizations, Dispute Resolution Center, Institute for the Arts of Democracy, Planning Council and a Business Owner's Guide*

Report of the Committee on Citizen Participation, *Making Democracy Work: A Process for Citizen Participation*, City of St. Paul, Department of Planning and Economic Development, 1973

Stutz, Robert M., *Successful Citizen Participation Techniques in Ohio*, Office of Local Government Services, Community Development Division, Ohio Department of Economic and Community Development, Columbus, 6/1978

ASCD, *Public School of Choice*, Alexandria, VA: Association for Supervision and Curiculum Development, 1990

Community Economic Development Strategies, Chicago: UIC Center for Urban Economic Development,1987.

Ford Foundation, *The Common Good:Social Welfare and the American Future*, New York: The Ford Foundation, 1989

Community-Based Development:Investing in Renewal, The Report of the Task Force, 9/1987, Washington D.C.: National Congress of Community Economic Development, 1987

Clay, Philip L., "Capacity-Building for Urban Economic Development: The Community-Based Organization," in *Blacks and Public/Private Partnerships*, Washington, D.C: HUD and Howard University, 1985

Home Sales, Vol. 4 # 12, Washington DC: National Association of Realtors, Dec. 1990.

Peirce, Neal L. and Steinbach, Carol F., *Corrective Capitalism: The Rise of America's Community Developmnt Corporation*, New York: The Ford Foundation, 1987

, *Enterprising Communities: Community Based Development in America, 1990*, Washington, D,C: Council for Community-Based Development, 1990

Real Estate Outlook, Vol. 3 # 11, Washington DC: National Association of Realtors, Nov. 1990.

The Paterson Habitat for Humanity, *Fact Sheet for Buyer Applicants*, 12/1991

Working Neighborhoods, Chicago: Center for Neighborhood Technology, 1986

Journals and Magazines

Black World, Chicago: Johnson Publishing Co., 2/1973, 12/1973 and 11/1975

City Limits, New York, 1/1990

The New York Times Magazine, 6/17/1990

The Annals: Technology Transfer: New Issues, New Analysis, American Academy of Political and Social Science, Beverly Hills: Sage, 11/1981

The Review of Black Political Economy, Vol. 10, #1 and Vol. 2, #1, New York, 1979/1980

NorthStar: News and Ananlysis, Vol. 1, #2, Chicago, 8/1989

Newspapers

The Star Ledger, Newark, New Jersey

The Record, Hackensack, New Jersey

The New York Times, New York

Index

194
-in investing in people, 199
-in educational facilities, 201
-in entrepeneur-investors, 201
self-reliance, 4, 14, 124
-notion and practice of, 45
self support, 7, 11, 46-47
service records, 103
social and human services
-efforts to link welfare to work, 226-230
-involving residents, 233
-nature and reason for, 225
-neighborization, 232
-restructuring, service delivery, 230
-spill-over from, 244
South Bronxes, 4
sparklingly clean, 244
stakeholders, meaning of, 115-117, 184, 211
starting busines in poor neighborhood, 167
-safety, 168
-cleanliness and physical attraction, 169
-engage in a business with potential in your neighborhood, 170
-engage in supportive activities, 172
-patronize neighborhood businesses, 172
-hire neighboors, 173
-organize, join neighborhood groups, 174
-try work co-ops or buyouts, 175
structural attributes of the working poor neighborhood economy, 152
-low paying and menial jobs, 152
-higher paying and better jobs are-held by non-residents, 153
-most working poor are either

on partial/full public assistance, 153
-actual/apparent high consumption, 154
technoserve society, 150
themes and assumptions, 11
transitory, see neighborhood, 60
types and sources of investment, 181
-neighborhood credit unions, 194
-nonmonetary investment, 180-181
-nonprofit, 186
-rotational business loans, 198
-private, 185
-public, 183
-sweat equity, 190, 192-193
-syndication, 197
types of neighborhoods, 56
urbanization, 34
volunteer labor, 192
voting, 70, 241
waste disposal, 253
welfare, 10, 27
worker cooperatives, 175-176
working community, 5-6, 19
working poor, 5, 6, 8, 13, 19, 42
-counting, 42